Years of Darkness
The Troubles Remembered

Years of Darkness

The Troubles Remembered

Gordon Gillespie

Gill & Macmillan

Gill & Macmillan Ltd
Hume Avenue, Park West, Dublin 12
with associated companies throughout the world
www.gillmacmillan.ie

978 07171 4226 2

Index compiled by Cover to Cover
Type design by Make Communication
Print origination by Carole Lynch
Printed and bound in Great Britain by
MPG Books Ltd, Bodmin, Cornwall

This book is typeset in Linotype Minion and Neue Helvetica.

The paper used in this book comes from the wood pulp of
managed forests. For every tree felled, at least one tree is
planted, thereby renewing natural resources.

A CIP catalogue record for this book is available
from the British Library.

5 4 3 2 1

This book is dedicated to Margaret, Roberta and Sandra

Contents

Foreword

It is a cliché that Ireland's present is made more difficult by the fact that too many people remember its past. In truth, the opposite would be nearer to the truth. Were we actually to remember the complexities and human details of Irish history, then our grasp of present politics in Ireland would be far more sure and our appreciation of the limits and opportunities around us would be all the richer.

The Northern Ireland Peace Process has now gone on for so long that it has eclipsed from many people's view the Violent Process that preceded and necessitated it. However, honestly remembering the bloody atrocities practised by all sides in the Troubles is vital, especially if we want the next forty years to be more fruitful and less bloodstained than the last.

It is one of the many merits of Gordon Gillespie's *Years of Darkness: The Troubles Remembered* that it calmly helps us with that process of remembering. In doing so, it reminds us of several key aspects of the North's violent past.

Despite talk of the Troubles as a 'war', for example, and of paramilitary killers as 'combatants', the reality that emerges from this book is that so many Troubles victims did not die in combat at all, but were targeted when they were defenceless. Again and again in these pages we read of the vulnerable being cruelly put to death by the clandestine and the violent.

The human awfulness of it all is stark and poignantly clear as Gillespie deploys eyewitness accounts that tell of personal horror on all sides. The Provisional IRA's Bloody Friday bombings of July 1972 killed nine people, some of them horrifically mutilated in the process; among those who died was fourteen-year-old Stephen Parker, whose father 'was only able to identify his son's remains by his hands, a box of trick matches found in his son's trouser pocket and a Scout belt he had been wearing at the time of his death'. Such images help to counteract celebratory or romantic renderings of the ghastly violence that characterised the North for so many years.

Again, twenty years after Bloody Friday, in February 1992, five Catholics were murdered by the loyalist Ulster Freedom Fighters at a crowded betting shop on Belfast's Ormeau Road. I myself clearly remember the news of this incident being reported and recall hearing, some days later, the appalling details—of blood-spattered walls and screaming people—as a friend told me of the scene she had witnessed in the aftermath. And these Ormeau Road killings represented loyalist revenge for an IRA landmine in Co. Tyrone the previous month, which itself had caused eight deaths. Cyclical, tit-for-tat atrocity.

Amid all this, Gordon Gillespie's account valiantly tries to avoid the danger of reinforcing hierarchies of victims. He is keen to remind us 'of some of the less high-profile casualties of the conflict—as well as those who are better known'. A longstanding expert on the politics of the Troubles, Dr Gillespie is aware of the need to embed these atrocities within a political and chronological context, and he does so deftly. Thus the preparedness of some IRA members to engage in brutal violence grew, in part, from their experience of internment interrogation at the hands of the British in the 1970s: both aspects of the story are presented here.

Are there wider lessons in all this for our twenty-first-century crisis of terrorism and state response? Perhaps. But, if so, they might not be especially encouraging. If the post-9/11 world is one in which terrorist provocation has jolted states into often counter-productive reaction and in which calm analysis has been drowned out by the simplicities of antiphonal abuse, then it is a picture well-known to experts on the Northern Ireland Troubles. And the implication here, from this book, is that current fires will take very many years to burn out. For longevity is one of the depressing features of this Ulster tale. Northern Ireland's First Minister at the time that I write this in 2008, Ian Paisley, is seen here at the start of Gordon Gillespie's story, conspicuous even back in 1969.

But perhaps we can all learn from the North's bloody, vicious past; maybe serious interrogation of the past can help us to avoid brutal means of settling differences in the future. If so, then it is important to remember the quiet human pain that is caused by political violence—and Gordon Gillespie's valuable book helps us to do just that.

Richard English
Author of *Armed Struggle: The History of the IRA* (2003) and *Irish Freedom: The History of Nationalism in Ireland* (2006)

Preface

I belong to the Troubles generation, the generation that grew up in the 1970s with little or no memory of what Northern Ireland was like before the outbreak of widespread sectarian violence in August 1969. None of us who lived through the first years of the Troubles could have imagined that the conflict would last for almost four decades. Looking back at newspaper reports of the time it is striking to note how, in the early days of the Troubles, many people believed that it would be impossible for the conflict to continue much longer. As the years passed, a more common view was that it would never end.

A frequent theme in newspaper reports during the early years of the Troubles was that no atrocity could be worse than that which had just taken place. Sadly, this often proved not to be the case. By the early 1970s, when one atrocity seemed to follow hard on the heels of the last, those who were lucky enough to be able to 'tune out' the Troubles often did so. This undoubtedly led to some incidents—in which significant numbers of people were killed or injured—being almost forgotten in the broader story of the Troubles.

Those deaths that received greater attention often did so because of the extent of the atrocity, the individuals involved or the time at which they took place. On the other hand, many deaths and injuries received less attention for the same reasons. This did not, in any sense, lessen the suffering of the individuals involved nor of their families and friends. For many people the most important day of the Troubles was the day they lost someone close to them.

In recent years there has been much discussion about the need to avoid 'a hierarchy of victims'. Ironically, however, by drawing attention to the deaths of some individuals in particularly disputed circumstances or those involved in incidents where large numbers of people were killed or injured, we have succeeded in doing just that.

One of the limitations of a comparatively short book, such as this, is that while it can highlight the main events of the Troubles in terms of political developments and security incidents, it inevitably misses some of the subtler political points. As well as this it is difficult to convey the impact of the slow trickle of deaths, in ones and twos, which provided the backdrop to much of the Troubles and made a political settlement more necessary, but equally more difficult, to achieve.

Although this book is significantly longer than I had originally intended, in many ways it is still too short. I have rarely been able to mention incidents in which there were fewer than six fatalities. Giving each individual case the merit it deserved would, unfortunately, have required a much larger book. Despite this it is hoped that the events mentioned here will remind people not just of the political events of the conflict but also of some of the less high-profile casualties of the conflict—as well as those who are better known.

In writing this book I have once again been reminded of how interconnected the events of the Troubles were—often in obvious ways, such as the actions and reactions of political and security events, but also in smaller, more coincidental occurrences. The *Belfast Telegraph* of 9 November 1972, for example, carried a full-page review of *The Autobiography of Terence O'Neill* by the veteran unionist Hugh Montgomery Hyde. On the following page was a short report headed 'Maze Court: More are Charged'. The article began: 'Robert Gerard Sands (18), an unemployed coach-builder, who claims to be a member of the Provisional IRA, was remanded in custody for a week when he appeared at the Maze Court, Hillsborough, yesterday, charged with armed robbery by stealing £220 from James Boyd, of Jafmine End, Killeaton, Antrim, by using force.'

Given the size and duration of the conflict in an area as small as Northern Ireland, the coincidental linkage of such important historical figures as O'Neill and Sands was, in some ways, almost inevitable.

Gordon Gillespie
Belfast
June 2008

Acknowledgments

I would like to thank Professor Richard English for his support and advice during the writing of this book. I would like to thank the staff of the Linen Hall Library, where much of the material from which this book is drawn is lodged. I would like to thank Alistair Gordon of the Library's Northern Ireland Political Collection for his patience as I wrote (and talked my way through) this book. Particularly, thanks are due to Dr Ross Moore for his many insightful comments and his work as an unofficial editor. I would also like to thank the numerous eye-witnesses and reporters of the events mentioned here without whom this book would not have been possible.

Abbreviations

AIA	Anglo-Irish Agreement
CID	Criminal Investigation Department (UK)
CLMC	Combined Loyalist Military Command
CSJ	Campaign for Social Justice
DCDA	Derry Citizens' Defence Association
DCDC	Derry Citizens' Defence Committee
DUP	Democratic Unionist Party
GFA	Good Friday Agreement
IICD	Independent International Commission on Decommissioning
IMC	Independent Monitoring Commission
INLA	Irish National Liberation Army
IRA	Irish Republican Army
LVF	Loyalist Volunteer Force
MP	Member of Parliament
NICRA	Northern Ireland Civil Rights Association
NILP	Northern Ireland Labour Party
NIO	Northern Ireland Office
OIRA	Official IRA
PD	People's Democracy
PIRA	Provisional IRA
PSNI	Police Service of Northern Ireland
PUP	Progressive Unionist Party
RTÉ	Radio Telefís Éireann (national broadcaster in the Republic of Ireland)
RUC	Royal Ulster Constabulary
RVH	Royal Victoria Hospital
SAS	Special Air Service
SDLP	Social Democratic and Labour Party
SF	Sinn Féin
UDA	Ulster Defence Association
UDR	Ulster Defence Regiment

UFF	Ulster Freedom Fighters
USC	Ulster Special Constabulary (B Specials)
UUP	Ulster Unionist Party
UUAC	United Unionist Action Council
UUUC	United Ulster Unionist Council
UVF	Ulster Volunteer Force
UWC	Ulster Workers' Council
UPNI	Unionist Party of Northern Ireland
WDA	Woodvale Defence Association

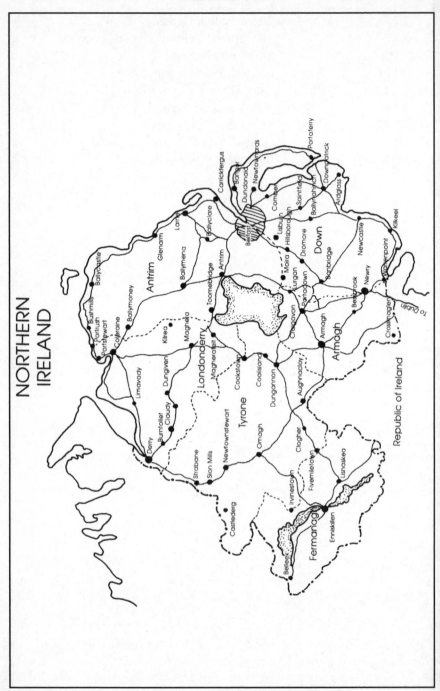

The Background to the Troubles

Although there had been significant sectarian conflict at the time of partition in the early 1920s, Northern Ireland experienced long periods of comparative peace for most of the fifty years that followed thereafter. There was a severe but short-lived outbreak of rioting in Belfast in July 1935 and a more prolonged, but low-key, Irish Republican Army (IRA) campaign along the border with the Republic between 1956 and 1962, but these events served more to keep Protestant–Catholic mutual suspicions alive rather than to pose a threat to the existence of Northern Ireland.

Throughout this period the Ulster Unionist Party (UUP) continued to provide the governing party in Northern Ireland, but the 1950s and early 1960s saw growing support for the Northern Ireland Labour Party (NILP) in Belfast, where the NILP threatened to displace the UUP as the largest political party. It was partly as a result of this that Terence O'Neill, UUP leader and Prime Minister of Northern Ireland from 1963, began a programme of economic reform allied to a policy aimed at improving relations with Catholics within Northern Ireland as well as with the Republic of Ireland.

Any move towards social and political reform inevitably risked a reaction from the right-wing of unionism, both from within the UUP itself and from outside—the latter represented most prominently by the firebrand Protestant fundamentalist minister Rev. Ian Paisley and also by the loyalist terrorist organisation taking the name Ulster Volunteer Force (UVF), which emerged in 1966. The hand of history also continued to play a part in the situation in that the celebrations of the fiftieth anniversary of the Easter Rising in 1916 strengthened both nationalist expectations and unionist fears of the prospect of a united Ireland. From this point pressure was increasingly brought to bear on O'Neill from those who, on one side, believed reform was going too slowly and, on the other, believed it was either unnecessary or moving too quickly.

O'Neill's position was further complicated by the return of a Labour government to power at Westminster in 1964, along with the expectation that Labour would be more sympathetic towards nationalist concerns than previous, Conservative governments had been. O'Neill was, therefore, caught between the need to continue political and economic reform while retaining party support for the UUP and maintaining political stability.

Nevertheless in March 1968 many believed that, despite some problems, Terence O'Neill was leading Northern Ireland towards a golden future. In a five-part assessment of O'Neill's first five years as Prime Minister conducted by the *Belfast Telegraph*, Roy Lilley commented:

> Despite the setbacks and uncertainties, the evidence of physical change on a massive scale is tangible. The motorways stretch out, the New University prepares for its initial student intake, houses and factories rise in Craigavon—five years after it was first proclaimed the new Ulster is gradually taking shape.
>
> (*Belfast Telegraph*, 12 March 1968)

Several days later he added:

> To-day there is an increasing public acceptance of the steps towards realisation of the vision which O'Neill held out when he came to power—and has held in his sights ever since. Physically the new Ulster is taking shape; socially the improving climate is perceptible and becoming more generally recognised. This is the measure of his achievement in five truly momentous years.
>
> (*Belfast Telegraph*, 15 March 1968)

Others had a more cynical view of life in Northern Ireland, however. The Campaign for Social Justice (CSJ) was formed in 1964 and began campaigning against discriminatory practices against Catholics in employment, public appointments, housing allocation, electoral boundaries and electoral practices.

The issue of discrimination in the allocation of public housing received particular attention in June 1968 when Dungannon Rural District Council allocated a house in Caledon, Co. Tyrone, to a nineteen-year-old Protestant woman ahead of other, obviously more deserving, cases on the waiting list. A Catholic family that was 'squatting' in a nearby house was evicted several days later. As the then Nationalist MP at Stormont Austin Currie later recalled:

> I had great difficulty believing the news when I heard it. The house was allocated to a nineteen-year-old, unmarried girl, of all the 269 people on the waiting list, probably the least deserving. Emily Beattie entered into the occupation of her new house on 13 June. Five days later, the Goodfellows were evicted from the house next door. The council bailiffs arrived, forced their way into the house and dragged Mrs Goodfellow and her mother out onto the street. Mrs Goodfellow clutched her nine-week-old baby to her as she was pulled along the ground. The whole sorry episode was caught by the TV cameras and press photographers, and had a major impact on public opinion, particularly when attention was drawn to the occupant of the house next door.
>
> (*All Hell Will Break Loose*, p. 94)

After the formation of the Northern Ireland Civil Rights Association (NICRA) in 1967 the campaign against discrimination was expanded, leading to a series of protest marches in 1968. The left-wing and republican connections of a number of those associated with NICRA inevitably led unionists to question whether the organisation's 'real' agenda was the reform of Northern Ireland or the destruction of the state.

While the first civil rights protests occurred in Catholic areas, where they received greater support, the security situation began to deteriorate when marches were planned to pass through what were perceived to be Protestant areas. In this arena, as in so many others associated with the Northern Ireland conflict, perception was a highly important factor. While most Protestants viewed these marches as nationalist and republican protests, most Catholics saw them as protests for civil rights and against discrimination. The use of force by the Royal Ulster Constabulary (RUC) against civil rights marchers in the Waterside area of Derry in October 1968 helped harden attitudes on both sides. For nationalists, the 'Orange State' had shown that it was incapable of providing equal treatment for Catholics; for unionists, demands for 'civil rights' were merely a front for an attack on Northern Ireland itself. A march by the radical students' group People's Democracy in January 1969, which was attacked by loyalists near Derry, strengthened these opposing views and was arguably the point of no return from which major sectarian conflict became inevitable.

Under increasing pressure O'Neill called a General Election for the Northern Ireland Parliament in February 1969, but failed to see off the critics of his moderate reformist policies. Instead, the outcome of the election served only to highlight the political divisions within unionism between the more liberal and conservative wings; it was followed by O'Neill's resignation.

There had been rumblings of discontent and protest during the spring of 1969, but the advent of the Orange Order's marching season heightened tension even further, with rioting breaking out on the Twelfth of July. Up to this time the RUC had generally been able to contain violence, but the riots that followed an Orange parade in Derry on 12 August (the 'Battle of the Bogside') spread to Belfast and other areas and disintegrated into open sectarian conflict. The deployment of soldiers on the streets of Derry and Belfast in support of the RUC in the following days was the beginning of a British Army operation that would continue for more than three decades.

Despite the outbreak of serious conflict, throughout the years that followed the vast majority of people continued to get on with their lives as best they could: going to work or school, attending or taking part in sporting events or perhaps watching television or going to the cinema. On 15 August 1969, the day when troops were deployed on the streets of Belfast, the city-centre cinemas were showing *Once Upon a Time in the West, The Longest Day, Dr No*, and, perhaps most ironically, *The Love Bug*.

The 1960s

5 OCTOBER 1968: THE DERRY CIVIL RIGHTS MARCH

On 3 October 1968 the Stormont Minister of Home Affairs, William Craig, banned a civil rights march and an Apprentice Boys of Derry parade—both of which were due to be held in Derry two days later—on the grounds that they could lead to serious public disorder. Nationalists in general saw this ban on all parades as a spurious attempt to prevent the civil rights march taking place. NICRA announced its intention to proceed with the march.

On 5 October the civil rights march formed up at the railway station in the Waterside area of Derry, headed by West Belfast MP Gerry Fitt and Nationalist MPs at Stormont Eddie McAteer and Austin Currie. Fitt had arrived from the Labour party conference in Blackpool and with him were three Labour MPs, invited by NICRA to act as observers. Austin Currie later recalled:

> The march started off, but the road ahead was blocked by two police tenders with RUC personnel standing in front of and between them. I couldn't see any way of getting through, so I assumed that we would process as far as we could and then there would be a stand-off. Suddenly, the policeman in front of me had a baton in his hand and was moving forward. I ducked and felt a blow on my shoulder that was presumably aimed at my head. The Telefís Éireann film shows me, with my hand up to protect my head, actually getting through the police cordon and then coming back again. After being hit I just kept going until stopped by a tender, and then came back to rejoin the marchers from the other side. I was extremely lucky not to be clobbered again, but I preferred that chance to being caught on my own between the tenders and the police. All was, of course, utter confusion at this stage, but I did see Gerry Fitt with blood running down his face being half carried away.
>
> (*All Hell Will Break Loose*, pp 110–11)

A number of the marchers began a sit-down protest in front of the police and an impromptu meeting was held by some of the protestors.

As sections of the crowd began to sing 'We Shall Overcome', the RUC ordered them to disperse. Some of the marchers began to retrace their steps, but trouble broke out again. Members of the Young Socialists threw placards at the RUC officers, who advanced on them with batons. The marchers were unable to retreat, however, because of a second police cordon behind them, which moved towards the marchers and began to attack them with batons. Eamonn McCann later described the events of the day:

> We marched into the police cordon but failed to force a way through. Gerry Fitt's head was bloodied by the first baton blow of the day. We noticed that another police cordon had moved in from the rear and cut us off from behind. There were no exits from Duke Street in the stretch between the two cordons. So we were trapped. The crowd milled around for a few minutes, no one knowing quite what to do. Then a chair was produced and Miss Betty Sinclair [of NICRA] got up and made a speech ... 'There must be no violence,' shouted Miss Sinclair, to a barrage of disagreement. But the decision as to whether there would be violence was soon taken out of our hands.
>
> The two police cordons moved simultaneously on the crowd. Men, women and children were clubbed to the ground. People were fleeing down the street from the front cordon, crashing into one another, stumbling over one another, huddling in doorways, some screaming ... Most people ran the gauntlet of batons and reached Craigavon Bridge, at the head of Duke Street. A water cannon, the first we had ever seen, appeared and hosed them across the bridge. The rest of the crowd went back down Duke Street, crouched, and heads covered for protection from the police, ran through side streets and made a roundabout way back home. About a hundred had to go to hospital for treatment.
>
> (*War and an Irish Town*, pp 42–3)

After the march had been broken up some of those involved crossed the River Foyle to the city centre and reassembled at the Diamond, where another confrontation with the police took place. The situation then gradually deteriorated into a confrontation between the RUC and youths from the Bogside estate.

Future events were undoubtedly influenced by the impact of television as RTÉ's coverage of RUC attacks on demonstrators, including MPs, conveyed the impression that the Stormont regime was a repressive government, opposed to reform. On the Monday after the Derry civil rights march the *News Letter*'s editorial recognised the importance of the television coverage, commenting:

> People whose ambition is to have Ulster shown up in a bad light must have felt a real sense of satisfaction on Saturday night. For in full view of millions throughout the British Isles this country has never, never looked uglier. The television film of riot scenes in Derry was so "good" it will surely find a ready market in other places across the world ...
>
> Northern Ireland has had its fill of civil strife, and not even on the wildest lunatic fringe should there be a desire to have us embroiled once more in acts of self-destruction. If we are not to put back the clock in Derry and indeed throughout the Province, there can now be recourse to one source and one source only—the law of the land. There is no other tribunal from which we can expect to obtain an impartial assessment of what and who went wrong in Derry and how.
>
> (*News Letter*, 7 October 1968)

In the *Daily Mail*, Pearson Philips reported on what he saw as the mood of Catholics in Derry, and Northern Ireland, in the aftermath of the march:

> The one-third of Ulster's population which "digs with the wrong foot"—as they say here—has been discriminated against in voting, housing and employment ever since the government of Northern Ireland was set up. They have been treated as second class citizens.
>
> After years of taking this with a kind of resigned placidity—typical of Irish Catholics—it looks as if they have at last found the will and the leadership to make affective resistance. But the leaders who have brought them to this position do not much like the violent turn events are taking. "Oh God," says Mrs Patricia McCluskey—one of the few Catholic town councillors in the predominantly Catholic western counties of Ulster—"I just don't like to think what could happen next." ...
>
> "The Unionists here have a siege mentality," says Mrs McCluskey. "They see themselves surrounded by all these awful Catholics

breeding away with the power of Eire behind them and they just dig themselves in. It is nonsense, of course, to claim that we are trying to wrest Ulster away from the United Kingdom. All we want is for the discrimination to stop. I think the only way this could happen is for the Wilson Government to step in and do something— I dread to think what might happen here now if they don't."

(*Daily Mail*, 10 October 1968)

1 JANUARY 1969: THE PEOPLE'S DEMOCRACY (PD) MARCH

By January 1969 one of the main concerns of unionists was that the Labour government at Westminster would become more closely involved in Northern Ireland matters. In early November, Terence O'Neill, William Craig and Brian Faulkner met Prime Minister Harold Wilson in London for talks. Wilson warned the unionists that if reforms were not continued, the government might consider the 'complete liquidation of all financial agreements with Northern Ireland'. In December O'Neill stated that 'Mr Wilson made it absolutely clear to us that if we did not face up to our problems, the Westminster Parliament might well decide to act over our heads. Where would our constitution be then?' The fear of greater involvement from London also betrayed the growing tensions within unionism. Craig, who had been sacked just days earlier from his post as Minister for Home Affairs, believed: 'There has never been any cause to suggest that Northern Ireland has used improperly its powers. If Mr Wilson or anyone else should threaten to interfere in the exercise of our proper jurisdiction, it is your duty and that of every Unionist to resist' (*Belfast Telegraph*, 17 December 1968).

It was against this background that the radical left-wing organisation People's Democracy announced, on 20 December 1968, that it was going to undertake a four-day protest march from Belfast to Derry. Fearing that it might inflame an already tense situation, both NICRA and nationalist politicians warned against holding the march. However, on 1 January 1969 the *News Letter* argued that the new Minister of Home Affairs, Captain William Long, had been right not to ban the march, saying that this would have granted it an importance it did not deserve. The newspaper added:

If 100 students want to walk to Derry along the raw, wind-blown highways and to brave the rigours of the Glenshane Pass they should be allowed to do so without let or hindrance. We may be sure that they will then arrive in Derry, if not unnoticed, at least with no fanfare or trumpets or the attention of the world.

(*News Letter*, 1 January 1969)

On 1 January 1969 about forty PD members began the march from Belfast City Hall to Derry. The marchers were harried by loyalists at various stages along the route and their presence undoubtedly heightened sectarian tensions. On the morning of 3 January Maghera's Main Street witnessed a sectarian riot that lasted two hours and involved up to 1,000 people, armed with sticks and tree branches. The marchers were shuttled past Maghera along quiet side-roads in cars and minibuses provided by supporters. Later that night trouble broke out in Derry when Ian Paisley and his supporters held a meeting in the Guildhall. The *News Letter* reported the incident as follows:

A water cannon, with both hoses going, drove round the hall in an attempt to disperse crowds. The hall was surrounded by Paisley opponents but his supporters armed themselves with sticks and clubs and burst out—attacking the crowd. Mr Paisley, with Major Ronald Bunting, finally left the building around 1 am. They had been inside for four and a half hours.

During the clashes at the Guildhall police and opposing groups fought running battles at the back of the hall. Several people were beaten up and at times the police were beaten back by an angry crowd. ...

A newspaper reporter who did manage to get inside the Guildhall was forcibly removed by stewards, assaulted and thrown down stairs into the street.

Civil rights supporters outside pulled down electricity cables cutting off power to a 29 foot Christmas tree in the square. They then shook the tree, knocking off bulbs and began using them as ammunition against the hall.

(*News Letter*, 4 January 1969)

On 4 January the march, now comprising several hundred people, was attacked by loyalists at Burntollet bridge, near Derry. Significantly, a number of those who attacked the marchers were identified as off-duty members of the Ulster Special Constabulary (B Specials). When the marchers reached Derry they were welcomed by nationalists, but stoned as they passed through Protestant areas of the city.

In the aftermath of the People's Democracy march, journalist Rob Batsford wrote:

> As I stood in Derry on Saturday a People's Democracy marcher fell like a log at my feet when a stone bigger than a man's fist smashed onto his head and blood poured down the side of his face. From a vantage point I saw the stone throwers, mainly children and young men, hurling their murderous missiles onto the marchers. Many adults were there too, urging them on to the attack. How do you explain the attitude of a mother who encourages her son to keep on?
>
> And once started, a riot is almost impossible to quell. Like an animal that has smelled blood, the crazy urge for more grows until it envelops the whole mass of people. …
>
> Looking back again I will never forget the old women who come to the demonstrations, wearing their prejudices like crowns, openly encouraging the men to violence. The women are as responsible as the men for the tragic scenes that have placed Ulster on the rack again. They shout and abuse, encourage and vilify, and should they perchance be injured themselves, evoke more pity and anger from the men. …
>
> And so, tragically, it seems the end is nowhere in sight. The riots, the beatings, the marches will go on. More people will be hurt, some badly. Some may even be killed. Once again Ulster's history has been coloured crimson with blood. The question is how much more must be spilt before the anger and hatred of her people has been assuaged.
>
> (*News Letter*, 6 January 1969)

The rapid change in mainstream nationalist opinion was clear in the editorials of the *Irish News*. On the first day of the new year, when the People's Democracy march set out, the newspaper noted:

> If the events in Derry on October 5, and similar expressions of belief in human rights have caught the footnotes of history, the tangible achievements which followed, and Westminster's own

declared interest in what the Stormont government was about, have generated a widespread optimism that O'Neill and his government really mean business.

(*Irish News*, 1 January 1969)

Three days later the newspaper's editorial commented:

Well, we in the minority have always known that there was not one law obtaining in these Six Counties but two—one for Unionists and another for non-Unionists. That fact is being made manifest by every mile traversed by these Civil Rights marchers of the People's Democracy. And that is why this march had to be held. Since the start of his Premiership Mr Terence O'Neill has made promises, talked soft—and done nothing.

(*Irish News*, 4 January 1969)

The general response to the march, and the reaction to it, was that it had had a devastating effect on community relations. As one Randalstown resident said, 'this has roused old feelings among neighbours and the tragedy now is that it could end up in sectarian war'.

A year after the march the PD held meetings in Dungiven and Derry, at which new branches of the organisation were established. At the City Hotel in Derry, Michael Farrell told an audience of 400 people that the struggle for civil rights in the North was far from over and that the struggle for socialism had hardly begun. A year after Burntollet, he said, the Special Powers Act was still in force and the Public Order Bill was being re-introduced in the Stormont Senate:

The violence of Burntollet and in Derry has been magnified and repeated on the Falls Road and Ardoyne, in Armagh and in the Bogside again. Yet the same tainted government is in power, ruling in the same partisan way.

(*Irish Press*, 5 January 1970)

24 FEBRUARY 1969: THE 'CROSSROADS' ELECTION

It was clear in late 1968 that not everyone had been won over by O'Neill's moves towards reform. On 13 November he faced a protest by several hundred students while attending the Methodist College prize-day ceremony, which was held in the Whitla Hall at Queen's University, Belfast. O'Neill was mobbed by the protesting students when he arrived and was helped into the building by police officers, who then had to call for support. Neil Johnston reported on what had now become almost a clash of cultures:

> Inside, as the assembled audience sang the first hymn, the strains of "We Shall Overcome" could be heard from the outside. But all the doors into the Whitla Hall had been closed and the prize distribution went off smoothly and without interruption.
>
> It ended after two hours by which time students, some of whom had remained outside, had begun to gather again in force. When the Prime Minister left by the same side entrance to walk the few yards to an adjoining building where tea was being provided, police had to hold back students and form a pathway for him and others, and there were several scuffles.
>
> When the Prime Minister and Mrs O'Neill emerged their car had to be protected by a ring of police, and there were more scuffles as the car was driven off. There was a rush to the university gateway, but the car got away without being stopped.
>
> That left another confrontation between the police and the students, and for a while the situation looked extremely unpleasant. As the rush hour traffic streamed up University Road most of the police climbed back into their waiting tender. As they did so there were shouts of "SS Special Branch", "Go Home RUC" and "Police violence on the campus."
>
> (*News Letter*, 14 November 1968)

On 9 December 1968 O'Neill attempted to go over the heads of unionist critics of his reformist policies and garner support by appealing directly to the public via television. In that broadcast he uttered the words that have become synonymous with that watershed moment in Northern Irish politics: 'Ulster stands at the crossroads ... What kind of Ulster do you want? A happy and respected province in good standing with the rest of the United Kingdom or a place continually torn apart by riots and demonstrations and regarded by the rest of Britain as a political outcast?'

The journalist Mervyn Pauley commented:

He took the dramatic step of appealing to mass opinion, the man in the street, to weigh in with his views and to stand up and be counted. And last night there were indications that this is what the public intend doing through various media of communication and their public representatives. Captain O'Neill's speech will undoubtedly please the broad mass of moderate intellectual opinion in Northern Ireland. Whether, as the Premier clearly hoped, it will jolt the lunatic fringes on both sides into a reassessment of attitudes, remains to be seen.

(*News Letter,* 10 December 1968)

The broadcast did win O'Neill much public support, but in the months that followed the crisis within the Unionist Party, and outside, deepened. On 24 January 1969 Brian Faulkner resigned from the Unionist government in protest against O'Neill's policies; a second minister resigned two days later. On 30 January twelve backbench Unionist MPs called for O'Neill to be removed as Prime Minister in a bid to maintain party unity. The following day the *Daily Mail* reported:

To an outsider it is barely credible that O'Neill should have to contemplate the possibility of getting the sack less than 24 hours after Parliament appeared to back his brand of tolerant Unionism without even the formality of a vote.

The sad fact is that, though O'Neill has shown he can carry the moderate mass of his countrymen with him—Catholics as well as Protestants—he is as dependent as any politician on those who put him in power.

He is especially vulnerable because he leads from one wingtip of the party rather than the centre. And the desire of some in the centre and on the right of the parliamentary party to get him out has not been abated by all the fair words of yesterday's debate.

Even after the debate some of his closest political allies were speculating openly how long he would hang on to an increasingly intolerable position.

(*Daily Mail,* 31 January 1969)

On 3 February 1969, O'Neill responded to the challenge to his leadership by calling a General Election to the Northern Ireland Parliament for 24 February. By announcing the election he hoped to demonstrate the degree of public support for his policies and isolate his critics. In a reference to O'Neill's December 1968 speech, this election came to be known as 'the crossroads election'.

With a turnout of just under 72 per cent, the election returned thirty-nine unionists (twenty-four official unionists and three unofficial unionists supporting O'Neill; ten official Ulster Unionists opposing O'Neill; and two undecided), six members of the Nationalist Party, three civil rights candidates, two Republican Labour and two members of the Northern Ireland Labour Party.

Although O'Neill and his supporters won an overall majority of seats, he failed to rout his critics. Instead, the election served mainly to demonstrate the divisions within the unionist political bloc. Official Unionist supporters of O'Neill won 31.1 per cent of the poll and unofficial unionist supporters of O'Neill a further 12.9 per cent. However, anti-O'Neill Official Unionists won 17.1 per cent of the poll. Signposting future developments, there was also a shift in voting in the nationalist bloc away from the Nationalist Party and towards individuals connected with the civil rights movement.

The election also saw the emergence of a number of figures who would dominate Northern Ireland politics for the next three decades, not least John Hume (who was elected for the Foyle constituency) and the Rev. Ian Paisley (who provided a strong challenge, but lost, to O'Neill in Bannside).

Unable to see off the opposition stemming from within his party and from outside, O'Neill resigned on 28 April 1969. The following day HC McDowell assessed the career of 'the crossroads Premier':

Teetering on a razor's edge ever since he took over the Premiership from Lord Brookeborough six years ago, Captain O'Neill did not gain many friends on his own side by initiating face-to-face discussions with Mr Sean Lemass, the then Premier of Eire. This proved to be his Achilles heel, for the Rev. Ian Paisley seized the opportunity to denigrate the Premier for alleged "traitorous conduct" and to mount a vicious campaign which has not ceased yet.

Despite a few bruises and not a lot of vilification from the keepers of the Protestant conscience, Captain O'Neill held steadfastly on until the civil righters and their more aggressive auxiliaries added to the heat of an already hot situation.

(*News Letter*, 29 April 1969)

In November 1970 O'Neill, now in the House of Lords, claimed that
he had 'had approaches suggesting that I should allow my name to go
forward as the next President of the Republic when Mr de Valera
retires'. In response, the *Irish News* was both irritated and slightly
amused by O'Neill's comments and critical of his achievements while
Prime Minister of Northern Ireland:

> Why, during his six years of Premiership at Stormont, did he do so
> little to ensure that Catholics could get houses and jobs, in his
> anxiety to have them live like Protestants? When houses and jobs
> were going, even then, Lord O'Neill's henchmen saw to it that, if
> possible, they were denied to Catholics. Unionists frankly advocated
> discrimination (and many still do) in pursuit of the preservation of
> their Protestant privilege. Did their view conflict with that of Prime
> Minister O'Neill?
>
> (*Irish News*, 9 November 1970)

12 AUGUST 1969: THE BATTLE OF THE BOGSIDE

By August 1969 the first deaths of the Troubles had already taken
place. On 14 July sixty-seven-year-old Francis McCloskey died after
sustaining injuries during a crowd attack on an Orange Hall at
Dungiven, Co. Londonderry. There were conflicting arguments as to
whether or not he had been struck by the police.

Samuel Devenney died on 17 July after suffering a heart attack. He
had been beaten by police officers at his home in Derry on 19 April
during an incident in which RUC officers broke into the Devenney
home in pursuit of a number of youths who had run through the house
to escape the police. Although an inquest found that Mr Devenney had
died of natural causes, a subsequent investigation by British police
officers led one senior officer to comment that there had been 'a conspiracy of silence' surrounding the attack on Samuel Devenney.

Despite the deaths of Francis McCloskey and Samuel Devenney the
British government remained cautious about intervening in Northern
Ireland matters. On 29 July Home Secretary James Callaghan met
Gerry Fitt and three Labour MPs who were worried about the possi-
bility of trouble at the Apprentice Boys march in Derry on 12 August.
Callaghan said that he shared their concern about the situation, but

'pointed out to the MPs the "extensive" programme of reforms under-taken by the Northern Ireland government and said that the problems of the North should be solved without outside intervention. However, he is also believed to have said that the Northern Ireland reforms were largely the result of pressure applied from Westminster' (*The Irish Times*, 30 July 1969).

On 12 August 1969 severe rioting broke out on the edge of the Bogside area following a march through the city by the Apprentice Boys of Derry. The rioting would continue for three days in what became known as the 'Battle of the Bogside'. Trouble broke out at 3.00pm as the Apprentice Boys parade passed through Waterloo Place, in the city centre. Rival crowds of Protestants and Catholics began taunting each other, then stones and bottles were thrown. The *Irish News* reported on subsequent developments:

A 30-strong force of riot police in the centre of Waterloo Place also came in for some stoning, but it was not until the parade had passed and Civil Rights leaders had moved the Catholic crowds back from the square that the familiar police versus Catholic picture began to emerge. ...

A police water cannon was called in but was found to be in-effective in dispersing the crowds. It was, however, used to put out fires in two William Street shops.

Shortly after 7 pm police mounted a massive attack using heavy armoured vehicles and smashed the Rossville Street barricade. At the same time other police rushed through Chamberlain Street, off William Street, and forced the crowd there into the car park in the centre of the Rossville Street multi-storey flats block. There, the police were showered with bottles, petrol bombs and stones and they moved back into Chamberlain Street.

Police at the front of the flats rushed up Rossville Street behind Land Rovers and armoured vehicles. When the retreat from the barricade was halted a very large crowd of men from the St Columb's Wells area began forcing the police back.

It was at this stage that police vehicles were set on fire and a policeman was set alight by a petrol bomb. His colleagues rolled him over on the ground and as a section of the crowd moved towards them one policeman drew his revolver to keep the crowd at bay.

(*Irish News*, 13 August 1969)

The Derry Citizens' Defence Association, a local vigilante group, was involved in co-ordinating opposition to the police by erecting barricades, patrolling the streets and helping counter the effects of cs gas. These actions eventually led to the creation of the 'no-go area' known as Free Derry. Derry man Eddie Harrigan later recalled the strategic significance of the Rossville flats during the Battle of the Bogside:

> It was really from there that the control of the Battle of the Bogside was centred. You could get up there through the lift system. From the lifts there was a ladder up to the roof for the workmen, so we made use of it. There was quite a few people up there, but if you take everybody that tells you they've been on the roof of the flats during the battle it would have been three-quarters of Derry there. There was between 70 to 100 people on there regularly. I went up a few times but I've a fear of heights—it got to me after a time.
>
> People made the petrol bombs on the flats and sometimes in the garages of the flats. They were brought up in milk crates. The average age of people on the roof was 16 to 25, but even younger people played a role in bringing the petrol bombs up. This organisation developed spontaneously but it worked. Everybody was behind what was going on.
>
> The police tried to fire tear gas on to the roof but the breeze usually worked to our advantage. People had different theories about how to protect themselves from the gas. Some people used vinegar and handkerchiefs. It seemed to work but it could have been just psychological. Others put their heads in basins of water. People were still choking and had sore eyes.
>
> (*Living Marxism*, August 1989)

The decision to allow the Apprentice Boys' march to proceed, and the outcome of that decision, highlighted the gulf in attitudes between nationalists and unionists. The *News Letter* believed that:

> The youths who threw stones and other missiles at the Apprentice Boys got their "protest" in, but it is one that is likely to burst from them at any time, whether a parade is being held or not. Clearly no country can allow hooligans to dictate, by threats and by actual violence, what is to be permitted and what is to be banned. The

decision to allow the Apprentice Boys' demonstration go on was
the correct one, since, of itself, it carried no threat to peace.

(News Letter, 13 August 1969)

For the Irish News, on the other hand:

> The shambles of yesterday and the inevitable confrontation
> between police and the people of the Bogside are another proof, as
> if one was needed, that if ever there is to be a normal society in this
> area, the unionists must shed the idea that they own the North; and
> that even a move in the interests of peace, is a concession to the
> minority and unthinkable ... Without yesterday's assertion of
> power, Derry could well have been at peace, instead of entering
> again on another period of self-destruction.

(Irish News, 13 August 1969)

An intervention by Taoiseach Jack Lynch, in which he claimed that the
Unionist government was no longer in control of the situation and
called for United Nations soldiers to be sent to Northern Ireland, did
nothing to calm the situation. Northern Ireland Prime Minister James
Chichester-Clark said the Taoiseach's remarks were 'inflammatory
and ill-considered' and that he would hold Lynch personally responsible for any worsening of feeling.

Chichester-Clark called up the Ulster Special Constabulary to
provide support to the RUC, but this proved insufficient to contain the
situation. With police resources exhausted, Chichester-Clark
requested British Army support to maintain law and order. At 5.15pm
on 14 August soldiers of the Prince of Wales Own Regiment and the
Queen's Regiment were deployed to relieve the police.

14 AUGUST 1969: RIOTS IN BELFAST

As rioting spread beyond Derry the situation quickly deteriorated
into open sectarian conflict, and many Protestants believed that the
very existence of Northern Ireland was under threat. In Belfast, fires
destroyed hundreds of houses, leaving thousands of people—pre-
dominantly Catholics—homeless.

George Hamilton reported on the impact of the violence on the
Falls Road. Among other developments, he noted that men claiming

to be members of the IRA had taken over the Broadway Cinema and turned it into a refugee centre, and that some people had moved mattresses into the cinema. His report continued:

> Every street running off the Falls Road is barricaded. Groups of people, many of them wearing crash helmets and carrying dustbin lid shields, were stopping traffic and diverting it away from the Falls Road area. At North Howard Street a six-wheel lorry had been turned on its side and set on fire. Other streets in the area had been cordoned off with telegraph poles, lamp-posts and paving stones.
>
> Meanwhile, dozens of houses in the area were being evacuated and self-appointed peace stewards were loading dozens of lorries with families' furniture and belongings. A building between Dover Street and the Divis Tower block of flats was set on fire and a bull-dozer had been used to block off Dover Street ...
>
> A mob at the junction of Falls Road and Grosvenor Road stopped a corporation bus and asked all passengers to leave. The driver ran to safety but the mob commandeered the bus which they pushed down the Falls Road. Several police armoured vehicles were seen to approach the top of the Falls Road and a large contingent of police are believed to be stationed in back streets.
>
> Later Cupar Street was dotted with blazing barricades which were set up about every five yards along the street.
>
> Lorries toured the Argyle Street area today selling sheets of plywood for six pence each. Nearly every house in the area has been boarded up and a number of small children are collecting and storing empty bottles in milk crates.
>
> (*Belfast Telegraph*, 15 August 1969)

The newspaper also reported that a petrol-tanker had been hijacked at the corner of the Grosvenor and Falls roads.

On Saturday 16 August the *News Letter* described the dramatic impact of the violence on the city of Belfast:

> It was walk it home for thousands of Belfast citizens early last night—and they left behind them a city bereft of transport, enter-tainment and the solace of picture houses and public houses. "The town is dead," said one reporter who had just toured the city before 10 pm. Belfast Corporation transport ceased functioning in the

Falls Road area from 2 pm onwards after a number of buses had
been "hi-jacked" by armed men ... They were followed around
6 pm by the Donegall Road, Springfield Road, Shankill Road and
Crumlin Road services.

Around 8.30 pm Mr Max Hale, Corporation transport officer,
on the instructions of the general transport manager, Mr R.W.
Adams withdrew services from the east end of the city.

The city centre cinemas shut their doors early and did not have
evening performances. Some of the staffs were forced to stay
overnight because of trouble in certain areas of the city. Public
houses too suffered from the early closing time. They shut their
doors around 7 pm. Clubs, too, closed down.

(*News Letter*, 16 August 1969)

Over the following years public transport often became a prime target
for rioters during civil disturbances. Will Hughes noted:

Rioting was commonplace and vehicles were frequently seized by
mobs to form barricades, thus protecting themselves from rival
mobs or the authorities. Many of these vehicles were subsequently
set on fire making them an even more effective deterrent.

The size and availability of buses made them a popular choice
for barricades and between the outbreak of the Troubles in 1969
and the formation of Citybus in 1973, approximately 100 vehicles in
the Belfast Corporation Transport fleet were destroyed, with countless more suffering damage. As time progressed events were to take
a more sinister turn with vehicles being specifically targeted.
Frequently buses were simply stopped by mobs, some of which
were armed, and after the driver and passengers had been ordered
off, the vehicle was set on fire. In addition, depot installations were
firebombed resulting in large numbers of vehicles being destroyed
at a time. Between 1973 and 1987 approximately 500 more vehicles
were to be destroyed, averaging 32 a year.

(*Citybus: Belfast's buses 1973–1988*, p. 27)

In the days following the Battle of the Bogside and the deterioration
of relations between Protestants and Catholics there were a number
of new developments—some temporary, others more long-term. NICRA
set up its own radio station, Radio Free Belfast, to broadcast informa-

tion and a similar pirate radio station, Radio Free Derry, operated in that city. Within days more pirate radio stations, such as Radio Orange and Voice of Ulster, were broadcasting in Belfast, despite attempts by the authorities to block their signals. More significantly, during the course of the riots barricades were erected on both sides of Cupar Street, between the Falls and Shankill roads, to provide communal protection. When the Army erected iron sheets as a barrier in September, it was a physical recognition of a division that already existed. (By 2007 there were approximately forty peace walls in Belfast, stretching nearly 13 miles in total length.)

In the wake of the August riots and the deployment of troops on the streets of Belfast and Derry, the greater involvement of the British government in Northern Ireland affairs was now inevitable. On 27 August Home Secretary James Callaghan visited Northern Ireland for talks with the Unionist government and other groups. He put pressure on the Stormont government to introduce further reforms, including the restructuring of the RUC. By early September many believed the worst was now over. The *Financial Times* noted:

> Faced with the realisation that it was no longer able to control the situation by itself, the Northern Ireland Government had no other choice but to accept the intervention of the British Government. At the same time, the Catholic minority could only sigh with relief that British troops had come to protect it and even Dublin has reluctantly accepted the British military presence as a necessary short-term evil.
>
> It is a tribute to Mr Callaghan that, in such conditions, he managed to lay down the law without giving offence to either side, while at the same time creating a more favourable climate for the introduction of long overdue reforms.
>
> (*Financial Times*, 2 September 1969)

The Scarman tribunal was set up to examine the violence and civil disturbances that beset Northern Ireland in 1969. In April 1972, shortly after the Northern Ireland Parliament was suspended, the tribunal's report was published. The tribunal found that:

> Neither the IRA nor any Protestant organisation nor anybody else planned a campaign of riots. They were communal disturbances

arising from a complex political, social and economic situation.
More often than not they arose from slight beginnings: but the
communal tensions were such that, once begun, they could not be
controlled. Young men threw a few stones at some policemen or at
an Orange procession: there followed a confrontation between
police and stone-throwers now backed by a sympathetic crowd. On
one side people saw themselves, never "the others", charged by a
police force which they regarded as partisan: on the other, police
and people saw a violent challenge to the authority of the state.

(Scarman Report, para. 2.4)

Despite the accuracy of Scarman's assessment, the report failed to
convey the impact of the violence on individuals. Most of the damage
to property was to Catholic homes, particularly in Bombay Street,
where three-fifths of the houses were destroyed by fire. Of sixty-three
houses on Bombay Street, thirty-eight needed to be demolished, five
required major repairs and ten required minor repairs. By contrast,
few houses were damaged in Protestant areas.

The 1970s

7 MAY 1970: THE ARMS CRISIS

In May 1970 Taoiseach Jack Lynch sacked Finance Minister Charles Haughey and Agriculture Minister Neil Blaney following revelations of a plot to smuggle arms into the Republic of Ireland and send them on to Northern Ireland. Haughey and Blaney were accused of conspiring to import £100,000 worth of weapons, which allegedly were destined for the Provisional IRA. The transportation of the weapons was called off when it was decided that it was likely to be stopped by customs officials at Dublin Airport. A third minister, Kevin Boland, resigned from the government in protest against the sackings; Minister for Justice Micheál Ó Móráin also resigned.

John Healy reported on the events surrounding one of the most dramatic days in the Republic's history:

> The Longest Political Day had everything but sex—and, as one Fianna Fáil Deputy said halfway through it, we have enough on our mind without sex. It started in true Bond fashion when that most un-Bond-like of men, the Taoiseach, Mr Jack Lynch, set off the action with a statement phoned to the newspapers shortly before three in the morning: he had fired Neil Blaney and Charles J Haughey from his Cabinet and Kevin Boland had resigned because he disagreed with the Taoiseach's judgment.
>
> For the first time in the history of Fianna Fáil, the Cabinet was split wide open. Four ministers had resigned or been fired within 36 hours from the Cabinet of a party which had become a cliché for its monolithic structure and its permanence.
>
> Moran, Blaney, Boland and Haughey—the backbone of Lynch's Cabinet was gone and a stunned capital city, which had gone to bed arguing over whether Mick Moran had been pushed or had resigned—woke up with the answer: two more fired and a third departing of his own free will.
>
> (*The Irish Times*, 7 May 1970)

A two-day debate in the Dáil on the nomination of new ministers
followed on 9 and 10 May. On 11 May Christopher Warman wrote in
The Times:

> As the smoke clears from the battlefield of the Dáil, where
> Government and Opposition ended their fierce combat last night
> after 37 exhausting hours over gun-running allegations, Mr Lynch,
> the Prime Minister seems to have emerged the victor for the
> moment.
>
> The threat of a constitutional crisis has faded and fears that the
> ruling Fianna Fáil Party might disintegrate under the shock of the
> allegations and opposition attack have been allayed by Mr Lynch's
> firm voice of moderation. The party, which gave its leader a unan-
> imous vote of confidence on Wednesday after the dismissal of two
> Ministers and the resignation of a third, has held together in the
> face of tormenting interrogation from the Fine Gael and Labour
> opposition, whose members spent hour after hour seeking to
> widen the crack.
>
> Mr Lynch, in his reply to the debate last night, left no doubt that
> despite the shaking his party had had there was no thought in his
> mind to dissolve Parliament. The Government would continue to
> govern. His party was the only one capable of leading to the fulfil-
> ment of a united, peaceful and prosperous Ireland, he said.
>
> The Government won the vote at the end of the debate on the
> almost entirely forgotten issue of approving the nomination of
> three new Ministers, by 73 votes to 66.
>
> *(The Times, 11 May 1970)*

The *Financial Times* noted that the precise course of events surrounding the plan to import guns into the Republic remained far
from clear:

> Two important questions remain unanswered. Firstly, Mr Charles
> Haughey, the former Finance Minister, and Mr Neil Blaney, the ex-
> Minister for Agriculture, have categorically denied any personal
> involvement in the gun-running plot and Mr Lynch has failed to
> produce any concrete evidence to counteract these denials.
>
> Secondly, a former Irish army intelligence officer, Captain Jack
> Kelly, who has admitted having a "small part" in the arms plot,

persists in his claim that the then Minister for Defence, Mr James Gibbons, knew all about his actions. Mr Gibbons, who has now been moved to replace Mr Blaney, told the Dáil that he had no involvement whatsoever.

In the aftermath of this dramatic debate, it was clear that the Prime Minister was not misleading the House with intent, but rather that his omissions, for whatever reasons, have left the whole sorry affair very much wide open.

(*Financial Times*, 11 May 1970)

On 28 May Haughey and Blaney appeared in court on arms conspiracy charges; both men denied any involvement and were released on bail. Blaney was cleared of gun-running charges in July, and Haughey was cleared in October. The defence argued that the guns had been imported as part of an officially sanctioned operation on behalf of the Irish Army. The first trial of Haughey, Captain James Kelly, Belgian arms dealer Albert Luykx and Northern republican John Kelly lasted just six days, ending on 29 September when a defence counsel remarked that the judge was conducting the trial in an 'unfair tone'. Mr Justice Andreas O'Keefe said he could not continue when such an accusation had been made in open court and he discharged the jury. Luykx was ordered to pay the costs for all parties because the judge considered that 'It would be a great hardship for the other accused persons if they were to lose the "very considerable" fees which they had paid to counsel, solicitors and perhaps witnesses' (*The Irish Times*, 30 September 1970).

As with the aborted first trial, the second trial also carried a dramatic air of intrigue and international arms dealing. On 8 October the *Irish Times* reported:

Another witness yesterday was Hans Hasselsteiner, employed by Kirchner and Company of Vienna. Hans Hasselsteiner, who gave evidence through an interpreter, mentioned a meeting on Saturday 18th April last with three men in Vienna. Only one of the three men identified himself—Herr Schlueter from Hamburg. The other two introduced themselves as Mr Albert and Mr Kelly. Mr Kelly gave no other details about who he was or what he worked at. Hans Hasselsteiner said that he now recognised both men seated in the body of the Court and identified them as Mr Lukyx and Captain

Kelly. The three men wanted to take over a shipment of 10 crates of pistols and 72 cartons of ammunition which were stored in the Customs warehouse of Vienna airport.

(*The Irish Times*, 8 October 1970)

On 23 October Haughey and the other three accused were acquitted of the charges. The controversy rumbled on, however, with Taoiseach Jack Lynch insisting that there had been an attempt to import arms and that all of those charged had been involved.

3 JULY 1970: THE FALLS ROAD CURFEW

While it was the introduction of internment, in August 1971, that led to an upsurge in sustained violence which marked the worst years of the Troubles, the framework within which the increased level of violence would emerge had already been set by events of previous years. In this respect two separate events in 1970 helped set the tone for what was to come.

On 27 June 1970 there was a prolonged spate of violence in north and east Belfast. In north Belfast sectarian violence broke out after an Orange march, and three Protestants were shot dead by the IRA in the Crumlin Road area. Later that evening two more Protestants were shot dead by the Provisional IRA on the Newtownards Road in east Belfast. A number of the IRA men fired from the grounds of St Matthew's Catholic Church. A Catholic man was also shot dead by loyalists during the gun battle. It was an important moment because this incident marked the first appearance, in coherent form, of the Provisional IRA. The whole episode is bitterly contested. A loyalist booklet entitled 'Murder in Ballymacarret' saw it as an aggressive IRA action, pure and simple. Republicans in the Short Strand area, on the other hand, have always regarded it as a desperate and necessary defensive action against a marauding loyalist mob, and it has entered the nationalist memory as such.

Protestant anger at the events of 27 June was heightened by the fact that the RUC (which had been disarmed under the proposals of the Hunt Report in 1969) had been ineffective in dealing with the IRA gunmen and that when the Army had arrived, an hour-and-a-half after the violence broke out, their main concern appeared to be to protect the Catholic Short Strand area from Protestant reprisals rather than tracking down the IRA men responsible for the shootings. At Stormont, the Unionist MP for the area complained that the soldiers 'stood there like statues' and called for General Sir Ian Freeland to be removed as General Officer Commanding (GOC). This reflected the view of many unionists, who believed that the Army was unwilling to 'take on' the IRA (whether Provisional or Official). For republicans, what they called 'the Battle of Ballymacarrett' was a key moment for the IRA in its role as defender of the Catholic community. The lesson many loyalists took from the event, on the other hand, was that the security forces were either unwilling or unable to prevent republicans attacking Protestants and therefore a more organised loyalist paramilitary force was needed in the area.

Less than a week later another key event took place in west Belfast. At 4.30pm on 3 July the Army cordoned off Balkan Street, on the Falls Road, and searched one of the houses, where they found a small quantity of arms and ammunition. As the Army patrol withdrew an hour later stones were thrown at them and the soldiers replied with CS gas. The situation deteriorated rapidly. Just before 7.00pm home-made grenades were thrown at the troops. Most of the attacks on the 'army incursion' on the Lower Falls were carried out by the Official IRA, which remained strong in the area. Twenty-five minutes later the local army commander ordered all his units to prevent any movement into or out of the area. At 10.00pm the Army proclaimed a curfew, which was announced by loudspeaker from a helicopter flying overhead. On Saturday 4 July there was a two-hour break in the curfew between 5.00pm and 7.00pm, which allowed local people to go out and stock up on essentials. In the event the proclamation of a curfew was almost certainly illegal because it did not have the backing of the NI Minister of Home Affairs, who was the only person with the power to make such a declaration.

By the end of its search of the Lower Falls area the Army had recovered approximately 100 weapons and 25,000 rounds of ammunition. While this was a significant amount of weapons, the operation had involved 3,000 troops, who fired nearly 1,500 rounds of ammunition and used over 1,500 CS gas grenades or cartridges. Four civilians were killed and fifty-seven wounded; eighteen soldiers wounded. More than 300 people were arrested (Geoffrey Warner, 'The Falls Road

Curfew revisited', *Irish Studies Review* Vol.14, No.3, 2006, pp 325–42).
The four men killed by the Army were, to say the least, unlikely candidates as instigators of trouble. William Burns was a fifty-four-year-
old shopkeeper, thirty-six-year-old Charles O'Neill was reportedly
attempting to speak to the soldiers when he was run down by an
armoured car, twenty-four-year-old Zbigniew Uglik was a freelance
journalist and sixty-two-year-old Patrick Elliman was a former
labourer and cobbler. Beyond these tragedies the behaviour of some
of the soldiers during the course of the searches did nothing to win
the 'hearts and minds' battle on the Falls Road. One soldier later
recalled the antagonism between the troops and residents, which was
heightened by the curfew:

> A guy still in his pyjamas came out cursing, wielding a lamp and
> whacked Stan across the head. Stan dodged the next one and
> decked the bloke with his rifle butt. I knew full well that a lot of
> the lads were taking this opportunity to vent their anger over
> things already done. Heads were being cracked and houses trashed
> from top to bottom. Everything in the houses became a mass of
> rubble but, out of the blur, little, sharp details still cut through:
> school photos; smiley family pictures (cracked); trinkets and cruci-
> fixes (snapped); kids crying; crunching on the glass of the Pope's
> picture … a body in the hall, flattened against the wall.
>
> (Nicky Curtis, *Faith and Duty*, p. 35)

The curfew was eventually lifted at 9.00am on 5 July. Shortly afterwards a 'Bread March' of several hundred women and children, led by
Provisional Sinn Féin member Maire Drumm, carried food into the
area.

The subsequent decision by Army officers to allow two Northern
Ireland government ministers to accompany the press on a tour of the
area on the afternoon of 4 July seemed a further, calculated insult.
One commentator subsequently remarked: 'As far as the inhabitants
of the lower Falls were concerned, the sight of these two men, riding
around the district in army vehicles, could only be seen as a symbol of
the unionist establishment lording it over its Catholic "subjects"'
(Warner, p. 327). Meanwhile Gerry Fitt, the Westminster MP for West
Belfast, was prevented from entering the area. Under political pressure
to take some action on Northern Ireland, the Irish Minister for

External Affairs, Patrick Hillery, made a secret visit to the Falls on 6 July, which led to a further dispute between London and Dublin.

Although referred to as 'the Balkan Street search' by British officials, in republican circles the event became known as 'the rape of the Falls'. In retrospect, even the British Army recognised the incident as a pyrrhic victory:

> The Army had been under significant pressure to "sort out" the lower Falls. "Sorting out" was taken to mean imposing law and order and enabling the RUC to patrol without assistance. The army had relatively few options open to it other than house searches. Tactically the Balkan Street search was a limited success. However, it was a significant reverse at the operational level. It handed a significant information opportunity to the IRA and this was exploited to the full.
>
> (*Operation Banner*, para. 217)

The Falls curfew, if not a turning-point in relations between the Catholic working class and the Army, did mark an important point in the growing antagonism between the two. Taken together with the events of the previous week it highlighted the widening gulf between the views and expectations of the various political actors, which was exacerbated by the increasing tension and violence.

9 MARCH 1971: THE SHOOTING OF THREE SCOTTISH SOLDIERS

On 6 February 1971 twenty-year-old Gunner Robert Curtis was fatally wounded by a sniper in the New Lodge area of Belfast. Several days later the *Daily Mirror*, which was often critical of the deployment of troops in Northern Ireland, asked: 'How much more can they take?'

> Gunner Robert Curtis stepped into military history at the weekend. In the streets of Belfast he became the first British soldier to fall to enemy fire since the Aden battle of 1967. His father, Mr Matthew Curtis, summed up the feelings of many parents: "Why," he asked, "should the lives of our troops be endangered in this way? Why don't we pull out and let the mobs fight on."

The fact is that in doing one of the dirtiest jobs in their history the Army find it difficult to justify their presence, not only to their enemies but to the folks back home.

Meanwhile the military commitment steadily increases. In April 1969 the normal Ulster garrison of around 2,400 was reinforced to guard essential installations. Then, politicians seemed sure that troops would never be seen in the streets. Four months later soldiers were in Belfast. By last July emergency forces had reached their peak at 11,500—approaching the biggest trouble-spot force that Britain had ever deployed.

(Daily Mirror, 10 February 1971)

By 1 March two more soldiers had died, but the response to these deaths paled into insignificance when compared to the reaction to the murder of three Scottish soldiers, aged 17, 18 and 23, on 9 March 1971. The News Letter's report on the murders, entitled 'Slaughter', noted:

Three young soldiers were found shot dead on a lonely road at Ligoniel overlooking Belfast last night. They were the victims of the most cold-blooded act of violence yet perpetrated by IRA terrorists in Northern Ireland.

The men, all Royal Highland Fusiliers, were shot through the head at point-blank range and their crumpled bodies were found lying in a ditch. Two of them were brothers. The triple murder, which has outraged the Province, is believed to have taken place at around 7.30.

The alarm was raised by two schoolchildren who stumbled on the bodies on the way to their nearby home. An eye-witness who was also early on the scene said of the grim discovery, "It first seemed to me that I was looking at a bundle of rags. The bodies were lying on the side of the ditch."

This man told me that he ran down the road to a public house to telephone the police.

The murdered men were named early today as Fusilier John Boland McCaig, Fusilier Joseph McCaig (brothers), and Fusilier Dougald [sic] Purdon McCaughey. At the time they met their death they were wearing civilian clothes, having an off-duty spell from riot patrol in the New Lodge Road area.

(News Letter, 11 March 1971)

Adding to the general sense of horror, the bodies were first discovered
by a group of children:

> Two children Robert Brown, aged 12, and his cousin Brenda Irvine,
> aged 15, stood on their own beside the three bodies while a third,
> Eileen Brown, Robert's sister, aged 15, ran for help. They had heard
> the shots and saw a grey van being driven down the lane towards
> Ligoniel.
>
> "Two men came on the scene." Robert said today, "We were just
> standing there frightened and not knowing what to do. One of the
> men touched the head of a man lying over another. His head fell
> back and the man who had come on the scene said, "They are stone
> dead."
>
> (*Belfast Telegraph*, 11 March 1971)

A theory soon emerged that the soldiers had been lured from a pub
by IRA members, in the belief that they were going to a party. Instead
they were shot dead on the Ligoniel Road. The *Irish Times* reported
that five beer glasses, some with beer still in them, were found near the
bodies. Public opinion was outraged by the circumstances in which
the soldiers had been murdered, and the fact that two were brothers.
The degree of condemnation of the murders was such that the
Provisional IRA issued a categorical denial that it was responsible (*The
Irish Times*, 12 March 1971). Loyalist youth gangs were later reputed to
have adopted tartan scarves as forms of identification in response to
the killings, thereby becoming known as Tartan Gangs.

Belfast Telegraph correspondent Arthur Williamson saw a deeper
motive behind the murders:

> Was the intention of the murderers to provoke British public
> opinion into a demand that Ulster should be left to its own devices
> and therefore the mercy of the terrorist infiltrators? This was the
> question facing the Prime Minister and the Cabinet as they met to
> assess the implications of the horrifying news.
>
> It was immediately recognised that precipitate action would pro-
> duce just the kind of situation the killers were anxious to exploit.
> Reprisals would lead to a bloodbath in which more innocent people
> would be the victims and intensify hatred for the security forces,
> while withdrawals would be an abdication of responsibility.

However outraged public opinion may be, the Government has constantly to bear in mind the strife-torn area is a part of the British Isles, and not a mandated or colonial territory.

(Belfast Telegraph, 13 March 1971)

The murders had several immediate consequences. On 12 March 5,000 shipyard workers marched to the Ulster Unionist Party headquarters in Glengall Street and called for the introduction of internment. Two days later it was announced that soldiers under the age of eighteen would be withdrawn from Northern Ireland.

In Ayr, 15,000 people attended the funerals of brothers John and Joseph McCaig, while in Northern Ireland there were also tributes to the Scottish soldiers:

Almost 20,000 Ulster people today paid their last respects to the three young Scottish soldiers found shot dead at Ligoniel last week, in processions through the streets of Belfast and Carrickfergus.

The biggest crowd, estimated by police at more than 10,000 gathered in silent tribute around the Cenotaph at Belfast City Hall. The city centre ground to a halt as men, women and children collected from all parts of the city. Later, another crowd of mourners walked with wreaths from the York Street area.

And as the first victim, Fusilier Dougald McCaughey, was buried in Glasgow about 6,000 people, many of them workers from local factories, took to the streets of Carrickfergus. Workers from ICI, Courtaulds and Carreras marched to the Town Hall to hand in a petition protesting about the law and order situation.

Flags on public buildings and ships in the harbour were flying at half-mast, as the crowd stood in silence.

(Belfast Telegraph, 16 March 1971)

Speaking at Stormont on 11 March the Northern Ireland Prime Minister, James Chichester-Clark, warned of the danger of over-reacting to the murders:

Quite the worst thing that could happen as a result of these murders would be for ill-disposed persons to encourage actions or even the expression of views which might open the path to reprisals. Many of us have memories long enough to warn us not only of the appalling consequences of murder and outrage but also of the risks of revenge and the chain reaction that follows.

Sadly, Chichester-Clark's warning would prove accurate on many occasions over the coming years. In the aftermath of the murders Chichester-Clark failed to persuade the British government that a tougher security policy was required in Northern Ireland, and he resigned on 20 March.

9 AUGUST 1971: THE INTRODUCTION OF INTERNMENT

On 9 August 1971 Operation Demetrius saw the introduction of internment without trial in Northern Ireland. In an early morning operation the Army arrested 342 Republicans, mainly from the Official IRA, from a list of 452 persons sought. No loyalists were arrested. It soon became clear that security information on republican activists was hopelessly out of date. Of those who were arrested, 105 were released within two days. A week after internment was introduced, the Provisional IRA's Chief of Staff claimed that only thirty of its members had been interned.

On the morning after internment was introduced the *Daily Mail* reported:

> Hundreds of Ulster families had a shock awakening just before dawn yesterday—at the point of a gun held by tight-faced British troops. A four-year-old girl was carried off with her father because there was no-one else at home to look after her. It was hours before the tearful child was reunited with her mother.
>
> Throughout the Province it was the same picture of hundreds of husbands and sons being frogmarched off—many of them without time even to put on their shoes. It could be years before many of them are free again. Yet in defiance of all British traditions of justice these men have not been tried or convicted.
>
> (*Daily Mail*, 10 August 1971)

People's Democracy member John McGuffin was one of those arrested on Monday 9 August. He later recalled:

A crashing on the door awoke me. It was 4.45 o'clock. I went down-
stairs in my pyjamas to answer. As I opened the door I was forced
back against the wall by two soldiers who screamed at me, "Do you
live here?" Overwhelmed by their perspicacity I admitted that this
was so, whereupon they ordered me to get dressed. I foolishly asked
why. "Under the Special Powers Act we don't have to give a reason
for anything," an officer said. "You have two minutes to get
dressed." Through the window I could see in the dawn light half a
dozen armed men skulking in our tiny front garden.

I was given exactly two minutes to get dressed while a young soldier boosted his ego by sticking an SLR up my nose. My wife, not
surprisingly, was almost in tears as I was dragged down the stairs
and into the street. She ran after me to give me my jacket and was
roughly ordered back into the house. Our quiet residential
bourgeois neighbourhood hadn't seen such excitement in years as
I was frogmarched and escorted at the double down the avenue by
eight soldiers. As we sped down we were joined by a dozen more
who were hiding in nearby gardens, wreaking havoc on the horti-
cultural efforts of various OAPS.

(John McGuffin, *Internment*, p. 9)

The introduction of internment was criticised by nationalists of all
shades, as well as by civil rights organisations. Rather than reducing
the level of violence, as unionists had hoped, internment had the
opposite effect: there was a massive upsurge—thirty-four people died
in Northern Ireland in 1971 before 9 August; 140 were killed in the rest
of that year. The introduction of internment marked the beginning of
the worst period of violence of the Troubles, which persisted until
1977. Even after this, the anniversary of the introduction of internment became associated with severe rioting in nationalist areas of
Northern Ireland for many years afterwards. The famous West Belfast
Festival (Féile an Phobail), which coincides with this date, was established partly to provide more positive activities at this time of year.

The men arrested on 9 August were subjected to 'deep interrogation' techniques by the Army in an attempt to disorientate them
before they were questioned. The experience of Joe Clarke was similar
to that of many others who were handcuffed and hooded during the
process:

My position was the same as for other men—fully stretched, hands as far apart as humanly possible and feet as far from the wall as possible. Back rigid and head held up. Not allowed to relax any of the joints at all. If any relaxation of limbs—arms, elbow joints, legs, knee joints—someone came along and grabbed the limb in a rough manner and put it back into position again.

… I closed my fist only to find that my hands were beaten against the wall until I opened my fingers again and put my hands back into position. On the other occasion I tried to rest by leaning my head against the wall but the response to this was my head was "banged" on the wall and shaken about until I resumed my position. All the time there was the constant whirring noise like helicopter blades going around. From the sound of this noise I would say that it was played into the room where I was because on the occasions that I was taken from this room even outside the door of the room the noise was noticeably vague almost to be inaudible.

(Quoted in *The Guineapigs*, John McGuffin, pp 57–8)

As well as the negative political and security fallout, the mistreatment of internees became a major issue of concern. In February 1972 a report from a committee of British Privy Councillors, headed by Lord Parker, recorded the use of five techniques used in 'deep interrogation' and concluded that the methods could be justified under exceptional circumstances only. Importantly, however, one member of the committee, Lord Gardiner, stated that the interrogation techniques were not justifiable. In 1978 the European Court of Human Rights ruled that the internees had been subjected to 'inhuman and degrading treatment'.

Despite these dramatic events Belfast city centre was surprisingly quiet, partly because bus services had been withdrawn. *News Letter* columnist Ken Nixon wrote:

Two bewildered American tourists strolled, hand in hand, along an alley in Smithfield Market, strangely unbusy yesterday. A bomb went off, some distance away and they darted into a junk-shop, looking startled. The man there calmed them. "It is far from here, sir. And it sounded like a wee one. Not more than five pounds."

By lunchtime the city centre people—the shop girls, the sales-men, the junior executives, the waiters, the barmen, the puzzled, edgy people who keep Belfast's heart working had become used to the day.

It was a day of violence but unlike many other days of violence. There was something extra-ordinary about it. The usual rumours had unsettled the morning so they crowded around radios at one o'clock to hear what had really happened.

(*News Letter*, 10 August 1971)

In 1988, when internment was again being suggested as a means to reduce paramilitary activity, former Prime Minister Edward Heath came out strongly against the suggestion:

Looking back on it, we very quickly realised it was a mistake. Firstly, there was the way in which it was handled. The people who were interned really bore very little resemblance to those out to cause damage.

Secondly, the way people were arrested by police and the army caused reactions not only throughout the whole of Ireland, but throughout the United States and the rest of the world, which was very damaging to us.

Thirdly, it gave the IRA a way to recruit from amongst people who had been interned, and training them, which proved impossible to stop.

Fourthly, it gave the IRA something that they have been able to celebrate ever since—the anniversary of the introduction of internment.

(*The Guardian*, 22 August 1988)

The British Army later admitted that it recognised the difficulties associated with internment:

A considerable number of terrorist suspects were interned: the net total of active IRA terrorists still at large decreased by about 400 between July and December 1971. A very large amount of intelligence had been gained: the number of terrorists arrested doubled in six months. However, the information operations opportunity handed to the republican movement was enormous. Both the introduction of internment and the use of deep interrogation techniques had a major impact on popular opinion across Ireland, in Europe and the US. Put simply, on balance and with the benefit of hindsight, it was a major mistake.

(*Operation Banner*, para. 220)

4 DECEMBER 1971: THE McGURK'S BAR BOMB

On 4 December 1971 a 50 lb Ulster Volunteer Force bomb exploded in McGurk's Bar in Belfast killing fifteen people, all Catholics, and injuring a dozen more. The McGurk family lived above the bar and the owner's wife, Philomena, and fourteen-year-old daughter, Maria, were among those killed. Others who died in the explosion included thirteen-year-old Jimmy Cromie, a friend of the bar-owner's sons, and Philip Garry, a seventy-three-year-old school crossing patrolman.

Although the bomb was planted near the doorway, the explosion reduced the entire building to rubble. Eight of the victims were crushed to death, three died from burns, two from multiple injuries, one from the blast and crushing and one from carbon monoxide poisoning.

The *Daily Mirror* reported:

The Saturday night crowd in the pub were given no chance. The explosion ripped through the bar scything down unsuspecting drinkers. And then the first floor home of the McGurk family collapsed on top of those who survived the blast.

Among the dead were Mr McGurk's wife Phyllis, 46, and 14-year-old daughter Marie. He and his sons Gerald, 15, Patrick, 11, and John, 9, were injured.

Ironically the pub itself was regarded as one of the safest and best conducted in the Catholic area. For Mr McGurk had a rule which forbade the singing of any songs with a political or religious theme.

The bomb caught the pub with even more than its usual Saturday crowd. Two other pubs nearby had closed down early in case of violence in the troublesome area. When the explosion came, little Marie McGurk and a young friend killed with her were playing cards in a flat above the pub.

(*Daily Mirror*, 6 December 1971)

Eyewitness Martin Kelly recalled:

> I had just passed the pub and was 20 yards away when the explosion happened. I was hurled off my feet but rushed over to help. I saw a man, obviously dead, lying on the ground. Both his legs had been blown off.
>
> I dived into the rubble with hundreds of other people from the flats across the road. We dug for the victims with our hands bleeding but nobody gave it a thought.

Belfast Telegraph reporters described the scene after the explosion:

> Troops and police rushed to the scene where some of the injured were already crawling from the debris. Immediately, along with people who streamed from nearby houses, they began digging in the rubble with their bare hands as screams were heard in the darkness.
>
> As they came across bodies stretchers were called for. Military and civilian ambulances were used to ferry the 13 injured to the Mater and Royal Victoria Hospitals. Within half an hour 800 people had arrived on the scene to help in the rescue. They were organised into human chains by troops who issued commands through loud-hailers. The debris was removed virtually brick by brick. Later an Army mechanical digger was called in to speed up the operation.
>
> At one point there was the threat of another explosion from a severed gas main. But the rescuers worked on as small fires broke out in the rubble all around them. Firemen used foam to douse the flames.
>
> Several of the rescuers were violently sick as badly mutilated bodies were uncovered. A team of surgeons from a Belfast hospital rushed to the scene and treated the injured on the spot.
>
> (*Belfast Telegraph*, 6 December 1971)

One of the survivors of the explosion was John McGurk, whose mother and sister were killed. In an interview with the *Irish News* in December 1996, he recalled the night of the explosion:

> It really wasn't a case of the lights going off, it was like something out of a really bad horror film. I remember tumbling in air and space amid this massive rush of wind and noise. It must have been a matter of seconds. I couldn't remember anything else because I

must have been unconscious for a while but I don't know how long it was. ...

It was miraculous for me because a person, Jimmy, who was just a few feet away from me was killed. I woke up and I didn't really know what had happened. There was then the realisation that the building had collapsed and I was stuck ... I thought I smelt gas and I was completely terrified. My first instinct was of complete and utter survival and wondering how I would get out of this. The worst thing about it was that I'm nearly sure that I heard my sister crying for help, because there wouldn't have been any other young female stuck there. It's possible that it was my imagination. It's possible that she was already dead, but that's what I remember.

For some years after the event there continued to be a dispute as to whether the bombing had been conducted by loyalists or was the result of the premature explosion of an IRA bomb. Republican Labour MP at Stormont Paddy Kennedy suggested that British military intelligence or the British Army's Special Air Service (SAS) was responsible because in his opinion, 'not even the UVF could have been responsible as they would not have the heart to carry out an explosion of that kind' (*The Irish Times*, 6 December 1971).

At the time the explosion was claimed by 'The Empire Loyalists', but seven years later a UVF member was convicted of the bombing and received fifteen life sentences. In 1978 journalist David McKittrick suggested that the bomb had been planted by loyalists attempting to bomb another pub further along the same street, but being unable to get to their original target, they left the device at McGurk's instead.

An hour after the bombing sectarian rioting broke out in north Belfast and a gun battle took place between the Army and the IRA. In the course of the shooting British Army Major Jeremy Snow was fatally wounded; two police officers and five civilians were also shot and injured.

Six of the victims of the bombing were buried on 7 December; one of them was James Cromie. The *Belfast Telegraph* reported:

About 600 people walked silently behind the coffin as it made its way up North Queen Street. The funeral paused briefly as it passed the tangled wreckage of the public house where 15 people died when a bomb exploded on Saturday.

James Cromie was playing table football in an upstairs room with the proprietor's son and friends when the bomb went off. He died instantly …

Black flags fluttered from many houses in North Queen Street and Unity Flats. Several shops in the area closed briefly, as the funerals passed. A large force of police and troops stood by in case of trouble, but there were no incidents.

(*Belfast Telegraph*, 7 December 1971)

The bombing of McGurk's Bar led to the greatest loss of civilian life in any one incident of the Troubles in the North until the Omagh bomb in 1998. Despite this the atrocity has never received as much attention as other incidents with fewer casualties. As Malachi O'Doherty later noted:

Many people believed that the carnage in McGurk's was an "own goal", and this was plausible because so many IRA bombers were dying in accidents at the time.

Dr William Rutherford was the head of Casualty at the Royal Victoria Hospital. On that night, he later told me, he moved the whole unit up to the bar to treat the injuries. "I brought morphine to treat the pain, but we didn't need it. People were in such shock that they felt nothing. I had never seen that before."

A police officer has told me that his father brought him into the hospital to see the injured, to impress upon him the damage that political violence was doing. One of the survivors, John McGurk, became a journalist in Belfast himself. John grieves that his family got little sympathy because the bombing was reported, even years later, as an IRA own goal.

(*The Telling Year: Belfast 1972*, pp 79–80)

30 JANUARY 1972: BLOODY SUNDAY

On 30 January 1972 thirteen men were killed and another fatally wounded when soldiers from the British Army's Parachute Regiment opened fire at the end of a civil rights march in Derry city. Although it had been declared illegal, the march had generally been peaceful until it reached its destination, at which point a section of the crowd attempted to climb over a street barrier and were forced back by the

Army with rubber bullets and water cannons. More than 100 youths threw stones and iron bars at the soldiers and a running battle ensued for more than ten minutes. The question of whether soldiers opened fire first or whether they were fired on by republican gunmen, or believed they were being fired on, remains a source of great controversy. Whatever the truth of the matter, Bloody Sunday was one of the key events of the Troubles—it hardened attitudes in the Catholic community and strengthened support for the IRA, as well as causing damage to Britain's reputation internationally. In Dublin, on 2 February, anti-British demonstrations were followed by an attack on the British Embassy and the burning of the building. Bloody Sunday also encouraged the British government to move towards taking full control of security policy in Northern Ireland, which in turn would lead to the introduction of Direct Rule.

The civil rights march of up to 20,000 people was believed to be the largest since November 1968. The Army had cordoned off an area near the bottom of William Street. After stones were thrown, the Army used CS gas and dye to break up the crowd. The march organisers called on people to go to Free Derry corner, 400 yards away, where they would hold a public meeting. It took the crowd approximately twenty minutes to assemble at this point. Ivan Cooper recalled:

Just as Miss [Bernadette] Devlin started to speak—she had only uttered about two sentences—when the Army opened fire. The speakers and everyone around the platform fell on their stomachs.

I could see from where I was lying, people being selectively shot down by the Army. I saw people trying to go to the assistance of others being shot down themselves. People were in a terrible panic and dispersing everywhere.

At one point I went with a friend of mine to go to the assistance of two people lying shot on the ground. I had a white pillow case in my hand. Both of us were fired on and my friend was struck on the side of the mouth by a bullet.

(*Irish News*, 31 January 1972)

Ivan Cooper insisted that the Army had not been fired on at that stage, that the soldiers were not fired on until ten minutes later. The Army was adamant that they had been fired on first and had only opened fire when they saw a man preparing to throw a nail bomb.

The Army had erected a number of manned barriers to prevent the march entering Protestant areas. They also claimed that they had planned to arrest a number of those they saw as 'ringleaders' as the march began to disperse. According to an official document produced by the Army:

> The Brigade operation order said it was anticipated that the arrest operation would take place on foot. However, one battalion commander decided to use a mixture of armoured and softskin vehicles to carry his men right up to the rioting marchers, before they debussed and started making arrests. A few moments before the operation was mounted a high velocity shot was fired at the soldiers from the area of the rioters. The operation went ahead and three platoons debussed in three different areas in the immediate vicinity of the rioters. Almost immediately shots were fired and within minutes 12 civilians were dead.
>
> (*Operation Banner*, para. 222)

The Guardian responded to events in Derry in a qualified manner by stating:

> The disaster in Londonderry last night dwarfs all that has gone before in Northern Ireland. The march was illegal. Warnings had been given of the danger implicit in continuing with it. Even so, the deaths stun the mind and must fill all reasonable people with horror.
>
> (*The Guardian*, 31 January 1972)

John Hume compared the killings with the Sharpeville massacre in South Africa in 1960 and called the Army's actions 'nothing short of mass murder—another Sharpeville, another Bloody Sunday'. He added that he wanted the strongest action taken, 'including the immediate withdrawal of these uniformed murderers from our streets'.

A tribunal of inquiry, headed by Lord Chief Justice Widgery, was quickly established to look into the events surrounding Bloody Sunday, and produced a report in April 1972. The Widgery Report found that there would not have been any deaths if the organisers of the march had not created a dangerous situation. It stated that some soldiers showed a high degree of responsibility, but the behaviour of others bordered on the reckless. Many nationalists viewed the report as an attempt to whitewash the guilt of the Army, which did little to abate their anger. Father Edward Daly, later Bishop of Derry, who attended many of the dead and dying on Bloody Sunday, said that the Widgery Report 'found the innocent guilty and the guilty innocent'. In August 1973 Coroner Hubert O'Neill described the deaths of those killed on Bloody Sunday as 'sheer unadulterated murder'.

The sense of injustice continued for decades after the events of Bloody Sunday. In 1997 one eyewitness, Eamonn MacDermott, recalled how Bloody Sunday had left him with three abiding impressions—incomprehensibility, fear and anger:

> It was just too much to believe that they could really be firing live rounds into a crowd that big. My ears and eyes were telling me that these soldiers were standing there firing at us. We had all become too well accustomed to the different sounds made by different guns not to immediately recognise the distinctive crack of the SLR. But my brain would not accept it.
>
> There had been many marches and riots in the past but they had never ended like this, this was no gun battle, this was all one way traffic.
>
> Then as reality took hold I can still remember the fear, the sheer unadulterated terror. I had been scared before that day and many times after it but unless you have experienced a crowd of 15,000 people in the grip of sheer terror, desperately trying to run anywhere to get out of the line of fire, you cannot imagine what it feels like.
>
> Then on reaching the relative safety of my father's car, the terror mounted as we got stuck in the middle of Rossville Street. From my seat in the back I could see the Paras clearly standing firing as the crowd ran in blind panic. There were bodies lying there, whether shot or simply taking cover I never found out.
>
> Then the most lasting impression a deep, deep sense of anger. An anger that even today, twenty-five years later, is never far from the surface when that day is mentioned.
>
> (Bloody Sunday Supplement, *Derry Journal*, January 1997)

Throughout the 1990s there were appeals for a fresh inquiry, and in January 1998 Prime Minister Tony Blair announced a new investigation into Bloody Sunday. Ten years on, however, the inquiry team under Lord Saville has still not produced a final report, provoking criticisms of the duration and cost of the inquiry.

22 FEBRUARY 1972: THE ALDERSHOT BARRACKS BOMB

On 22 February 1972 a 50 lb bomb in a stolen car exploded at Aldershot military barracks, headquarters of the 16th Parachute Brigade, killing five women workers on the domestic staff, a gardener and Captain Gerry Weston, a Catholic army priest. Thirteen other Army and RAF personnel were injured. The Official IRA claimed the attack, stating that it was a response to the deaths on Bloody Sunday. Shortly after the bombing the Official IRA issued a statement:

A unit of the Irish Republican Army carried out a successful retaliatory operation at the headquarters of 16 Parachute Brigade at Aldershot. The operation took place at the officers' quarters of the brigade. The operation, which resulted in the deaths of several high-ranking officers of the brigade, was carried out as a reprisal for the murderous killings perpetrated by troops under the control of this brigade when they fired without provocation on unarmed civilians in Derry.

On the day after the Aldershot bombing the Official IRA persisted with its claim that at least twelve military officers had been killed. In fact, Fr Gerry Weston was the only member of the armed forces to be killed in the bombing. While serving with the Parachute Regiment in Belfast he had worked in Ballymurphy, where he tried to improve relations between the Army and the local community. He had been awarded a MBE for his 'efforts to reduce tension and prevent rioting— at considerable personal risk over a period of time and often in a situation where it would have been impossible to send armed soldiers without inflaming the situation' (*News Letter*, 23 February 1972).

When Noel Jenkinson was convicted of the Aldershot murders, the *Daily Telegraph* reported:

Early on Tuesday, February 22, Jenkinson and another man not caught set out from London on their diabolical mission. To allay suspicion as they drove through the sprawling barracks at

Aldershot they wore khaki camouflaged uniforms. Those who vaguely noticed a car on its way to the mess took little notice, seeing men inside dressed in Army type uniforms.

The peg-timing device to set off the bomb packed with 200 lbs [sic] of stolen gelignite substitute was timed for 1 pm when the mess should have been crowded. But it went off at 12.40, causing the seven deaths and damage estimated at £90,000. It was the worst act of IRA terrorism in Britain since the infamous bicycle bomb explosion at Coventry in 1939 when five people died.

(*Daily Telegraph*, 15 November 1972)

Police were eventually able to arrest some of the bombers by tracking down the owner of the car used in the explosion through the numbers left on the remains of the car engine and chassis.

On the morning after the explosion Martin Woollacott reported for the *Guardian*:

The blast which tore apart the headquarters mess of the 16th Parachute Brigade came at 12.40 pm on a grey, drizzly day. A few officers were having drinks in the bar at the back of the building. The blast ... brought soldiers and civilians rushing from all over the town. They found the dead and some of the injured still trapped in the debris.

The mess is a three-storey concrete and glass building set with four similar other buildings amid green lawns. It is very much of a piece with the rest of Aldershot's new "open-plan" military area which, with its park-like open spaces and the pleasing mixture of modern blocks with the best bits of the old Victorian barracks and buildings, looks like a particularly lavishly planned new town ...

One side of the mess's middle floor had simply been punched out by the explosion. Slab concrete hangs down by its reinforcement rods, entangled with sodden red curtains. All glass in nearby buildings was blown out.

(*The Guardian*, 23 February 1972)

The *Daily Mirror* described the bombing as 'Senseless, monstrous, cowardly!' and added:

The IRA bombers in Aldershot add one more senseless brutality to their murderous record in Ulster. When the smoke cleared at the

paratroopers' mess, who were the maimed and mangled victims?
Five waitresses. One other civilian. One Roman Catholic padre.
Will this monstrous episode be enshrined in song and legend with
all the bitter chants of the past?

No doubt this cowardly outrage was intended as a reprisal for
the events of "Bloody Sunday" in Londonderry. The IRA say so.
Almost unbelievably, their first reaction was to describe it as "a successful retaliatory operation." So you massacre five women and an
Army padre—and you call that success. God help us all.

(*Daily Mirror*, 23 February 1972)

Inevitably the editorials of many other newspapers also made connections with Bloody Sunday. The *Irish Independent* commented:

The Aldershot killings were the result of a savage, stupid and cowardly act of violence divorced from any genuine feeling of patriotism
and motivated only by a lust for revenge which is utterly primitive.
Whoever planned and perpetrated the killings brought about the
deaths of people innocent of any crime against the Irish people.
And even if these unfortunate men and women had been guilty of
crimes, who gave the bombers the right to take their lives? Not the
people of this country who are as appalled as the rest of the world
is at the seven tragic deaths. The answer is that, again, we are presented with the work of self-appointed executioners acting in no
one's name but their own.

Just as horrible as their deeds is their demonstration of a belief
that one death cancels out a previous death, that the dead of Derry
are atoned for by the deaths at Aldershot. They claim that they
regret civilian deaths, ignoring the basic truth that they have no
right whatsoever to deal out death to anyone. They are in the way
of peace because their every act is a further attempt to involve us
all in the whirlpool of violence.

(*Irish Independent*, 23 February 1972)

Some of the most stinging criticism came from Bishop Cahal Daly,
who told an audience in Longford:

This evil thing could be authorised, planned and executed and
can now be approved only by men who have let their minds be

perverted by an evil philosophy. For it is a barbaric code which holds that innocent lives can be taken to avenge life and it is an un-Christian and a radically evil principle to say that the end justifies the means. This indeed is the most immoral of all immoral principles.

May this horrific crime at least have one good effect, of bringing about a final repudiation of all our people of such evil means.

(*Belfast Telegraph*, 24 February 1972)

4 MARCH 1972: THE ABERCORN RESTAURANT BOMB

On Saturday 4 March 1972 a 6 lb bomb exploded in the Abercorn Restaurant in Belfast city centre, killing two people and injuring more than 100 others.

Ann Owens (22) and Janet Bereen (21) were killed in the explosion. Sisters Rosaleen and Jennifer McNern, who had stopped in the restaurant after shopping for wedding outfits, both lost their legs in the explosion. Among the other people in the restaurant who were severely injured were Jimmy Stewart and Irene Arnold, both of whom also lost their legs in the explosion.

A witness later told the inquest that shortly before the explosion she had seen two teenage girls walk out of the restaurant, leaving a bag behind.

Just before 4.30pm the Post Office telephone headquarters received a phone call from a person who claimed that a bomb would explode in Castle Lane in five minutes, but failed to give a precise location. The bomb exploded just one minute later.

On the Monday after the explosion (6 March) the *Irish News* quoted an ambulance paramedic who had witnessed the aftermath of the bomb:

Castle Lane and the wreckage of the Abercorn were awash with blood after the explosion and so were the ambulances. It was the most distressing scene I have ever witnessed. There were bloody mangled bodies lying everywhere and some women were walking around in a daze with their clothing ripped to shreds and blood pouring from their faces and from body wounds.

(*Irish News*, 6 March 1972)

The paper went on to report that:

> Doctors and nurses who were off duty were called to both the RVH
> [Royal Victoria Hospital] and the City Hospital to help with the
> casualties. A fleet of ambulances operated a shuttle service between
> Castle Lane, scene of the explosion, and the hospitals. As blood
> soaked bodies were carried from the ambulances they were taken
> straight to the operating theatres. Many of the 136 casualties—102
> of them women and girls—were suffering from shock and lacera-
> tions caused by flying glass and masonry and were discharged
> within hours.

Janet Bereen's father, a senior anaesthetist at the Royal Victoria
Hospital, was involved in operations on victims of the bomb, unaware
that his daughter had been killed in the explosion.

Staff at the RVH described the hours following the explosion as the
'most appalling since the Blitz'. One surgeon described it as 'the most
dreadful night since the Troubles started'. The coroner subsequently
described the incident as 'pathological murder of the most depraved
kind'.

In the aftermath of the explosion there was some confusion as to
who was responsible for the bomb. At one point the Provisional IRA
claimed that the Woodvale Defence Association (WDA) was responsible, claiming that the WDA had threatened the restaurant because it
did not play 'God Save the Queen' at the end of events held in the
building. A statement from the Provisional IRA denied responsibility
for the explosion: 'This terrible act was undoubtedly the work of
Unionist extremists who fear that their position of privilege is now
seriously threatened by the resistance of the Nationalist people.' Later,
it emerged that the IRA had been responsible.

Surgeon Dr John Robb, who had treated some of the injured, asked
of the bombers: 'What do they think they are going to achieve? When
it is over do they believe that they can put the bits of our society
together any more than we surgeons can put the bits of a human body
together when they have been destroyed irrevocably.' Dr Robb said he
doubted whether the surgeon on duty at the hospital would ever get
over the experience of dealing with the injuries of those caught in the
bomb. And of those injured in the bomb he said, 'People losing, one,
two and in one case three limbs—what do you say to these people?

What do you say to the relatives? What is the sense of it?' (*Belfast Telegraph*, 6 March 1972).

The *Belfast Telegraph* spoke of people being united in grief:

> Two days after it happened, the horror of the Abercorn Restaurant blast is still uppermost in everyone's mind. The knowledge that for some people, the effects will not last for days, or months but 20, 30, 40 or 50 years is simply appalling. Such tragic injuries have been inflicted before … but never have they been detailed so quickly and to such effect. … Even the breakdown of a BBC reporter, as he tried to tell the story on TV of the disaster, conveyed more of the human misery than any words could have.
>
> This is one disaster which, because of men who reacted with their hearts as well as their heads, will not be forgotten.
>
> (*Belfast Telegraph*, 6 March 1972)

Despite the general revulsion at the carnage of the Abercorn bomb, less than two weeks later, on 20 March, the IRA caused more devastation when it exploded a car bomb in Donegall Street, Belfast. Three Belfast Corporation workers were killed while working at the back of a bin lorry, another man was killed while driving along the street and two police officers were killed when the 200 lb car bomb exploded as they were examining the car. The final victim, seventy-nine-year-old Henry Millar, died in hospital two weeks later from injuries sustained in the explosion. Nearly 150 other people were injured.

The first bomb warning, shortly before 11.30am, said that a bomb had been planted in Church Street, off Donegall Street. At 11.55am another call was received by the *Belfast Telegraph,* claiming there was a bomb in a building in Donegall Street. In the meantime, the security forces had moved people from Church Street into Donegall Street.

George Robb, the driver of the bin lorry, was injured in the explosion. At the inquest he recalled how he had been suspicious of the car and the man who had parked it:

> I watched him get out of the car. He kept his face to the wall because he knew I was watching him. I turned to several people and warned them that there could be a bomb in that car, but they never paid any attention to me ….
>
> A few seconds went by—then bang. I was lying on the road. I got

up and I could see a workmate. His arm was so many feet away from him and he was shouting, "help me, help me".

On 21 March the *News Letter* reported:

> It was business as usual until the bomb exploded. For it was not in Church Street but in the street into which so many of the innocent had been lured.
>
> Suddenly a street full of people had become a front-line battlefield. No one knew where the blast had taken place. All they knew was the tons of glass and rubble crashing round them where they fell.
>
> Choking smoke and dust filled the air and even before it had started to settle the screaming began. The bleeding, twisted bodies of men and women were strewn about the street.
>
> Others began to pour out of the nearby premises. The walking wounded helped to carry the others. People carried out searches of their offices and found more injured, some screaming with shock rather than pain.
>
> (*News Letter*, 21 March 1972)

One eyewitness told the *News Letter*: 'All I could hear after the explosion were women screaming hysterically as they were being taken out of offices.'

On the day after the explosion the *Belfast Telegraph* commented on the event and noted that members of the Parachute Regiment had been among the first to come to the aid of the injured:

> As in every tragedy there were examples of selfishness and charity as the rescuers tried to comfort the wounded. The faces of the young paratroopers and policemen in the midst of the carnage were unforgettable. These were men hardened by their job to face the worst of the battle. But they looked stunned. The pictures told the story.
>
> Unhappily, the public must face the realities. After the Abercorn and the other atrocities this was not an isolated incident. It could happen again.
>
> (*Belfast Telegraph*, 5 March 1972)

Three days after the explosion the Provisional IRA claimed that 'proper and adequate warnings have been given before all bombing operations that could cause loss of life or injury to civilians.' The statement continued:

> Several warnings this week have been changed and confused by the British security forces in order to deliberately cause the maximum civilian casualties. This was the principal factor for the tragic loss of life and heavy civilian casualties in Donegall Street on Monday last.

28 MARCH 1972: THE INTRODUCTION OF DIRECT RULE

The suspension of the Northern Ireland Parliament in March 1972 was one of the key events in the course of the Troubles. In a matter of hours a system of government that had lasted for half-a-century was ended by the Westminster Parliament and replaced by a system of Direct Rule from London and an administration headed by the new Secretary of State for Northern Ireland, William Whitelaw.

In the days before the suspension of the Northern Ireland Parliament was announced, Northern Ireland Prime Minister Brian Faulkner appeared to be in an exceptionally belligerent mood. In an interview with the German magazine *Der Spiegel* he was scathing of the Irish government and Taoiseach Jack Lynch, in particular: 'Lynch could destroy the IRA and he could hand over to us the people who carry out their dirty work in the North and then flee to the South. Lynch is morally responsible for these acts of terror in our country' (*News Letter*, 21 March 1972).

Faulkner was also coming under pressure from right-wing unionists, including Vanguard leader William Craig. On 18 March a Vanguard rally in Belfast's Ormeau Park attracted a crowd estimated variously at between 50,000 and 90,000 people, but which the *News Letter* described as the biggest rally since the days of Lord Carson.

Henry Kelly reported for the *Irish Times*:

> Crowds were pouring into Ormeau Park from shortly after midday. Flags, Ulster and British, and bunting hung from poles were displayed around the gates and main platform. Contingents of young men from the main Protestant areas of Belfast arrived, marching in

step behind banners. One large contingent arrived in fairly strict
military formation; about 100 men, wearing dark glasses and berets
and answering orders shouted to them by a leader. There was a
special contingent of women too; dressed in blue anoraks and
wearing blue slacks and blue hats with the badge of the Loyalist
Association of Workers. These women marched and carried flags.

By shortly after 2.30 pm, the park was a massive sea of waving
flags, banners and posters. Groups from various parts of the North
were drawn up under the main platform and the chairman
announced that there would be a token review of some lines of
men drawn up in semi-military fashion. Mr William Craig and the
Rev. Martin Smyth, county grand master of the Orange Order in
Belfast, and other platform speakers, then inspected ranks. A
special contingent of former B Specials formed a colour-party and
they were brought to attention by the chairman of the meeting, Mr
George Allport, prospective Unionist candidate for Bangor.

(*The Irish Times*, 20 March 1972)

In the most controversial segment of his speech to the crowd, Craig
stated:

We are firmly decided to defeat anyone who tries to subvert our
constitution. And we must build up the dossier on those men and
women in this country who are a menace to this country, because
one of these days, if and when the politicians fail us, it may be our
job to liquidate the enemy.

At a meeting in 10 Downing Street on 22 March, Edward Heath told
Faulkner that the British government was taking control of security
in Northern Ireland. Three weeks later Faulkner was interviewed on
television and he recalled what may have been the crucial exchange
between the two men:

Mr Faulkner said he had asked Mr Heath if he had any criticism of
the Stormont administration and he had said "none at all." It was
then he asked Mr Heath why he was wanting to take the decision
he was proposing, and Mr Heath replied: "Because it seems this is
what is required by the opponents of Northern Ireland." Mr Faulkner
said he found this an extraordinary situation, and something no

honourable Prime Minister could accept and he had refused to accept it.

One of the principal aims of the IRA was the suspension of Stormont and since Mr Heath's decision had been announced they had thrown their hats in the air and said they had achieved one of the things they wanted.

(*News Letter*, 11 April 1972)

The announcement of the introduction of Direct Rule from Westminster brought a furious response from unionists. Shipyard workers marched to Belfast city centre in protest and ground crews at Aldergrove Airport, near Belfast, refused to refuel planes.

The first day of a two-day protest strike called by Vanguard on 27 and 28 March saw riots by loyalists in Portadown and sectarian clashes in Lurgan. Power-station workers joined the strike and power cuts lasted for up to six hours at a time. At an ICI plant near Kilroot, loyalists damaged twenty-five cars belonging to Catholic workers who refused to join the strike. In a television interview Craig forecast: 'When the bombing campaign transfers itself to English towns and cities, British politicians, in the interests of expediency, will do a deal with Dublin at our expense' (*Daily Mail*, 28 March 1972). At Belfast City Hall 25,000 gathered to hear an address by Craig. The *Daily Express* reported:

Queen Victoria stood stonily unmoved in a sea of Protestants who thundered applause at fiery words. This crowd was in fact a tenth of the force that stopped work and stopped the province—which not all the guns and bombs of the IRA has succeeded in doing. Hardly a soldier or a policeman as the mass of people wearing "Outlaw Whitelaw" buttons cheered the raising of the loyalist [Ulster] flag above the Union Jack on City Hall.

(*Daily Express*, 28 March 1972)

The *Irish News* reported that 'tens of thousands of Catholic workers' were forced to leave their jobs at the start of the Vanguard strike.

On the second day of the strike the centrepiece was intended to be a rally at Stormont, with another speech by Craig. As the event progressed this developed into a unionist show of unity in opposition to the incoming Direct Rule administration. The *Belfast Telegraph* noted:

The Prime Minister, Mr Brian Faulkner, stood side by side with Vanguard leader Mr William Craig on a Stormont balcony yesterday and addressed the biggest rally of Protestants in Ulster for more than half a century.

Between 150,000 and 200,000 people, many carrying Ulster flags and Union Jacks, cheered the two men and the whole Cabinet when they appeared on the balcony. Most of them never heard the speeches of the Premier and Mr Craig, probably only about the ten or 12,000 nearest the loudspeakers—but for them it was enough to be there to show a solid front.

Thousands had arrived by car and traffic was brought to a near standstill in a wide area around Knock and Dundonald. Many more had walked several miles to be there. Most sported Vanguard badges of some kind and some girls stuck Vanguard labels on their foreheads.

Mr Craig was delayed by the traffic congestion but when the Prime Minister appeared on the balcony and was later followed by the entire Ulster Cabinet, there was a burst of ear-splitting cheering—and a special cheer for Mr John Taylor, who is still recovering from an IRA assassination attempt.

There were more cheers when Mr Craig arrived and he and Mr Faulkner shook hands warmly.

(*Belfast Telegraph*, 29 March 1972)

Despite the ending of the Stormont administration, the Provisional IRA seemed in no mood to compromise. In Free Derry on 8 April, for instance, the local Provisional commander, Martin McGuinness, told a meeting of IRA men in Brandywell that the Social Democratic and Labour Party (SDLP) was 'wasting its time going around seeking for peace. We are fighting on until we get a united Ireland' (quoted in Deutsch and Magowan, Vol.2, p. 169).

21 MAY 1972: THE MURDER OF RANGER WILLIAM BEST

On Sunday 21 May the Official IRA kidnapped and shot dead William Best, a nineteen-year-old member of the Royal Irish Rangers. He was on two weeks' leave from a posting in Germany and had returned home to the Creggan, in Derry, where he was kidnapped and shot dead by the Officials. He had originally intended to stay with his girl-friend in Maghera, but had become worried about his family and so went back to Derry.

According to one source, on the day before his death Best was reported to have been seen near what would later be called 'recreational rioting', or the Saturday afternoon 'teatime riot' as it was known in Derry, which by this time had almost become a local tradition. Colin Smith reported:

> The participants are almost entirely teenage boys (some youngsters who usually have none of the tearful rage of real Irish gut reaction). Most of the rioters seem to regard it as a marginally more attractive proposition than "Match of the Day".
>
> The main object is to provoke the Army into firing rubber bullets which can be sold to American tourists, reporters, and those rare Bogsiders who haven't already got one standing on the mantelpiece.
>
> (*The Observer*, 28 May 1972)

Part of the reason for the Officials' decision to murder William Best may have been rivalry with the Provisional IRA. Less than two weeks before Bloody Sunday the Officials had captured a member of the Royal Scots Regiment, who was visiting his girlfriend. The Officials interrogated the soldier for four hours and then released him. The decision was scoffed at by the Provisionals, who portrayed it as weakness on the Officials' part. After Bloody Sunday the Officials' policy was to kill British soldiers whenever possible. The temptation for some of the Officials was to believe that by murdering a soldier from Derry, they were proving that they were even harder than the Provisionals. Tension had also been heightened in Derry by the death of fifteen-year-old Manus Deery, who had been killed by a ricocheting bullet from an Army sniper on 19 May.

Best was picked up in the Creggan and taken to the Bogside, where he was interrogated. The *Sunday Press* reported:

> As he walked through the streets near the family house he was spotted by two Officials, former school pals of his. They stopped him and put him into a car which brought him to the Officials centre in Meenan Park in the heart of the Bogside. The hooded

Best was brought in, accompanied by two masked men. People walking past the Centre, which serves as an area HQ, believed the hooded figure was to be interrogated for some misdemeanour.

Minutes later, shortly before 10 pm, members of the Official Command Staff began to arrive for a hastily convened meeting. According to a senior Official officer who was present, Best's British Army passbook was examined closely, it revealed that he had joined the Army in March 1971 and had served in Cyprus with the Royal Irish Rangers, before being posted to Germany.

(*Sunday Press*, 28 February 1972)

He was kicked and allegedly burned with cigarettes (after Best's death, in response to this, some women attacked Officials in Derry with lighted cigarettes). Later he was taken to an Official IRA safe house, where a two-hour 'court martial' was held. One of the five members of the Officials' court martial said: 'He told us that he liked the Army. He had just come back from Cyprus and he enjoyed that. He was asked if he would come over here if his regiment was sent and he said "yes".'

William Best was not aware that he was to be killed when he was taken from the house. One of those directly involved in his death said:

We told him he was going to be moved to another house to see a higher authority. We drove him to the top of William Street where there's some waste ground. We put a hood over him and told him that this was because we didn't want him to see the house.

We took him outside the car and told him to mind the step just as if there was a door there, but there wasn't a door or a step there at all. There was nothing. Then we hit him. I know it sounds callous but at least he had no anguish.

(*The Observer*, 28 May 1972)

A statement from the Official IRA in Derry said: 'The soldier in question was apprehended in suspicious circumstances. He was taken and tried by an IRA court and sentenced to death.'

Five Bogside women started a peace campaign in response to the murder. They included Margaret Doherty, a sister of one of those killed on Bloody Sunday. They organised a march of 500 women to the local Official IRA headquarters to protest about the murder. At one point, when an Official IRA spokesman claimed that William Best had been killed as a response to Bloody Sunday, Margaret Doherty responded angrily, 'My brother was one of 13 shot that day and none of those 13 families wanted another killing in the name of the dead' (quoted in Sean Swan, *Official Irish Republicanism 1969 to 1972*, p. 354). However, the women also made it clear that they did not want the barricades removed around no-go areas and did not want the IRA men to leave Free Derry.

The public response to the murder of William Best (on top of the Aldershot bomb) played an important part in the Officials' decision to call an end to their campaign. On 29 May 1972 the Officials declared an indefinite ceasefire, with the qualification that they retained the right to defend themselves against attacks by the British Army 'or by the sectarian forces on either side'.

On 30 May Republican Clubs Chairman Ivan Barr argued that his organisation had approached the Official IRA four weeks earlier about calling a ceasefire because they believed the situation was close to a massive sectarian confrontation. Executive member Malachy McGurran said that 'the Provisionals' campaign seemed calculated to upset Protestants. Factories and shops had been blown up and many Protestant workers had been put out of jobs. The Provisionals by their actions brought to the fore reactionary people and organisations like Mr William Craig and the Vanguard Movement' (*The Irish Times*, 31 May 1972).

While the reaction to the murder of William Best helped lead to a substantial reduction in Official IRA activity, in retrospect the *Belfast Telegraph*'s editorial seems unduly optimistic:

Private Willie Best is dead. How and why he died has helped change the face of not only his native Londonderry but of Ulster as well. The horror of his killing is swinging people towards peace. Last Saturday, the last day in Private Best's life, Ulster seemed on the verge of civil conflict. There had been days of hideous sectarian incidents. The IRA seemed resolved to shoot and bomb the province towards a Protestant backlash.

To-day we can look back on the most encouraging week the peace-seekers have had. There will be setbacks like yesterday's explosion. It has been a long haul. But, at last, more and more people are shaking off the shackles, standing up and being counted, marching, talking, begging the men of violence to stop.

What has happened should be an inspiration to others who may have given up hope that sanity and reason could defeat the gunmen.

(Belfast Telegraph, 27 May 1972)

28 MAY 1972: IRA BOMB KILLS EIGHT IN SHORT STRAND

On 28 May 1972 a bomb that was being moved by IRA members exploded prematurely. The explosion came on a day when loyalists had erected street barricades in an attempt to force the British government to take action against republican no-go areas, and there was some speculation that loyalists might have been responsible for the Short Strand bomb.

The car being used to transport the device, and which was wrecked by the explosion, had been hi-jacked at gunpoint in the Ardoyne area the previous day and the owner warned not to report the theft until 11.00am the next day.

The bomb exploded in Anderson Street, in the Short Strand area, killing eight people. Early reports suggested that six people had died and eighteen were injured. Four of those killed were IRA members. It was several days before a number of the bodies could be identified, and as late as 31 May the *News Letter* was speculating that there may be a ninth victim.

The *Belfast Telegraph* reported:

At least six people died when a bomb exploded in a narrow residential street in the Short Strand area, three car bombs blasted Belfast city centre and a man was shot dead from a passing car as the violence continued over the weekend.

Elsewhere in the city Protestants erected barricades in the Willowfield district as a protest against no-go areas, a 12-year-old English girl holidaying in Belfast was seriously wounded during shooting in the Oldpark area and several other people received gunshot wounds.

But the worst casualty toll was when a 20–40 lb bomb, which the security forces believe was in transit, went off early on Sunday morning at Anderson Street in the Short Strand area.

At least six people died and 18 were injured when the blast ripped through the narrow residential street. Many of the bodies were badly mutilated and it is feared that the final death toll may be even higher. Two houses were demolished by the force of the explosion and at least 50 others were extensively damaged. Security forces said a loaded revolver was found among the debris after the bomb went off.

(*Belfast Telegraph*, 29 May 1972)

Initially there was confusion as to who was responsible for the bomb. The *Daily Telegraph* stated that:

There were conflicting accounts of activity in the street before the bomb exploded, shortly before 3 am. Many local residents were adamant that the attack must have been the work of Protestants. Some said they spotted men in khaki anoraks walking away from the car after parking it, while others said they saw two cars, one apparently a getaway vehicle, driven into the street. The Army said later, however, that a sentry who was at a post nearby did not report any vehicles moving into the street at that time.

(*Daily Telegraph*, 29 May 1972)

In Dublin a Provisional Sinn Féin spokesman claimed that the bomb had been the work of 'British secret service agents'. A statement from the Provisional IRA in Belfast repeated the claim that the bomb had been the work of outsiders:

The Belfast Brigade of the Provisionals, in a statement today, claimed that minutes before the bomb exploded two cars were seen to enter Anderson Street, and one was abandoned. Republicans in the area, added the statement, immediately alerted "an active service unit" and when members of the unit approached the vehicle it exploded.

(*Belfast Telegraph*, 29 May 1972)

In fact, the location of the crater caused by the blast suggested that the bomb had exploded between the vehicle and a house.

On 1 June the *Irish News*, reporting on the funerals of two of the IRA members killed in the explosion (Martin Engelen and Edward McDonnell), still referred to the explosion as being the result of a car bomb:

Included in the large funeral cortege were comrades of the deceased men and groups of young men from battalions and companies of Fianna Eireann, who wore black berets and dark glasses and marched in military style to orders given in Irish.

The Tricolour-draped coffins were carried for some distance along the route by the dead men's comrades and a guard of honour was provided by members of Fianna Eireann.

The funeral procession was led by members of Cumann Na mBan carrying the many floral tributes received by the families of the deceased.

As the funeral proceeded from the church to the cemetery between lines of people which extended for almost the entire route, the drone of a pair of Army helicopters could be heard overhead. There was a complete absence of military or police personnel in the vicinity of the funeral except where the procession turned into the cemetery. There the crowds were observed from the top of the Army post by soldiers with binoculars and cameras. Girls held open umbrellas in front of those taking part in the march to prevent them being identified.

(*Irish News*, 1 June 1972)

Two of the IRA members killed in the premature explosion, Joey Fitzsimmons and Jackie McIlhone, were seventeen years old at the time of their deaths. Later, a history of the Short Strand written from a republican perspective commented:

The young age of these "volunteers" and the engagements they were involved in, may in a sense reflect that the pressing situation at that time, did not allow for adequate training and whilst the commitment they showed could be in no way questioned, a cutting down of operations, and a more adaptable training programme may in the long term have been a better option. In fact in later years the IRA would re-organise itself into more effective cell units with a better standard of training and security awareness.

(Ballymacarrett Research Group, *Lagan Enclave*, p. 75)

What was often lost against the background of high-profile incidents in which large numbers of people were killed was the catalogue of sectarian killings (particularly by loyalists) that was being added to on an ongoing basis. As the journalist Malachi O'Doherty later noted:

In May [1972], loyalists had killed ten people, some of them just killed by trawling gun gangs and shot on the street. By the time of the Provo ceasefire [in June], these killings were routine, though not as frequent as killings by the IRA ... In fact it was not peace at all that was on offer but a phase in which the violence looked less like a liberation struggle against British forces and more like a murky war between Protestants and Catholics in which each side punished the other by killing randomly captured people in ones and twos.

(*The Telling Year: Belfast 1972*, p. 155)

3 JULY 1972: THE UDA CONFRONTS THE ARMY

On 27 June 1972 the IRA began a temporary ceasefire (lasting thirteen days) in the hope of drawing the British government into talks that would lead to a withdrawal from Northern Ireland. Unionists were particularly suspicious of British intentions at this time and loyalist paramilitaries began to set up barricades in certain areas as a response to what they saw as the government's indecisive security policy.

On 1 July 1972 the UDA began building four permanent no-go areas—three in Belfast (in the Woodvale, Oldpark and Shankill areas) and one in Portadown. Road gangs wearing masks and anoraks started breaking up road surfaces with pneumatic drills in streets around these areas and driving stakes and steel girders into the roads.

The situation escalated when residents of Ainsworth Street, on the borderline between the (Protestant) Shankill and (Catholic) Springfield roads, approached members of the UDA and asked for a permanent barricade to be set up in nearby March Street, effectively creating a no-go area. The residents feared that if the barricade was not set up, they would be fenced off from other Protestant areas and thereby left open to attack by republicans. The Army commander in the area agreed that barricades could be put up to seal off the area, except at specified junctions. However, when it became apparent that the barricades would enclose approximately fifty Catholic families inside a loyalist no-go area, the decision of the local commander was overruled by British Army Headquarters. Soldiers began to move in to stop loyalists, who were arriving with road drills to erect the barricade. On learning of the Army's about-face, the UDA sent out a general alarm to its members to assemble and in less than half-an-hour UDA men were pouring into the area from all over Belfast.

Things began to reach crisis-point at 7.00pm when a convoy of hijacked vehicles, including several buses, arrived on the Shankill Road and several hundred UDA men began to form ranks. All were masked, many wore hard hats and crash helmets. Some had walkie-talkie radios for communication and others had red crosses on their hats and carried first aid bags. As the rain began to pour down thousands more UDA men arrived and began forming ranks along Ainsworth Avenue and the surrounding streets. As tension mounted, UDA men continued to arrive from all over the city. One newspaper reported: 'The men marched in orderly fashion into Ainsworth Avenue, the vanguard taking up positions only a few yards from the [Army] troops at the junction of March Street. When all the companies of the UDA had arrived their ranks were so dense that they stretched almost to Shankill Road' (*News Letter*, 4 July 1972).

In less than ninety minutes the UDA had assembled 8,000 men in battledress, armed with iron bars and clubs. The men in the front ranks carried riot shields similar to those being used by the Army.

Women and children were evacuated from nearby houses in case of serious trouble. In March Street, at the centre of the confrontation, many residents left their homes as bands of youths broke paving stones to use as weapons. Crates of milk bottles were stacked up, to be used as petrol bombs. Lorry-loads of stones were driven up from the Shankill and stockpiled in nearby streets and hijacked vehicles were parked close by, ready to be used as barricades. The Army also suspected that a truck at the rear of the UDA ranks was filled with arms and ammunition and that the crew was ready to issue the weapons when they got the order.

On the Army side dozens of Saracen armoured cars, Ferret scout cars, Land Rovers and heavy vehicles brought soldiers, who took up positions facing the loyalists. Army marksmen carrying rifles fitted with night-sights were also deployed. As General Robert Ford, the Army commander, rushed to the scene, 250 troops faced the loyalist paramilitaries. A UDA officer in mask and dark glasses said: 'We don't want a confrontation with the army—but we will fight them if we have to. This whole thing is just about fifty spikes that we want to put in the road. If they don't let us, we will fight them all night and all day if necessary' (*News Letter*, 4 July 1972). At one point about two dozen women moved into the street and formed a thin line between the two groups.

Before meeting the UDA leaders General Ford telephoned William Whitelaw and warned him that if the UDA advanced on the Army, his men were likely to be overrun unless he had authority for the troops to fire. Whitelaw gave Ford permission for the troops to open fire, but only as a last resort (Whitelaw, p. 97).

A woman in one of the terrace houses off Ainsworth Avenue offered the use of her front room for the talks and it was here that Ford, accompanied by senior officials, two other officers and a military policeman, met UDA leaders Jim Anderson, Tommy Herron, David Fogel and Sammy Doyle. As the meeting in the terrace house continued, the paramilitaries massed along the Avenue beat their batons on their shields, chanted, 'UDA, UDA' and sang loyalist songs.

Talks between Ford and the UDA men continued for three hours, until just before 11.00pm, when agreement was reached—there would be no permanent barricade, but the Army would carry out patrols and set up a checkpoint at the disputed area. Unarmed UDA men would be allowed to move unhindered behind this checkpoint. News of the agreement was welcomed by the UDA rank-and-file with cheers and shouts; they clearly saw the outcome as a victory. They left in the commandeered vehicles, which were parked in nearby streets. As the cavalcade snaked down the Shankill Road, local residents came out of the side-streets to cheer the UDA members as they made their way home. When asked by the press if he had expected a confrontation, General Ford smiled but declined to answer (*News Letter*, 4 July 1972).

There is little doubt that the potential confrontation between the UDA and the Army was defused at the cost of some concessions on the part of the authorities as they could not afford an all-out conflict with loyalists, particularly at that time. This feeling was largely reciprocated by the loyalist paramilitaries. One UDA leader later commented: 'We did not confront British troops last night. It was a confrontation with the politicians. If violence had broken out, by sheer power of numbers the UDA would have won. But we consider we had a victory because violence did not occur' (*Belfast Telegraph*, 4 July 1972). The next day's *Belfast Telegraph* editorial summed up the outcome by stating:

The trial of strength in the area between the Shankill and Springfield Roads last night is as near as the UDA has come to a pitched battle with the army. It was averted only at the cost of the generals admitting that a private paramilitary group has the right, through might, to mount patrols in a sealed-off enclave of a British city. Both sides may claim a "victory" of sorts, with some justification, but in fact the losers are all those who value democratic rights.

(Belfast Telegraph, 4 July 1972)

21 JULY 1972: BLOODY FRIDAY

On Friday 21 July 1972 the Provisional IRA exploded twenty-six bombs across Belfast in just over an hour. Nine people were killed and 130 injured. A car bomb at Oxford Street bus station killed four Ulsterbus workers and two soldiers. Two women and a schoolboy were killed by another car bomb on the Cavehill Road, in north Belfast. Some of the bodies were so badly mutilated that it was initially thought that a greater number of people had died. Although telephone warnings were given by the IRA, the emergency services could not cope with the number of bombs and bomb scares. The day later came to be called 'Bloody Friday'.

One of those killed by the car bomb on the Cavehill Road was Stephen Parker, the fourteen-year-old son of Rev. Joseph Parker. Rev. Parker was only able to identify his son's remains by his hands, a box of trick matches found in his son's trouser pocket and a Scout belt he had been wearing at the time of his death.

On the day the 'bomb a minute blitz' took place, a *Belfast Telegraph* report conveyed something of its scale and the confusion it created:

… the police, the Army and a newspaper office were swamped with anonymous warning telephone calls but it is not known if all the streets were cleared in time.

Firemen were fighting a large fire in Donegall Street after a huge blast there. And firemen were also at the M2 flyover after a blast near Bellevue on the Antrim Road.

Two railway stations were among the targets of the bombers and by mid-afternoon the trail of destruction was pinpointed in these areas.

Botanic Avenue (bomb in a bread van); Garmoyle Street; Queen's Bridge (hole blown in structure by bomb); Donegall Street (huge explosion followed by raging fire which swamped city centre with smoke); Ormeau Avenue (explosion near the gas works); Smithfield (bus station damaged); York Street (railway station blasted); Bellevue (M2 flyover bridge damaged) ... Brookvale Avenue (hotel damaged by blast); Dundrod (police investigating reports of explosion near airport, but location not known); Twinbrook estate, Dunmurry (target not known).

(*Belfast Telegraph*, 21 July 1972)

Like many others, the *Guardian* initially reported that eleven people had been killed in Belfast's 'hour of terror'; the *Daily Telegraph* said thirteen had been killed. It was not until 24 July that the actual death toll of nine was confirmed. On 22 July the *Guardian* reported:

After 2.45pm, when the bombing began, and for much of the afternoon, Belfast was reduced to near total chaos and panic. Girls and men wept openly, hugging each other for safety in the main streets as plumes of smoke rose around them and dull thuds echoed from wall to wall.

It was impossible for anyone to feel perfectly safe. As each bomb exploded there were cries of terror from people who thought they had found sanctuary, but in fact were just as exposed as before.

People tried to leave the city centre as quickly as possible, leading to traffic jams. Many others were stranded when bus services were cancelled and either walked or hitch-hiked home.

The *Guardian* report added ominously that if William Whitelaw did not act quickly, there could be a reaction from the UDA.

By the following day a clearer picture was beginning to emerge of the events of what was quickly dubbed 'Bloody Friday'. The first bomb exploded at a hotel in Brookvale Avenue just before 2.30pm, followed by twelve more explosions within the next fifteen minutes.

Within minutes of the opening onslaught scores of ambulances, their sirens wailing, were struggling through heavy traffic. Soldiers and policemen fought vainly to get the rescue services through to the blast scenes.

Fires broke out after many of the bombs to add to the chaos. And weekend shoppers, who thronged many of the busy streets, rushed for cover as bomb after bomb shattered the city.

> The hub of Belfast resembled a disaster area with mutilated bodies, people with torn limbs, women and children in hysterics and bombed buildings engulfed in flames.
>
> (*News Letter*, 22 July 1972)

In all, more than twenty bombs exploded across Belfast in less than ninety minutes. Some of the most horrific scenes were at Oxford Street bus station. One of those present, Patrick McKee, was sitting in a bar opposite the station when the bomb went off:

> An explosion blew out all the windows. I jumped through one of them and ran across into the bus station which was wrecked and blazing. People were running out screaming in sheer panic. I fought my way through the crowd and the scene in the waiting rooms, the café and the loading bays was sickening. People with awful injuries were lying everywhere. A young girl aged about 18 badly bleeding from a wound in her stomach staggered up moaning, "Please help me". I carried her out and laid her on the floor of the bar. I ran back four more times and each time picked up an injured woman and took them across to the hotel.

Roisin Burns was waiting for a bus home when the explosion occurred:

> I was crushed to the floor by people being blown off their feet. I was frantic. My legs were trapped as I tried to scramble out. I thought it was the end. I helped an elderly woman to her feet, then rushed to where the door had been.
>
> My eyes were filled with smoke and I couldn't stop coughing. It was blind panic by everybody. Suddenly a policeman grabbed me and helped me out. People were scrambling about everywhere. In the panic people were getting trampled. I rushed to try to help. One woman was kneeling over a small child crying and sobbing for help. Her face was covered in blood and the child looked lifeless. I offered to carry the child away but got knocked down again in the scramble by other people to get away.
>
> Through the smoke I saw torn pieces of bodies between twisted metal, bricks and shattered glass. I thought, "Oh my God" and was sick. A soldier grabbed me, helped me to my feet and told me to get out quick because another blast was expected.
>
> (*Daily Express*, 22 July 1972)

The *Belfast Telegraph* reported of the 'Death Terminal':

> The scene inside the bus station was one of devastation. The bomb had apparently been placed near the depot manager's office; the nearby cafeteria was a burned out shell and glass was everywhere. Police and troops carried plastic bags as they went about the gruesome task of collecting the mutilated bodies, parts of which were flung up to 30 yards away by the blast.
>
> (*Belfast Telegraph*, 22 July 1972)

Like almost every other source, the *Irish Times* was scathing of what it saw as the Provisionals' 'Nazi-style disregard for life'. The newspaper's editorial added:

> We might at least be spared the excuse that adequate warnings were given, and the regrets that life was lost. While yesterday's events were worse in degree than usual, they were the same in nature as many before them. The chief injury is not to the British Army, to the establishment or to big business, but to the plain people of Belfast and of Ireland.
>
> (*The Irish Times*, 22 July 1972)

31 JULY 1972: OPERATION MOTORMAN

On 7 July 1972 Secretary of State William Whitelaw and Northern Ireland Office (NIO) ministers had met Provisional IRA leaders for discussions during a temporary IRA ceasefire, but there had been no areas of agreement between the two groups. The ending of the IRA ceasefire brought an increase in violence, and after Bloody Friday there was even greater pressure for action to be taken against the Provisionals, and particularly against no-go areas.

In the days before the Army's Operation Motorman was mounted, troops were brought into Northern Ireland from Britain and West Germany. Hercules transport planes flew 1,000 soldiers into Aldergrove Airport, the assault ship *Fearless* brought 600 members of the Royals Scots Regiment and the *Intrepid* brought a dozen heavily armoured Centurion tanks fitted with bulldozer blades. On the eve of Operation Motorman there was amassed over 28,000 soldiers, including 5,300 members of the UDR, as well as armoured vehicles and a troop of armoured bulldozers to clear barricades, making it the largest concentration of troops in Northern Ireland since the end of the Second World War.

On 20 July more than 250 soldiers had moved into the former Grand Central Hotel in Belfast's Royal Avenue. The hotel had closed in September 1971 because of the fall off in business caused by the Troubles. Security in Belfast city centre had also been stepped up, as the *News of the World* reported:

> An uneasy calm pervaded Belfast. Soldiers stood guard at almost every street corner, stopping women to search their shopping bags, and frisking men. And road blocks were set up to stop motorists and check their identities in a new bid to prevent the bombers infiltrating the city centre.
>
> (*News of the World*, 23 July 1972)

Almost lost in the background were the numerous incidents in which one or two individuals were murdered. Among these were the cases of Patrick O'Neill, Rose McCartney and Francis Arthurs, who were murdered by the UDA on 22 July. The *Irish Times* reported:

> On Saturday morning the bodies of Miss Rose McCartney of 87 Irish Street in the Falls area and her fiancé, Mr Patrick O'Neill (26) from Havana Street in the Ardoyne were found in a car at Forthriver Road near the Protestant Glencairn estate. Miss McCartney and her fiancé had both been shot dead. She was a well known folk singer in Belfast.
>
> The body of Mr Francis McArthurs [sic] (34) of Fallswater Street was found in a stolen car at Liffey Street in the Oldpark area on Saturday. He was badly beaten before being shot, police said, and it was understood that Mr McArthurs had been travelling to the Ardoyne area in a taxi when the vehicle was stopped by Protestant vigilantes. Mr McArthurs was taken from the taxi but the driver and girl were allowed to go on.
>
> (*The Irish Times*, 24 July 1972)

On 25 July the funeral took place of eighteen-year-old James Joseph Jones, the one hundredth soldier to be killed during the Troubles.

In advance of Operation Motorman, on 26 July troops removed barricades in Andersonstown. The *Belfast Telegraph* reported:

> Barricades surrounding the Andersonstown area of Belfast were ripped down when more than 600 troops mounted a three-hour operation early today. Five hundred men of the Prince of Wales' Own Regiment of Yorkshire, backed by men of the Royal Engineers and 19 Field Squadron, moved into the area at exactly midnight.
>
> The troops took over the area within a matter of minutes, but when they moved in to tackle the barricades their arrival was heralded by a "bush telegraph" of civilians banging on dustbin lids and blowing whistles.
>
> The troops were almost certain that they would come under fire. Army marksmen moved in to cover the engineers, and troops travelling through the area in Saracen carriers were told to batten down their vehicles. As they moved deeper into the area, however, the attack was in the form of petrol bombs and missiles. The soldiers were attacked by youths with petrol bombs and stones in the Derrin Park–Fruithill area and they replied with rubber bullets.
>
> (*Belfast Telegraph*, 26 July 1972)

Army engineers used bulldozers to rip out the barriers and roadblocks and a number of obstructions were checked for booby-traps.

On 28 July the number of troops in Northern Ireland continued to build towards nearly 30,000, and an Army move against no-go areas was heavily telegraphed. However, SDLP leader Gerry Fitt commented:

> I would hope that these troops have been brought in to protect the lives of innocent Catholics in Belfast which have been at risk in recent weeks and months … People have called for moves against the Bogside and Creggan. I would point out that the barricades there have not been the cause of desperate and bloody sectarian murders. While in Belfast, for example, it is quite obvious that innocent Catholics are being caught at UDA roadblocks and murdered.
>
> (*The Irish Times*, 28 July 1972)

The operation began at 4.00am on Monday 31 July. The Army set up an outer cordon around Belfast and Derry. In Derry the Bogside and Creggan estates were sealed off, as were Andersonstown and

Ballymurphy in Belfast. Troops moved in to clear the barricades and had claimed control of the area by 7.00am. The Army suffered no casualties, but two Catholic youths were killed in Derry. The operation was formally ended on 1 December 1972.

Operation Motorman was heralded as a success by the British government and media. On the morning after the operation the *Daily Telegraph* reported:

> All the former no-go areas in Northern Ireland were last night controlled by the Army. About 13,000 troops taking part in Operation Motorman had established their ascendancy after a dawn action in which specially equipped tanks rooted out barricades and soldiers moved in with little resistance.
>
> The Army had no casualties. In Belfast not a shot was fired, but in Londonderry five people were hit during short gunfights. A 16-year-old youth and a man of 19 were killed ...
>
> Operation Motorman began at 4 am. Tanks with their guns trained to the rear moved up to barricades. Most of the barriers round Catholic no-go areas had to be destroyed by troops, but in some places they were helped by Catholic residents. Protestant militants of the Ulster Defence Association helped to remove their own barricades. In Belfast, about 5,500 troops took part in the operation. Four thousand were employed in Londonderry and about 3,000 in other areas, including Lurgan, Armagh, Coalisland, Cookstown, Portadown and Dungannon.
>
> After the troops took over they carried out small-scale searches at secluded addresses. Twenty-four people were arrested and 20 of them were still being interviewed last night. Weapons, ammunition and explosives were found.
>
> By last night men of the Royal Ulster Constabulary were again on patrol in the Bogside and Creggan areas of Londonderry and in parts of Belfast which they had been unable to enter for months.
>
> (*Daily Telegraph*, 1 August 1972)

The *Irish News* pointed out that the seizure of a number of community halls in Catholic areas of west Belfast to provide accommodation for troops had had a serious impact on social activities. The newspaper also painted a less glowing portrait of house searches, noting that:

In the Spamount Street home of a man alleged to be a member of the Provisional IRA the alcove walls around the fireplace were ripped open by the troops, the television smashed and four puppies taken away by the soldiers. Other residents in the street said that soldiers came around the houses shouting obscenities and kicking in the back doors.

(*Irish News*, 1 August 1972)

In the wake of the Army's largest single operation of the Troubles there were still areas in which the security forces found it difficult to operate, but these were no longer in the form of the overt no-go areas that had existed before Motorman.

31 JULY 1972: THE CLAUDY BOMBS

At 10.20am on the same morning as Operation Motorman was initiated, a car bomb exploded at McElhinney's pub in Claudy, Co. Londonderry. Five minutes later, as people were running to escape the explosion, a second car bomb exploded at Beaufort Arms Hotel, then a third car bomb exploded outside the village post office. From the village's population of less than 1,000, six people died immediately and three more died later from injuries they received in the blasts. The explosions injured fifty others and damaged most of the shops and houses in the village.

Among those who died were nine-year-old Kathryn Eakin, who was killed by shrapnel from the first explosion while playing outside her family's shop. Fifty-nine-year-old Elizabeth McElhinney was killed while serving petrol at a street petrol pump. Sixteen-year-old Willie Temple had just started a job on a milk delivery round. Sixty-year-old David Miller died while helping people injured in the first explosion to the medical centre when he was caught by the second blast. As police officers tried to move people away from the second bomb, many walked directly towards the third.

The bombing of Claudy was widely viewed as an attempt by the IRA to draw soldiers away from the Bogside in the wake of Operation Motorman. It was subsequently revealed that the telephone the bombers had intended to use to deliver a warning was not working because the telephone exchange was out of order as the result of an earlier explosion. Although most believed that the Provisional IRA planted the bombs, on the night of the bombings Seán McStiofáin, the Provisionals' Chief of Staff, denied the IRA was responsible, stating, 'obviously such action can only suit the British military to divert attention from the massive invasion of the Nationalist areas in Derry, Belfast and other Northern towns' (*Belfast Telegraph*, 1 August 1972). Though few believed the Provisionals' statement, another categorical denial was issued a week later.

At the inquest in September 1973 Londonderry coroner Hubert O'Neill (who a month earlier had presided over the Bloody Sunday inquests) described the deaths as 'sheer unadulterated, cold, calculating, fiendish murder'.

Counsel for the Ministry of Home Affairs, Robert McCartney, told the inquest that the first bomb exploded at 10.20am, adding, 'You will hear evidence of the scenes of confusion and horror after this village had been literally ripped apart from the explosion.' Joseph McCloskey, who was killed in the explosion, was talking to Patrick O'Donnell, who was thrown from the car he was sitting in by the blast. Rose McLaughlin was killed while in her husband's café talking to a neighbour and fifteen-year-old Patrick Joseph Connolly and Arthur Hone were killed in the street by shrapnel.

After the first bomb went off police shouted to people to move away from a suspicious van parked outside the post office. In doing so, they unwittingly moved towards a third bomb, in a van parked outside the Beaufort Hotel. The third bomb exploded, killing David Miller, James McClelland and William Temple. McCartney said that they had been 'literally torn apart by metal and shrapnel'.

RUC Inspector Andrew McCarter told the inquest that after the first explosion he saw smoke belching from the village and heard people scream. As he rushed to the village by car he tried, but failed because of poor radio reception, to inform police in Derry about the explosion. After moving his car to higher ground he eventually got through to the authorities and asked for the fire service, ambulances and help to be sent immediately by the police.

Inspector McCarter told the inquest that he suspected there were other bombs and warned people to clear away, but as people had relatives killed or injured it was difficult to convince them that they were still in danger:

When Sergeant Jones told him there was a car bomb outside the post office he said he shouted a warning and told people to get out of the way. A constable shouted to him that there were two more bombs and he again shouted to the people saying, "There are two more bombs in this car. For God's sake get out." Just then there was a loud explosion, and he expected not to see the van outside the post office. It was still there but then suddenly there was a flash of light and the van disintegrated. He went to Church Street and saw that the second bomb had exploded outside the hotel and he found the bodies of two people at the rear of a milk lorry and one at the opposite side of the street.

(*The Irish Times*, 26 September 1973)

In the wake of the bombs there was immense sympathy for the town and grandiose plans were made by official sources to 'get Claudy back on its feet', but these ambitions took years to come to fruition, as did payment of compensation, which inevitably created a feeling among the villagers that they had been forgotten. Three years after the bombing of Claudy local shoemaker Johnny Burke expressed the dis-illusionment of many of those who survived:'The people here were too grief-stricken at the time to do anything, or really care about things like money. When, nine months or a year later the grief sub-sided, they found that nobody was really interested anymore' ('Claudy—three years after', *Sunday Press*, 27 July 1975).

In September 2002 there was renewed interest in the events sur-rounding the bombing of Claudy when police began a review of the investigation and an anonymous letter to a UUP councillor, Mary Hamilton (who had been injured in the Claudy explosions), claimed that a Catholic priest, later named as James Chesney, had played a central role in bombing Claudy. It was also revealed that Secretary of State William Whitelaw had met Cardinal William Conway, the head of the Catholic Church in Ireland, in December 1972 and discussed Fr Chesney's activities. The priest was subsequently transferred to Co. Donegal, where he died of cancer in 1980. SDLP member Ivan Cooper supported the view that Chesney was a central figure in the bombing:

Within a couple of days, a man lurked like a scared rabbit outside one of my constituency offices. He told me the IRA was behind the bomb and I had every reason to believe him. He gave no names and

I asked no names. That is the way it was then. It was dangerous to know too much. But several months later, I became aware of the identities and I have absolutely no doubt that Father Chesney was involved.

(*The Guardian*, 21 September 2002)

If Chesney was involved in the bombing of Claudy (as seems as least possible), then the decision to remove him from Northern Ireland appears to have been a decision to pursue pragmatism over justice. It requires little speculation to suggest that the decision not to interview or charge Chesney with involvement in the bombing was taken at a senior level, motivated by the view that this was a lesser evil than revealing the involvement of a Catholic priest in such an atrocity. The revelation would undoubtedly have heightened sectarian tensions and could have made Catholic priests targets for loyalist paramilitaries. In effect, then, it appears that the decision to cover up Chesney's alleged role in Claudy was an entirely political one.

22 AUGUST 1972: NEWRY CUSTOMS OFFICE BOMB

By mid-1972 the security situation appeared to be out of control and Northern Ireland society was tearing itself apart. On 21 August the *News Letter* reported on 'another weekend of torment in Ulster', outlining the main security incidents that had taken place over the previous two days:

A gunman was shot by troops; two men were assassinated by murder squads; bombs wrecked an electricity sub-station, two public houses, a café and hotel, and a massive bomb was planted in chapel grounds. This was the pattern of round-the-clock violence which rocked Ulster during the weekend.

The bombing campaign in Belfast heralded the start of a week-end in which there were 21 major incidents leading up to a half-hour vicious gun battle in the Lower Falls area last night when troops shot one gunman after an attack on a mobile patrol and observation post in North Howard Street.

(*News Letter*, 21 August 1972)

On 21 August there were bomb explosions in Belfast at a Lisburn Road paint depot and at the GPO sorting office in Pilot Street, as well as a series of armed robberies in Belfast, Castlewellan and Armagh. Three separate post offices were raided in Co. Tyrone, an eighty-six-year-old man narrowly escaped injury when three youths threw a can of petrol through his window in Westland Street and the device failed to ignite. An incendiary device in Wellworth's store in Strabane also failed to ignite, but was thrown into the street where it burst into flames. In Derry shots were fired at an Army foot patrol; the Army returned fire, but no one was hit.

As was often the case at this time, just when it seemed that things could get no worse another major incident occurred.

The bomb at Newry Customs Office exploded at 9.45am on 22 August, moments after one of the customs officers pressed the alarm button, setting off a siren. Eight people in the room were killed instantly, and another died in hospital. One of the customs officers killed, thirty-one-year-old Marshall Lawrence, had been due to return to Scotland with his wife and five children the following week.

Three of those killed were IRA members who had brought the bomb into the customs post (at first, the bodies of only two could be identified), four were customs officers and two were lorry drivers waiting for clearance at the post. Twelve other people were injured.

Peter Chippindale reported for the *Guardian*:

Yesterday's bomb was brought to the customs station by three men in a black car. Two men, one armed with a Thompson sub-machine gun and the other with a revolver, carried the bomb in the box round to the back of the building, where they met one of the Customs marshallers who supervise the movement of lorries at the station. They forced him to go into the building at gunpoint, but one of the Customs officers inside managed to sound the alarm siren.

Police said the bomb went off five seconds later, before anyone had a chance to get out of the building. The explosion, at one end of the building in the entrance hall, blew out the end wall and parts of the front and back walls. Half the inside of the building was wrecked and parts of the ceiling came down. Troops and firemen found three of the bodies piled together in the heaps of rubble and shattered filing cabinets.

An Army spokesman said that the third man, who had stayed in the car at the front building, drove off immediately the bomb exploded but crashed his car into a lorry outside. He then ran off. Troops from the Argyll and Sutherland Highlanders who arrived at the scene minutes afterwards threw a security cordon round the area, but the man escaped and is believed to have crossed the border into the Republic.

(*The Guardian*, 23 August 1972)

The *Irish Press* reported:

Immediately after the explosion security forces rushed to the scene and started rescue work. Their job was a grisly one as most of the bodies had been blown apart. Rescue workers reported finding human limbs in fields up to 100 yards away. Teams of ambulances arrived at the post to take the injured people to hospital and soldiers tried to piece together the bodies to find out how many people had been killed.

At first only five could be found, but then a sixth was discovered. Later in the day a seventh body was pieced together and it was learned that customs officer Lawrence had died in hospital, bringing the total to eight.

(*Irish Press*, 23 August 1972)

The SDLP's Paddy O'Hanlon commented:

This explosion, in which eight people have died, must rank with Claudy, Bloody Friday and Bloody Sunday as one of the most tragic events in the history of a community in which tragedy has become a daily occurrence. What contribution—save to the spiralling statistics of death—does this instance make towards solving the problems of this community?

Meanwhile, a statement from the Official IRA called on rank-and-file members of the Provisionals to 'refuse to allow their dedication and patriotism to be exploited in pursuance of a campaign which is anti-national, anti-people and against all the principles of genuine Republican traditions and ideals'.

The Provisionals claimed responsibility for the bomb and expressed regret for the 'unintentional loss of life', but ultimately seemed more concerned with criticising the Officials:

In their very prompt statement condemning this morning's accidental explosion in Newry, the National Liberation Movement (Official IRA) have once more joined in the Imperialist chorus led by British Government members. Their attitude in these matters contrasts sharply with that of the Provisional IRA last February when the NLM themselves accidentally killed seven non-combatants at Aldershot.

Hypocrisy and the advertising of their own alleged virtue are the hallmarks of these statements from the so-called officials.

On 27 August another two IRA members were killed by their own bomb in Downpatrick, leading the *Irish Times* to comment:

Bombing in the North has reached a new peak of destructiveness, and the death toll includes some of the bombing teams themselves. In reprisal there has come a wave of random assassinations. ...

If dislocation of commercial life is the aim of the Provisionals in the North, they are likely to be disappointed. If dislocation of communication is aimed at, the results will be patchy. And if World War Two is at all a model, civilian morale will not suffer under what is, by comparison, a pinprick.

The analogy is not exact. In World War Two, groups of enemy countries were involved; in the North today the bombers are killing and injuring fellow countrymen with whom they say they hope to unite in a new Ireland.

The bombing in the North may go on for a long time. The same can be said for the campaign of assassination of Catholics. The police and British Army cannot stop it. And if the bombing did stop, is there any guarantee that the selective killings would cease on the other side? The Protestant killers may argue that they have leeway to make up.

(*The Irish Times*, 28 August 1972)

12 JUNE 1973: SIX PENSIONERS KILLED BY COLERAINE BOMB

One of the inevitable outcomes of the Troubles has been that some events have become central to the story of the conflict while others have been largely forgotten. One such 'forgotten massacre' took place in Coleraine, in 1973.

On 12 June 1973 two cars stolen in the south Londonderry area were used to carry bombs into the quiet town of Coleraine, Co. Londonderry. At 3.00pm, a 100–150 lb bomb, hidden in a Ford Cortina car, exploded outside a wine shop in Railway Road, killing six people and injuring thirty-three others, including a number of children returning home from school.

Seventy-year-old Francis Campbell, his seventy-two-year-old wife Dinah and seventy-six-year-old sister-in-law Elizabeth Craigmile were killed and the Campbell's daughter, Hilary, was severely injured by the explosion. They had been on holiday at Ballycastle and were shopping in Coleraine when the bomb exploded in Railway Road.

Sixty-year-old Elizabeth Palmer worked in the wine shop, which was hit by the explosion. She was found dead in the window of the store. Seventy-two-year-old Robert Scott was shopping in the town when he was caught in the explosion and killed. Widow Nan Davis was on her way to collect her pension allowance. She stopped to talk to her brother-in-law and was killed when the bomb exploded. *Times* correspondent Robert Fisk reported how, in the aftermath of the explosion, one man, with his arm severed, attempted to stand up and run from the area. Another person died on the pavement while being comforted by wounded civilians.

The only mitigating factor was that the carnage would undoubtedly have been much worse if the bomb had exploded fifteen minutes later when schoolgirls from the nearby high school would have been leaving school and walking along the street.

The second car bomb was left in a garage in Hanover Place and it exploded five minutes after the Railway Road bomb. Although the explosion wrecked the garage and destroyed a number of cars, no one was injured. That explosion did, however, add to the overall level of confusion and panic. A warning that another bomb had been left in Society Street proved to be a hoax. Although a warning had been given for the Hanover Place bomb, there was no warning given for the car bomb in Railway Road. This led many to speculate that the bombers' intention was to draw people towards the bomb in Railway Road and inflict as many casualties as possible.

Jarvis Grant, a reporter for the local newspaper, the *Northern Constitution*, whose offices were close to the scene of the explosion, described the scene immediately after the bomb exploded:

> When the smoke cleared the street was covered in debris. A
> number of bodies lay on the pavement and bystanders attended the
> injured. A temporary first aid post was set up in the nearby swim-
> ming pool and the injured, many of them still screaming from
> shock, were given first aid. Motorists took some of the injured to
> hospital and ambulances from outlying towns also assisted.
>
> Just after the bomb exploded I saw a woman with blood stream-
> ing from her face. She had a small child in her arms and blood was
> also coming from its face. Her other child, aged about two, was
> screaming. I helped to take some of the less seriously injured to the
> first aid centre. Many of them were severely shocked but uninjured.
>
> Minutes after the bomb exploded a fire broke out in a paint store
> and what seemed seconds later the second explosion in the garage
> sent people screaming in all directions. Rumours of further bombs
> spread rapidly and shoppers sped home out of the town as quickly
> as they could.
>
> (*The Irish Times*, 13 June 1973)

Others near the explosion were also injured. Victor McFadden was in
a car with his family when the bomb exploded nearby and his three-
year-old daughter Amanda was badly burned in the resulting fire. Mr
McFadden recalled:

> We were all driving to Portrush and were passing this car when
> everything seemed to go black. Amanda was sitting on my knee in
> the passenger seat and I jumped out of the car with her and ran.
> But I did not know where I was running to … It seemed as if a ball
> of fire had come right through the car. The passenger seat was
> badly burned and the sun visor was completely melted.
>
> When we got out there were bodies lying everywhere. I bundled
> Amanda into a police car and had her rushed up to the hospital.
> Her little face is badly burned and her hair has been completely
> burned away.
>
> (*Belfast Telegraph*, 13 June 1973)

In the aftermath of the event the local Presbyterian Minister, Rev. Brian
Kingsmore, remarked, 'Why these tragedies should be permitted by

God I do not know, but we are reminded in the Bible that "vengeance is mine saith the Lord" and some day these evil men will have to give an account to God.'

On 14 June the *Irish News* editorial spoke of the 'Horror in Coleraine' and said:

> There are no moral dimensions in these deaths by car bomb. Those who engineered or committed the Coleraine slaughter do not give a damn about the most basic of all rights: the right to life itself … After Coleraine, we are faced again with the terrible pathology of human beings who see nothing wrong in the routine of destruction by methods which can so quickly mean death and indescribable injury to innocent people. It is almost futile to say that despite Coleraine we must all try again for a return to sanity and the restoration of human reason. Otherwise, civilisation here is no more than an unpleasant joke and our humanity the thinnest of masquerades for the beasts of the jungle.
>
> (*Irish News*, 14 June 1973)

Later that month a coroner at the Coleraine inquest described 12 June 1973 as the worst day in the town's history. A police superintendent told the inquest jury that 'Six more innocent people could not have been selected from the whole of Northern Ireland to die in the blast that day.'

Although, as the *Irish Times* noted on the day after the explosion, the Coleraine bombing ranked with the worst atrocities seen in the Troubles, it has now largely been forgotten within the broader narrative of the conflict. That is possibly because the Coleraine bombing took place at the height of the Troubles, when such incidents were becoming all too familiar and the public was somewhat numbed by the frequency and randomness of the violence. It may also be because there was no question as to which organisation was responsible—the Provisional IRA. The fact that many politicians were more concerned with the outcome of the forthcoming Northern Ireland Assembly elections than with the impact of specific incidents on the ground may also have been a factor. Whatever the cause, the Coleraine bombing arguably deserves greater notice from historians than it has received to date, not least because its casualties were among the most vulnerable in society.

6 DECEMBER 1973: THE SUNNINGDALE CONFERENCE

Following the suspension of the Northern Ireland Parliament in March 1972 the British government began a process to try to find an alternative, locally elected administration for Northern Ireland. The preferred British option was for a nationalist–unionist power-sharing executive alongside an Irish dimension that would provide institutional links between Northern Ireland and the Republic. In October 1973 the Ulster Unionist Party, SDLP and Alliance agreed to form a power-sharing executive, provided the details of an Irish dimension—in reality a Council of Ireland—could also be agreed. This was set to be discussed by representatives of the British and Irish governments and Northern Ireland Executive at the Civil Service College at Sunningdale, in Berkshire, in December.

In the lead-up to the tripartite talks the *Irish News* believed that an agreement was inevitable, but added that 'there is a strong feeling—most intense in Whitehall, but largely shared in Dublin Government circles—that Mr Faulkner needs protection from the loyalist extremists, and that he, like other participants, will need substantial concessions to take home with him' (*Irish News*, 1 December 1973). The *News Letter* laid heavy emphasis on the importance to unionists of removing the Republic's constitutional claim to Northern Ireland:

> It is to be hoped that when the tripartite meeting assembles time and energy will not be spent discussing irrelevant minor subjects while this, the crucial issue, remains unresolved on the table.
>
> For the Unionist delegates it is a prerequisite that is absolutely vital. It is the make or break point and it will not be good enough, and it will not be accepted, if an attempt is made to delude the people of the Province with a form of words bearing a suggestion that "a very firm statement of recognition" is equivalent to the guarantee that is essential.
>
> (*News Letter*, 1 December 1973)

The replacement of William Whitelaw as Secretary of State in the days before the conference was almost universally criticised by those within Northern Ireland who wanted an agreement. The new Secretary of State, Francis Pym, only arrived in Northern Ireland on 4 December.

On that same day the *Times'* Stewart Tendler noted that 'the council of Ireland, and not power-sharing, is the raw nerve irritated by fear of the unknown quantity of the council and what it may entail.' Despite this, there seemed to be a daunting gulf between what the Ulster Unionists (supported by Alliance) required on the issue of the Republic's recognition of Northern Ireland and what the Irish government was prepared to offer, i.e. a 'firm recognition' of Northern Ireland.

In Northern Ireland loyalist tempers were running high. On 5 December Vanguard and DUP members tried to force some of Faulkner's supporters from the Assembly chamber, resulting in scuffles on the floor of the house. In the midst of the mêlée Vanguard member Kennedy Lindsay walked to a microphone on the floor of the Chamber and shouted, 'Have you got the message? No Assembly. No Executive' (*News Letter*, 6 December 1973).

The tripartite conference was held at the Civil Service College at Sunningdale Park, which had been selected because it had its own grounds, could be guarded thoroughly, had sufficient accommodation for the delegates and was near London. The Sunningdale conference began with statements from Heath, Cosgrave, Faulkner, Fitt and Oliver Napier. Discussion centred on the issues of policing, a Council of Ireland, regional development and joint enterprises. Many of the newspaper reports, particularly in the Republic, believed that the signing of an agreement would signal the end of violence, and that those who opposed it would be isolated because of overwhelming support for the agreement. Taoiseach Liam Cosgrave sounded a note of caution, however, warning against 'exaggerated hopes on what these talks can produce in the immediate future' (*The Guardian*, 6 December 1973).

The opening of the conference again highlighted the issue of the Republic's recognition of Northern Ireland, with Faulkner stating: 'One thing is essential if the majority in Northern Ireland is to have any confidence in the future. That is that the Republic must make clear its acceptance of the right of the people of Northern Ireland to order their own affairs' (*The Times*, 7 December 1973). Although there was no official chairman of the negotiations (which involved more than twenty-five people at the table), the role was effectively taken by Edward Heath. Discussions adjourned after six hours, before delegates dined with Heath at Downing Street.

The day was soured by leaks to the media from the Dublin delegation regarding the details of negotiations about the proposed Council of Ireland. The proposal was for a top tier of the Council to be made up of government representatives from the Northern Ireland Executive and the Irish government. A second, advisory tier would involve representatives from the Dáil and the Assembly. A rather cynical report in the *Guardian* added that, as well as the argument over leaks, 'on the other major issue discussed yesterday—law and order—the parties had done little more than state their positions and talk around them' (7 December 1973). Despite the recriminations over the leaking of information, an official statement at the end of the day stated that 'the atmosphere throughout was very friendly and constructive'. However, one report noted that 'When solemnly read out by an official, the statement was greeted with hoots of derision [by the press corps]' (*Daily Telegraph*, 7 December 1973).

On the second day the conference did not begin until almost noon while British and Irish experts examined legal aspects of the Council of Ireland, extradition and other issues. Informal sub-committees were formed to examine key issues, such as the recognition of Northern Ireland by the Republic, police co-operation, cross-border law enforcement, detention without trial and the functions of the Council of Ireland.

The *News Letter* pointed out the likely opposition to a Council of Ireland that made unionists a small minority in its overall composition: 'if the Province were to assent to the formation of an all-Ireland body on the basis of the figures suggested, it could be signing the death warrant of the Executive and the Assembly and, at a stroke, bringing to an end the shortest-lived experiment in devolved government Westminster has ever devised' (*News Letter*, 8 December 1973).

Most observers expected an announcement by midday on 8 December, although agreement now appeared less certain because there was no consensus on the issue of the recognition of Northern Ireland. Heath cancelled a meeting with the Italian Prime Minister and returned to the negotiations. Disputes also surrounded whether the Council of Ireland would have responsibility for policing and the need for all-Ireland courts to deal with terrorist-type crimes. On Sunday 9 December a communiqué was finally agreed by the participants. Almost half the text dealt solely with the Council of Ireland; other issues, including the Republic's recognition of Northern Ireland, were largely glossed over or were ambiguous.

While Irish republicans were critical of the agreement, the deal seemed likely to face its toughest challenge in trying to win the support of unionists, whose initial reaction was, at best, cautious. However, Faulkner claimed that the agreement 'provides an executive that has support in a way no other Northern Ireland government has ever had. Anybody who tried to break it would earn the disrespect of the whole world community' (*Irish News*, 10 December 1973). Nonetheless the following day Robert Fisk of *The Times* was already predicting the defeat of Faulkner at an Ulster Unionist Council meeting in January over the issue of support for the Sunningdale Agreement.

At the outset of the conference many commentators remarked on the fact that it began on the anniversary of the signing of the Anglo-Irish Treaty, fifty-two years earlier. Some hoped that the settlement would provide a more enduring settlement than its predecessor. In the event, their hopes would be thwarted and the package outlined at Sunningdale would collapse within six months.

4 FEBRUARY 1974: THE M62 BUS BOMB

On 4 February 1974 a bomb planted on a coach carrying soldiers and their families exploded on the M62 near Bradford, killing eight servicemen, Linda Houghton, wife of serviceman Clifford Houghton, who was also killed, and their two sons, aged five and two. The twelfth fatality of the bombing, nineteen-year-old Fusilier Stephen Whalley, died from his injuries three days after the explosion.

The privately owned 'servicemen's special' coach was packed with fifty-six passengers: forty-eight servicemen, four women and four children. The coach was scheduled to take servicemen and their families from Manchester to Catterick army base and to a RAF base at Leeming, near Darlington. At ten minutes after midnight a 50 lb bomb in the luggage boot in the rear of the coach exploded, leaving a 200-yard-long trail of debris and bodies. The driver managed to steer the damaged coach onto the hard shoulder.

There were no empty seats on the coach and Signalman Neville Maw was sitting on his kit-bag, beside the driver, when the bomb exploded. He climbed through the broken windscreen and ran back along the motorway to divert traffic around those who had been thrown from the coach.

The bomb was claimed by groups using the names Red Brigade and Saor Éire, but police believed these were cover names for the Provisional IRA.

In November 1974 Judith Ward was wrongly convicted for involvement in the bombing; the conviction was overturned in June 1992 when appeal court judges ruled that forensic scientists involved in the case had concealed evidence.

The *Belfast Telegraph* reported on the bus bomb:

The blast scene on the M62 was one of utter devastation. Tragic reminders—holdalls, Army caps and other personal effects—were scattered on the roadway for 300 yards. Burnt coach seats lay in the road along with scattered metal. A heavy mist and drizzle shrouded the scene as forensic experts combed the wreckage for clues.

The bomb exploded in the luggage compartment as the coach cruised up the motorway at about 50 mph, bound for the Army camp at Catterick and the RAF base at Leeming near Darlington.

Motorists and lorry drivers who were driving behind were faced with a harrowing sight. The rear of the bus, where many of the servicemen's wives and children were sitting, was a ball of flame. Passengers were screaming and bodies lay scattered on the carriageway.

Firemen set up high-powered lights to help them and police as they began the gruesome task of helping the injured and collecting the mutilated bodies. As a fleet of ambulances ferried casualties to several hospitals in the area, one policeman said, "I felt physically sick. This is something I will never forget the rest of my life."

West Yorkshire Chief Constable, Mr Gregory shook his head and said, "It was an inhuman thing to do. It's just terrible. It's an awful sight." A fireman said, "It was worse than anything I saw in France and Germany during the war. The bodies were literally torn apart."

A nationwide hunt for the bombers has been launched. Three other troop coaches on the road last night were stopped and searched but nothing was found.

(*Belfast Telegraph*, 4 February 1974)

The driver of the coach, Roland Handley, recalled:

'The midnight news had just finished and I was driving along with not a vehicle in sight. Suddenly all hell broke loose. There was a tremendous explosion—I slammed on the brakes and pulled the coach on to the hard shoulder.' He clambered out to find the rear of the coach had been blown off. 'The first thing I saw was a child lying among the wreckage. I picked it up. It was dead. I don't know whether it was a boy or a girl. I handed it to somebody. Another body was lying across the child. There was a jumble of bodies. It was a complete shambles—sickening and shocking.'

(*Daily Mirror*, 5 February 1974)

A number of other people on the bus narrowly avoided being killed. Corporal Jennifer McMahon fell through the coach floor after the explosion, was dragged along the road for 50 yards and suffered extensive bruising. 'Near the back of the coach a lance corporal from Stoke-on-Trent was asleep. He had just finished a tour of duty in the North and was dreaming that he had been trapped by an explosion. He woke to find it was real life. He was trapped and was dragged along the road. All those around him were killed or seriously injured' (*Irish Press*, 6 February 1974).

In an attempt to find those responsible for the bombing police interviewed nearly 2,500 people at Manchester's Chorlton Street bus station, from where the coach had departed. Two thousand copies of a poster showing the remains of the coach after the explosion were also released by the police in an effort to elicit information. The officer leading the investigation, Chief Superintendent George Oldfield of West Yorkshire CID, commented: 'If some people think the picture is gruesome, I make no apology. The men behind this mass murder have no regard for human life' (*Sunday People*, 10 February 1974).

On the day after the explosion the *Guardian* commented on the bombing and on the ongoing hunger strike campaign by republican prisoners in England who were demanding to be returned to jails in Northern Ireland:

The bombing of the M62 bus on Sunday night is a despicable act, in keeping with the practice of the IRA Provisionals though their involvement is not yet certain. To blind and indiscriminate murder, the terrorists have added the tactic of refusing to give warning. Yet they must have known that women and children would be in the coach. Among the 11 dead are a family of four, including two children aged five and two. If this is the start of the new IRA campaign promised last week—to force the Government to move eight Old Bailey bombers from English prisons to Northern Ireland prisons— the terrorists have misjudged the mood in Britain. ...

One reason why the eight should not be transferred is that it would be easier to arrange their escape from a Northern Ireland prison and to keep them out. The women's prison in Armagh, for example, is quite close to the border. A second and stronger reason is that Britain should not export its problems to Northern Ireland. The offences were committed in England, and the two prisons have quite separate administrations. There are no compelling compassionate reasons for changing the present rules nor is there any reason to allow the prisoners to qualify for a political amnesty, should pardons be introduced in Northern Ireland. Any transfer will be seen by the Provisionals as a preliminary to eventual release, and it will encourage them to extend their terrorism.

(*The Guardian*, 5 February 1974)

At the first day of the inquest coroner Bernard Little commented: 'Having seen the bodies of the victims, it is impossible to imagine the nature of the minds of the people who planned and executed this act of destruction.' The pathologist revealed that the deaths had been caused by blast injuries and x-rays showed that rivets from the coach had been blasted into some of the victims (*Belfast Telegraph*, 8 February 1974).

In the following months the IRA would continue its bombing campaign on high-profile and military targets. On 12 February ten people were injured by an IRA bomb at the National Defence College in Buckinghamshire. A catering manageress was also injured on 26 March by three explosions at an Army barracks in Ripon, Yorkshire.

28 FEBRUARY 1974: THE WESTMINSTER GENERAL ELECTION

The February 1974 Westminster general election proved to be a key turning-point in the first attempt to set up a new system of government after the abolition of Stormont. The ideas included in the White Paper *Northern Ireland Constitutional Proposals* suggested a Northern Ireland government that enjoyed 'widespread support' throughout the community and an Irish dimension but were still loosely defined. At the time of the elections to the Northern Ireland Assembly in June 1973, many unionists still saw a power-sharing executive as stretching only as far as to include Alliance and the NILP, but not the SDLP, some of whose members they viewed as the prime agitators in bringing down the Northern Ireland Parliament. While it was difficult to give a precise figure of the numbers who supported a power-sharing executive and some sort of North–South arrangement, *Fortnight* magazine estimated that the Assembly election had shown that approximately 393,000 voters were in favour and 318,000 against.

By the time of the February 1974 general election things had changed. The SDLP was part of the Executive, and the Sunningdale conference had proposed elaborate plans for a Council of Ireland. At the same time unionist demands for improved security, extradition of terrorist suspects from the Republic to Northern Ireland and a clear recognition of the constitutional status of Northern Ireland by the Republic had come to nothing. That unionist opinion had turned against the Sunningdale package was clear, but the extent of the opposition was still a shock to the pro-Sunningdale lobby when the result of the February 1974 election emerged.

In the week before the election the usually politically astute *Fortnight* magazine predicted that anti-Sunningdale candidates would win seven of Northern Ireland's twelve Westminster seats and that pro-Sunningdale candidates would take five. The *Irish Times* also over-estimated support for pro-Sunningdale candidates, predicting that Ivan Cooper would win Mid-Ulster (Vanguard's John Dunlop won by nearly 7,000 votes on a split nationalist vote), David Bleakley could win East Belfast in a split unionist vote (William Craig won by nearly 8,000 votes), pro-Sunningdale unionist David Smyth would 'plod home' in North Belfast (John Carson won by nearly 9,000 votes) and that in North Down 'it should be a close-run thing' between James Kilfedder and Roy Bradford (Kilfedder won by more than 16,000 votes). In another constituency the newspaper's assessment was:

> Rafton Pounder is sitting pretty in South Belfast. Really, there is no-one to touch him. And within days of his election he should be back on the European circuit between Brussels, Strasbourg and London, and as far as possible from the vulgarities of Northern Ireland. He is a Unionist and he loves his British link.

If there is a cloud creeping across his red, white and blue skies, it is in the form of the Alliance candidate, Mr David Cook, an energetic and forthright city councillor who has pulled no punches in the course of a very personal campaign. He should, at least, eat deeply into Mr Pounder's majority.

The remaining candidates are the Rev. Robert Bradford (Vanguard and uuuc) a Methodist Minister, Mr Erskine Holmes (nilp) and Mr Ben Caraher for the sdlp. None of the three should have much bearing on the result.

(*The Irish Times*, 28 February 1974)

In the event Bradford received 22,083 votes, Pounder 18,085 and Cook 5,118 votes.

Despite the efforts of pro-Assembly candidates, the election was widely viewed as a referendum on Sunningdale. Many also feared that the election would give rise to violence across the region. On the morning of the election Mervyn Pauley wrote in the *News Letter*:

Northern Ireland's 1,000,000-strong electorate goes to the polls today to return 12 mps to Westminster in what has been dubbed the "sound-out Sunningdale" election. Right up to the last minute, the eve-of-poll air was filled with charge and counter-charge as various party spokesmen took their political rivals to task. The everpresent problem of violence—a key issue in the election platforms of several candidates—has been underlined by the decision to put 30,000 members of the security forces on full alert throughout the period of the count, which starts tomorrow.

(*News Letter*, 28 February 1974)

A number of commentators also feared that the election would see a large amount of sharp practice. Loudspeaker vans toured the Falls Road announcing (incorrectly) that Gerry Fitt would be disqualified from being an mp because of his position as Deputy Chief Executive. One commentator took a decidedly cynical look at the election in West Belfast:

Gerry Fitt, the most experienced electioneer in N. Ireland forecast that this election would be "the dirtiest yet" and he was right, but nowhere was it dirtier than in West Belfast. From early morning in little houses on the Falls, the Shankill, Andersonstown, Woodvale, Turf Lodge and "the Village" the personators were busy. In Andytown cars toured the streets exhorting the people to "Vote Price, Vote Twice" and they were being extremely modest. ...

In Andytown a young man came out of the booth only to bump into his father whom he'd just personated. Two 17-year-olds, on comparing voting cards, discovered that they were supposed to be a father and son. One glamorous granny, after a hard day's work, was claiming the Irish and all-comers record of having voted 103 times! ...

On the Shankill activity was frenzied also. With sustained hard work perhaps the hated Fitt could be defeated, allowing ex-para, ex-Chindit, ex-pugilist Johnny McQuade to get to Westminster where "he'd show them!" ... There were the usual stories of groups of ladies poured over the pile of wigs on kitchen tables: "Does this one suit me Sadie?" "Don't be stupid, Lily, you used that one an hour ago." "Never mind our kid, sure it's cousin Sammy on the booth."

('Vote early, vote often', *Fortnight*, 22 March 1974)

In Belfast, election day ended with a wave of bomb explosions. The *Irish News* reported:

Belfast was rocked by 10 major explosions in which one man died, a woman lost both legs, and three other men were injured, one seriously. Heavy damage was caused to buildings along a line from Upper Antrim Road through the city centre to the Shaftesbury Square area, taking in Great Victoria Street and Bedford Street.

A two-hour intensive blitz throughout the city was signalled by blast bomb explosions in litter bins in the Bedford Street area. Then a car blew up near the Ulster Hall. From then until the campaign ended as abruptly as it began, the city centre vibrated under the impact of exploding car bombs spaced sometimes only minutes apart.

The man who died was Mr Hugh Harvey, aged 30, of Third Street, Shankill Road, Belfast. He took the full force of the explosion after a bomb had been hurled into the Red Star Bar at Donegall Quay.

(*Irish News*, 1 March 1974)

The fact that this was Northern Ireland's fourth election in one year, coupled with persistent rain on the day, helped lead to a low turnout of just over 70 per cent. *Fortnight* estimated that just under 296,000 had voted in favour of Sunningdale, with just under 422,000 voting against. Significantly, the constituencies where its predictions were most inaccurate were in the safe unionist seats of North, South and East Belfast and North Down—like many others, the magazine had underestimated the sea-change in unionist opinion against Sunningdale.

One of the reasons why the Executive would fail to gain support in the following months was a renewed IRA bombing campaign. In the autumn of 1972, in an attempt to prevent major bomb explosions in Belfast city centre, a security zone had been set up and cars and pedestrians were searched by soldiers before they could enter the area. The first in a series of security gates had been erected at the junction of Fountain Street and Wellington Place on 30 October 1972, which succeeded in reducing the number of car bombs being planted in the city centre. Inevitably there was a compromise between exhaustive, but slow, security checks and the danger of bringing the city centre to a halt. In March 1974 journalist Sandra Chapman wrote:

> To get into some of the busiest shopping centres one has to submit oneself to security checks. Bags and parcels come under scrutiny and frisking is an accepted practice for men and women. Those who do the searching are backed up by their armed colleagues who stand a short distance from them, ready to challenge any person who is suspected of carrying a bomb or a weapon. ...
>
> Why then are shops being continually bombed and burned seemingly at the will of the terrorists? The answer is obvious. You could hide an incendiary device in your lipstick and you can be 99 percent certain it won't be detected. Your bottle of Coty L'Aimant could easily be inflammable liquid unless it is sniffed. And what about the shoulder padding which has become a fashionable point in to-day's dresses? That bump up there could be anything. It's enough to hide a small pistol.
>
> Last week I walked through nine checkpoints—there are 31 in the centre of Belfast—and in none of them was I thoroughly searched. Not one of them detected an object in my coat pocket which was as big and bulky as an average-sized pistol. In Cornmarket only one of the three paper bags in my shopping bag was opened.
>
> (*Belfast Telegraph*, 14 March 1974)

2 MAY 1974: THE ROSE AND CROWN BOMB

Six Catholic men were killed and eighteen other people injured in a
UVF bomb explosion (initially attributed to the UFF) at the Rose and
Crown pub on the Ormeau Road, Belfast. Sandwiched between the
political dramas of Sunningdale and the UWC strike, and overshadowed by the horrors of the Dublin and Monaghan bombs, the Rose
and Crown bomb has largely been ignored by history. Five of the
victims died almost immediately; the sixth victim, Rose and Crown
bar manager Francis Brennan, died from his injuries on 11 May. The
bombing of the Rose and Crown coincided with the death of UDR
member Eva Martin, killed in an IRA attack on a UDR base in Clogher.

William Kelly usually took a bus to visit his son before going to the
Rose and Crown for a beer. On the night of the explosion he drove
instead and arrived home fifteen minutes earlier than usual. He had
just ordered a drink in the bar when the bomb exploded. Frances
Morrissey (18) and her sixteen-year-old brother, Thomas, were among
the first to arrive on the scene. They discovered their father (also
called Thomas) under a pile of rubble and stayed with him until an
ambulance arrived. He died minutes later.

At 9.35pm three youths hijacked a car in the Stranmillis area and
dumped it at 10.15pm in the Botanic Avenue area, shortly after the
explosion. It was unclear at first whether the bomb had been thrown
from a passing car or planted at the door of the pub. The Rose and
Crown bar was used by both Catholics and Protestants and had
already suffered a bomb attack in November 1973. On that occasion
no one was injured. The day after the May 1974 attack, however, early
reports suggested four dead and twenty wounded. The *News Letter*
reported on the 'bomb raid slaughter':

> The wrecked bar was a scene of horror, with the dead and injured
> people in some cases half buried under rubble. The Army and RUC
> cordoned off the whole area, and kept at bay a large crowd of
> anxious spectators, some of whom were seeking news of relatives
> who had been in the bar.
>
> The bar, a popular rendezvous with both Roman Catholics and
> Protestants, was completely wrecked inside but the building
> itself—made of brick—took the blast well and may not have to be
> demolished.

Hair-raising accounts of what happened when the bomb was hurled without warning into the packed bar, were given by several people who escaped from the holocaust almost unhurt. An elderly man who received only slight cuts to the face said, "I was just about to put my glass to my mouth when there was a terrific explosion followed by a shattering of glass. I was blown off my feet and when I looked around I saw the place was full of people lying in the most gruesome positions imaginable. Some terribly injured—one man's leg was hanging by a thread—were moaning in pain and others were cursing the bastards who had bombed the place."

(*News Letter*, 3 May 1974)

The *Irish Independent* reported:

Hysterical women tried to fight their way into the bar to see if relatives were among the dead or injured. One of the injured had his legs blown off. When police arrived the man was sitting clutching a glass and was still conscious. Another man had his stomach blown away. Among the dead were a couple who were killed instantly as they sat drinking at a table.

Crowds of people stood in the roadway openly weeping as a senior police officer appealed for witnesses over a loud hailer and an information centre was established in the rear of an RUC Land Rover.

(*Irish Independent*, 3 May 1974)

The following day Denis Lehane wrote in the same newspaper:

As Belfast yesterday awoke from a ten-day lull in the violence to find six more deaths in overnight outrages, the death toll in four years of violence stood at the staggering peak of 1,010. And the figure could still rise within the next 48 hours as two of the 11 people detained in hospital following Thursday night's bomb "massacre" at a Catholic pub in the Ormeau Road were officially described last night as "seriously ill".

(*Irish Independent*, 4 May 1974)

The *Belfast Telegraph* noted that the blast had blown some of the dead and injured out into the street, while many of those inside were covered in rubble. It continued:

Women, some of them with children in their arms, rushed to the public house and stood crying and screaming for relatives who they believed were inside. One man was carried from the public house with both his legs blown off. Another had a foot nearly blown away.

One man was killed instantly as he sat at the doorway to the building and another victim was found with a glass still clutched in his hand. One woman told how she had rushed from her home to find a man dying on the pavement. She said: "I don't know whether he had been blown there or had crawled, but he died as I arrived. I could hear moaning from inside the building and then the Army and police arrived".

(*Belfast Telegraph*, 3 May 1974)

Basil Glass, an Alliance Party Assembly member for South Belfast, arrived on the scene twenty minutes after the explosion. He recalled:

There were four ambulances standing by and scores of security forces personnel were digging in the rubble for dead and injured … Indeed it was hard to tell the dead from the injured. I saw the bar owner with blood gushing down his face. It was a terrible sight.

The *Irish News* noted that almost every bar along the Ormeau Road had been attacked during the Troubles and that there had been approximately twenty-four murders in the area, including the shooting of five members of the same family in separate incidents.

(*Irish News*, 3 May 1974)

The *Belfast Telegraph*'s 'Viewpoint' undoubtedly reflected the opinions of many of its readers:

Once again the reality of a night of horror has dawned on a war-weary public. Five killed and eighteen injured in a Belfast pub, one woman killed and a man injured in an attack on Clogher police station—these are the continuing statistics of war.

It would be presumptuous to assume that words alone can convey the awful waste of human life. Politicians have had their say. So have church leaders, trade union leaders, the extremists, the moderates, the bereaved and the injured.

There will be a passing sympathy for the injured and for the relatives of those killed in the pub explosion. The Rose and Crown now joins the sombre list of McGurk's Bar, the Abercorn and a host of others. There will be passing sympathy for the woman UDR member who was killed and for the man injured at Clogher. How many people will remember last night's casualties this time next week?

(*Belfast Telegraph*, 3 May 1974)

14 MAY 1974: THE UWC STRIKE

In November 1973 Vanguard members and other unionists who opposed plans for power-sharing and a North–South body came together to form a new loyalist workers' organisation, the Ulster Workers' Council (UWC), chaired by Belfast shipyard worker Harry Murray. The UWC leaders spent the following months attempting to win over key workers to the idea of an all-out strike, if political opposition failed, in order to protest against the implementation of the proposals agreed at Sunningdale.

On 9 May the UWC began to prepare the public for the proposed strike by telling the media that if the Assembly voted to support the Sunningdale Agreement, there would be an all-out 'constitutional stoppage'. Loyalist paramilitary groups still conducted activities based around their own particular concerns, however, and as late as 10 May the UDA and UVF blocked roads in Belfast for an hour as a protest against visiting arrangements for loyalist prisoners.

On Tuesday 14 May a long-running debate in the Assembly on whether to continue support for Sunningdale drew to a conclusion, with the Assembly rejecting a motion condemning power-sharing and the Council of Ireland by 44 votes to 28. Harry Murray met loyalist politicians at Stormont and asked them to support the strike. Even though he was not convinced that they would back his 'constitutional stoppage', he decided to announce an all-out strike, beginning with a cut-back in power generation to hit industry.

On 15 May the first power-cuts occurred and UDA leader Andy Tyrie decided to throw the weight of his organisation behind the strike. This was followed by the use of tactics in which roads were blocked, and in some cases people were threatened to prevent them going to work.

While the NIO and the Executive continued to believe that the stoppage would fizzle out, strike leaders began organising a co-ordinating committee to make their efforts more effective. The strike committee was chaired by Vanguard Assembly man and UDA member Glen Barr and included UWC, paramilitary and political representatives. Significantly, issues involving the use of road-blocks or intimidation tended to be dealt with separately by the paramilitary groups, providing the workers and politicians with 'plausible deniability' on these matters.

Mainstream unionist political opinion also seemed to support the strikers' objectives. On 16 May the *News Letter* titled its editorial 'When the people are ignored' and stated:

> No reasonable person deliberately goes out of his way to embark on a destructive course unless all other options have been closed. And in Ulster the options have been closed. The voice that sounded so loudly and so clearly last February fell on deaf ears. Today it is being raised again and it is inevitable this time that it should be accompanied by protest of a different form.
>
> (*News Letter*, 16 May 1974)

On Friday 17 May loyalist bombs (not claimed by the UVF until 1993) exploded in Dublin and Monaghan killing thirty-three people—the greatest loss of life on any single day of the Troubles. Despite the shock, carnage and loss of life, the atrocity had remarkably little impact on events in Northern Ireland at the time.

By Sunday 19 May unionist support for the strike was becoming firmer. The UUUC steering committee gave public support to the stoppage and unionist politicians took out a half-page advertisement in the *News Letter* calling for support for the strike the following day. The Executive, on the other hand, appeared to be tearing itself apart. When unionist Roy Bradford (Minister of the Environment) called on the Secretary of State to negotiate with the UWC, the SDLP's Seamus Mallon responded that Bradford should no longer be a member of the Executive.

On 21 May there was a high-profile 'back to work' march in Belfast, led by Trades Union Congress General Secretary Len Murray, but it attracted only 250 people, many of them politicians and peace campaigners. They found themselves being barracked by supporters of the strike—many of them women. The failure of the 'back to work' marches highlighted the fact that the initiative now lay with the strikers. The strike leaders increased the pressure on the government and Northern Ireland Executive by reducing petrol supplies, claiming that the Executive had misused the electricity they were supplying by not cutting power to industry.

On 22 May the Executive agreed to the Council of Ireland being 'phased in' after SDLP Assembly members reluctantly voted by 11–8 to accept the revised plan. By this time, however, events were largely beyond the control of the Executive, which looked to the British government to forcibly defeat the strike in the belief that this would lead to a reversal in unionist opinion.

On 24 May Harold Wilson met Faulkner, Fitt and Alliance leader Oliver Napier for emergency talks at Chequers. The following evening Wilson made a television broadcast in which he attacked the strikers and spoke of people 'spending their lives sponging on Westminster and British democracy'. Many unionists took Wilson's remarks as an attack on them and the speech effectively became the final nail in the coffin of the Executive. The Executive members did persuade Wilson to use troops to take over the distribution of fuel, but when the Army took control of twenty-one filling stations on 27 May in an attempt to weaken the strike's stranglehold, this measure proved to be ineffective. The UWC in turn retaliated by threatening a complete shutdown of industry. Ann Batt captured something of the atmosphere of the time:

> Little children, some of whom can't get to school because of the barricades, are having a whale of a time playing with the smashed bottles, old tin cans, sodden paper cartons and mouldering vegetables that choke the gutters.
>
> So your wee Belfast Johnny is going to go home filthy tonight. But you can't bath him. No hot water.
>
> Can't read him a bed-time story. No lights. Can't cheer yourself up with a fire. No coal.
>
> Can't make a hot drink. No electricity. Can't pop out to the pictures or bingo. They are either burned down, bombed out or closed.
>
> You can't catch a bus. There aren't any. Can't post a letter. It won't arrive. Can't make a local phone call without being deafened

by crackles. Can't fill a carrier bag with shopping without queuing for hours. Can't use your car for pleasure. Petrol's so scarce some ingenious folk are trying to run their cars on paint thinners.

You can't even rely on the old man's dole money coming in this week. What with 250,000 on strike. Giro cheques held up in the post and staff not coming in to work because of picketing and the petrol situation, the emergency security offices are all at sea.

Whatever happens politically, Belfast teeters on the abyss of total administrative collapse today.

(*Daily Mail*, 28 May 1974)

On 28 May electricity generation was expected to cease, with widespread effects on industry as well as domestic users. The sewage system was also deteriorating. Faulkner asked the NIO to open talks with the strike leaders; Rees refused. Faulkner and the other unionist ministers resigned from the Executive. The SDLP wanted to continue the Executive without unionist representation, but were dismissed by the Secretary of State. News of the collapse of the Executive was welcomed with bonfires and dancing in the streets in Protestant areas of Belfast and across Northern Ireland. However, with Faulkner's resignation the impetus had also gone out of the strike, and support for it began to collapse. The strike leaders therefore took the pragmatic decision to call off the strike, even though they had not achieved their objective of new Assembly elections.

17 MAY 1974: DUBLIN AND MONAGHAN CAR BOMBS

On Friday 17 May 1974 thirty-three people were killed and nearly 250 injured when four car bombs exploded in Dublin and in the town of Monaghan in the Republic of Ireland. Three car bombs in Dublin—placed in Parnell Street, Talbot Street and South Leinster Street—exploded without warning within minutes of each other, at approximately 5.30pm. As a result, twenty-six people and an unborn child were killed. Just before 7.00pm a fourth no-warning bomb exploded in Monaghan town, resulting in the deaths of seven more people. Two of the three cars used in the Dublin bombings had been stolen earlier in Protestant areas of Belfast; all four cars had Northern Ireland registrations. Both the UDA and the UVF denied responsibility for the bombings, but in July 1993 the UVF eventually admitted that it had carried out the attacks. (In March 1985 the *Irish Times* was still attributing the bombings to the UDA (*The Irish Times*, 1 March 1985).)

On the morning of Friday 17 May 1974 three cars were hijacked in Protestant areas of Belfast. In two of the three cases the drivers were held captive until later in the day, by which time the cars had been loaded with bombs and parked in the centre of Dublin. At 5.30pm there were three explosions in quick succession, at Parnell Street, Talbot Street at the junction of Gardiner Street, and in South Leinster Street near the junction of Kildare Street (within 300 yards of Leinster House). No warnings were given.

The largest bomb, that at Talbot Street, immediately killed seven people and injured thirty others. A bomb outside the Welcome Inn in Parnell Street killed five people. Among those killed in Parnell Street were a married couple and their two daughters.

The third bomb, in South Leinster Street, killed three others.

After the bombs exploded the city was rife with rumours that there were more bombs. The Irish Army bomb squad set off several controlled explosions on packages and cases outside buildings. Some streets were blocked off as suspect cars were kept under surveillance. In the aftermath of the explosions the *Cork Examiner* reported:

Even some veteran reporters who have covered many horrific tragedies in the North said it was the worst carnage they had ever seen. Two visibly shaken Gardai could not hold back the tears as they endeavoured to do everything possible for the maimed and horribly injured victims.

Large crowds converged on Talbot Street within minutes of the explosion there. Despite persistent appeals from the Gardai many people insisted on walking towards the area causing difficulties for ambulances. A passerby in Talbot Street, Francis Brennan, said:

"I have never witnessed scenes of carnage like I saw tonight. There were at least five dead that I could see. One woman was dreadfully mutilated. There were limbs and bits of clothing scattered around the street and things hanging on telephone wires. One woman was trying to move her leg where her foot had been. Another woman was rushing with her child to a police car, and I saw another man being carried away by his arms and legs with blood pouring from his face and chest. I saw another woman obviously

dead and yet another younger woman covered by tarpaulin. A man
lay half through a shop window and half on the pavement. I could
hear women and children weeping in hysterics."

(*Cork Examiner*, 18 May 1974)

At 7.00pm another car bomb exploded outside Graecen's bar on North
Road in the town of Monaghan, killing five people and injuring
twenty others. Josie McCormick, who worked in the bar, was injured
and taken to hospital. Later she recalled:

I'll never forget that night in hospital wondering [about] all the
people that we knew so well—how were they? Dead or alive? The
next day we came down the town coming home. It was just terrible
to see the extent of damage the bomb had done. We were so glad to
get out of town. I was so nervous for months and months after. I
was so glad to be alive, to get back to my husband and child. I felt
so very sorry for the people who had lost their loved ones.

(quoted in Don Mullan, *The Dublin and Monaghan Bombings*, p. 83)

The explosions triggered a deep sense of shock throughout Ireland
(though perhaps less so in Northern Ireland, which was absorbed
by the UWC strike) and abroad, and the UDA was viewed as the most
likely suspect. The UDA denied responsibility for the explosions, but
its press officer, Sammy Smyth, added: 'I am very happy about the
bombings in Dublin. There is a war with the Free State and now we
are laughing at them.' A UVF statement said:

We want to make it clear that we are appalled by these explosions.
It is indiscriminate and definitely against our policy. At the present
time the UVF have made a firm declaration that we will not engage
in any physical activities including bombings or shootings.

(*The Irish Times*, 18 May 1974)

The eventual death toll of thirty-three remains the highest number of
people killed on any single day of the Troubles.

In the months that followed the bombings many of the relatives of
those killed or injured felt that the government had down-played
or forgotten the atrocity. Over the years a number of them also came
to question the State's actions in pursuing those responsible, the

integrity of the RUC investigations, the possible involvement of British state forces in the bombings and the possibility that known suspects were not pursued.

Although the UVF admitted responsibility for the bombs in July 1993, speculation as to whether the organisation acted alone has continued. Fred Holroyd, a British Army intelligence officer operating in Co. Armagh at the time, suggested that the bombs were planted by loyalists based in Portadown, who had links with an MI6 officer through a RUC officer. Holroyd claimed that the loyalists were not aware that they were working for the Secret Service, which wanted to sway the Irish government into introducing tougher security legislation (*Sunday News*, 1 March 1987). In July 1993 a Yorkshire Television documentary, 'Hidden Hand—The Forgotten Massacre', suggested that loyalists had been assisted by British agents in carrying out the bombing. In May 1995 former British Army information officer Colin Wallace also suggested that the Army's 14 Intelligence Company had assisted the loyalist bombers. In particular, there were questions surrounding the issue of whether the UVF had the technical knowledge to make the type of bomb used in Dublin and Monaghan.

In 2004 an Irish parliamentary committee suggested that there had been collusion between loyalist paramilitaries and British security forces in relation to the Dublin and Monaghan bombs. The committee also suggested that a public inquiry into the bombings should be held in the UK.

In August 2006 the *Irish News* reported that it had obtained official documents relating to a meeting of British and Irish government officials in September 1974. At that meeting Northern Ireland Secretary of State Merlyn Rees had informed Irish ministers that the twenty-five people interned by the government during the UWC strike included those believed to be responsible for the Dublin bombings. In April 2007 an Irish commission of investigation report found no evidence of collusion in the winding-down of the Garda Síochána investigation into the bombings.

21 NOVEMBER 1974: THE BIRMINGHAM PUB BOMBS

On 21 November 1974 IRA bombs exploded at the Mulberry Bush and Tavern in the Town public houses in Birmingham. Nineteen people were killed and nearly 200 injured. Two more people died later. The explosions came on the day when the largest ever security operation in the West Midlands was being carried out in conjunction with the funeral of IRA man James McDade, whose body was being flown out of Birmingham airport.

As with many of the worst atrocities of the Troubles, a warning was given but came too late for any effective action to be taken to clear the pubs of customers and to prevent major loss of life. Other bombs did explode nearby, too, but caused no casualties. The horror of the bombings sparked a wave of anti-Irish sentiment, with attacks on Irish community centres, bars and businesses in England. In the wake of the attacks the British government rushed the Prevention of Terrorism Act into law. The Act included provisions for detention without charge for a period of seven days and expulsion from Great Britain to Northern Ireland or the Republic of Ireland.

In the immediate aftermath of the explosions the *Daily Express* reported:

People ran from the Odeon Cinema, which was rocked by the Mulberry Bush blast, and helped in a massive rescue operation. A detective, who was on duty at New Street station, was among the first on the scene. He said: "I couldn't begin to describe it. There was debris, glass and blood everywhere. I saw four bodies brought out." One eyewitness said: "This is a terrible scene of carnage." The entire ground floor of the pub was demolished. Glass and debris were shattered for hundreds of yards around.

A wounded man in a blood-stained shirt being helped away by two policemen, said: "The swine! The bastards! Everyone was talking quite happily and laughing and joking when suddenly we were all hit by a fantastic blast. There were women and young girls screaming, blood pouring everywhere. I saw one man who seemed to have half his body blown off. It was horrible."

Mrs Helen Whitehorn, of Lydon Road, Solihull, had just finished a meal in a city centre restaurant when the bombers struck. "Everybody ran out into the street," she said. "We just stood there not knowing what to do. The police shouted: 'Run away!' I ran down the street and into a doorway. Then I saw the front of the place almost opposite blow straight out."

(*Daily Express*, 22 November 1974)

Martin Cowley reported on the explosion at the other Birmingham pub:

> The licensee at the Tavern in the Town, Mr Dick Lawn, said he had been able to account for only one of the five staff who were on duty. He was on his way round to the Mulberry Bush, a short distance from his own pub, when the first bomb exploded at the Mulberry Bush. He then heard a bang and when he reached his own establishment he said it was "utter devastation." He saw one young girl being carried out.
>
> As police and firemen grappled with the fallen girders, a woman member of the St John's Ambulance told reporters that at least five dead had been carried from the pub. "It was like a slaughterhouse," she said.
>
> While she spoke, a dazed young man said his sister had been in the pub and the first-aid officers there advised him to contact the city's main hospital, the Birmingham Accident Hospital, where most of the victims were taken.
>
> An 18-year-old girl, who didn't want to give her name, was in the Tavern when the bomb went off. "Everybody was just drinking as normal. All of a sudden there was a bang and the lights went out. I didn't think it was an explosion. I put my head on my boy-friend's chest and he protected me. I thought I was injured, but I wasn't. I saw one girl who had completely lost her left foot."
>
> After the girl had told the story, she collapsed and had to be taken to an ambulance.
>
> (*The Irish Times*, 22 November 1974)

At Birmingham General Hospital staff worked to save the lives of those who were badly injured. But there were also more everyday concerns for the hospital workers:

> In the hospital reception area the acting hospital secretary, Mr Alan Bailey, helped to arrange for the safe keeping of an injured man's pay packet. There was £22 in the envelope, the blue fivers and green £1 notes dreadfully stained in blood. "It was chaotic for a while," said Mr Bailey, "but the staff were marvellous." Scores of them had heard of the outrage on the radio and raced unbidden to the hospital. Most had worked all day yesterday. They were still

drifting off home at 4 am. At breakfast time they will be back on duty.

(*Belfast Telegraph*, 22 November 1974)

The *Daily Mail* reflected general opinion in Britain when it called for a 'tough but calm' reaction:

> The bombing in Birmingham is the most horrible single act of terrorism ever committed in Great Britain—and ranks with the worst of atrocities carried out in Ireland itself. This is worse than war. By cold-bloodedly attacking civilians with no shadow of military justification, these bombers have placed themselves on a par with the death squads of Hitler and Stalin.
>
> The heavens cry out for vengeance for this sickening slaughter of innocent people. Yet we must react as a community with good sense as well as guts. Moral disgust is not enough. We must also try to reduce the chances of it happening again. Mr Roy Jenkins [Home Secretary] spoke with determination in Parliament yesterday. We trust that his actions will live up to his words.
>
> (*Daily Mail*, 23 November 1974)

There were also fears of a massive reaction against Irish people living in Britain. Mary Punch reported from Birmingham on the day after the explosions:

> As the city emerged under the chill grey skies there was open evidence of division: on the streets, in the shops, on the buses people were talking clearly of revenge on the Irish, a ban on the IRA and the death penalty.
>
> And, as the first numbness of shock wore off, thoughts and words tended to turn into action. Irish workers at British Leyland's Longbridge works were assaulted. Some 1,500 workers walked out while another 2,000 held a demonstration outside the gates. More than 1,000 workers from a frozen foods factory halted traffic at Aldridge, Staffs, during an anti-IRA march. Another 1,000 workers from the BRD Engineering company in the town joined in a march with 600 workers from McKechnie Metals Ltd.
>
> In Coventry a group of packers at Fords parts depot blacked all spare parts going to Northern Ireland. And during the night a large

piece of concrete was thrown though a window at the home of Brendan Magill, Sinn Féin's British organiser, at Richmond, Surrey. A phone caller later told him: "Next time it will be the real thing."

Loaders and traffic staff at Birmingham airport have grounded 17 domestic flights because they feel police security precautions there are "inadequate."

And while fear of a backlash in Britain was rising, Belfast had not long to wait for the real thing. Sectarian killers were quick to seize the excuse and invaded the Catholic Turf Lodge district in a car to murder a 17-year-old Catholic girl petrol attendant.

(*Irish Independent*, 23 November 1974)

12 APRIL 1975: UVF ATTACK ON THE STRAND BAR

On numerous occasions during the Troubles one atrocity followed another so quickly that the previous incident was quickly overshadowed. The first two weeks of April 1975 was one such period. The twenty-four hours after lunchtime on Saturday 5 April had seen seven dead and seventy-five wounded in two sectarian attacks on bars and two other men killed in separate incidents in Belfast. A loyalist paramilitary bomb attack on McLaughlin's Bar at the New Lodge Road (later attributed to the UVF) was followed hours later by a republican attack on the Mountainview Bar on the Shankill Road. Belfast appeared to be caught in an endless cycle of tit-for-tat loyalist and republican counterattacks. Derek Brown reported of the McLaughlin's Bar incident:

The bar was crowded with customers watching the Grand National on television. They had no chance to escape. The bomb, hurled at the front door from a car, exploded almost instantly killing two young men, wounding 15 other people and wrecking the inside of the bar.

Three hours later, in an act of vengeance by an unknown group, another bomb was thrown into the Mountainview Bar in the Protestant Shankill Road. Four men were killed and the hospital yesterday raised the death toll to five. Sixty people were hurt.

As the extent of the slaughter became known off-duty doctors and nurses volunteered for duty at the principal hospitals—Royal

Victoria, City and Mater. There is little information about the wounded but some have lost limbs and a high proportion will be scarred for life.

Four men were injured in new shootings last night. Three, believed to be Roman Catholics, were shot in the Moyard Social Club, Andersonstown. A 31-year-old Protestant was shot in the legs in Nixon Street, in the Shankill area.

(*The Guardian*, 7 April 1975)

Methodist Minister Rev. John Stewart lived close to the Mountainview Tavern and was on the scene minutes after the explosion. He remarked:

It was a harrowing experience. We pulled as many people out of the wreckage as we could. Some were not recognisable. They had been blown to pieces. Later, in the hospital, the injured were lying side by side with Catholics from the other blast. Those suffering are the innocents from both sides of the sectarian divide.

(*Daily Mirror*, 7 April 1975)

Over the period of 5–7 April, thirteen men died as a result of sectarian attacks or loyalist and republican paramilitary feuds and many others were injured. The future of the IRA's Truce also seemed to be in doubt after a fire-bomb attack on a Belfast city-centre store. The *Daily Mirror* angrily reported:

The Provos blasted the heart of Belfast again last night in "retaliation" for troops damaging houses raided in republican areas. One woman suffered a heart attack and two others were treated for shock as teatime shoppers evacuated a crowded store where three bombs had been planted. Fifty firemen fought the massive blaze that swept Bank Buildings at Castle Junction. The bombing was staged to ram home the Provo claim that the Army was jeopardising the fragile ceasefire.

(*Daily Mirror*, 9 April 1975)

On 11 April the Army shot dead one man and injured another after a failed UVF gun and bomb attack on the Catholic-owned Jubilee Bar in Lavinia Street, Ormeau Road. On the back of these atrocities followed another. Late on Saturday 12 April members of the Red Hand Commandos, which was linked to the UVF, drove to the Strand Bar in

Anderson Street in the Short Strand. The attackers fired shots into the bar and then threw in a 20 lb bomb, which exploded almost immediately. The car sped off towards the Newtownards Road. The Strand Bar was known to be a quiet bar and was popular with older people and with women.

The *Daily Telegraph* reported:

Saturday night's attack on the Strand Bar—a favourite haunt of local old age pensioners was made by Protestant militants who fired bullets through the window before throwing in the bomb. There was no chance for anyone in the crowded bar to escape, as the bomb went off immediately.

Rescue workers from nearby houses were reinforced by troops, police and firemen as they scrambled through the charred rubble for the victims. Groans and screams from the wounded, many of them elderly women, helped locate the injured buried under tons of masonry and wood. Some rescue workers were themselves buried when their struggle to hold up part of the collapsing roof proved impossible, and it fell down on top of them.

One of those killed was the mother of a large family of young children, who were not told of her death until they woke up yesterday morning. Among the 14 injured still in hospital yesterday was a woman of 86, who was said to be very seriously ill.

(*Daily Telegraph*, 14 April 1975)

The next morning the *Sunday News* described the scene after the explosion:

One side of the two storey building—on the corner of Anderson Street and the Short Strand—was completely demolished, and the full weight of the top storey crashed onto the people drinking below. Several police and firemen were trapped for a time when part of the roof and a wall collapsed in on them. Other rescuers pulled them free.

Local people formed human chains to pass out bodies—and parts of bodies—as the headlamps of police land rovers and private cars illuminated the grisly scene. Fire engines stood by to deal with a growing fire risk as broken gas pipes and electric cables were exposed.

Taxi loads of helpers arrived at the scene of the blast as rescuers deep within the wrecked building tore out mangled pieces of metal and splintered woodwork in their search for further bodies.

A local resident, who was helping to clear the wreckage, said, "What sort of people could do this? That bar was full of old age pensioners having a Saturday night drink. What sort of animals would do this to them?"

(*Sunday News*, 13 April 1975)

The victims of the bombing were Marie Bennett, a mother of seven children; Agnes McAnoy, a widow and mother of three children; Elizabeth Carson, aged sixty-four and the oldest victim; Mary McAleavey, mother of eleven children; and Arthur Penn, father of three children. Thirty-nine other people were injured and one of those, Michael Mulligan, died a week later.

Twenty minutes after the bombing of the Strand Bar, Stafford Mateer was shot dead by a gunman firing from the Short Strand in what was widely seen as a revenge attack. Another Protestant, Robert Kennedy, was found beaten to death the next day in another revenge killing for the bomb.

Cardinal Conway, the head of the Catholic Church in Ireland, and nine Northern Catholic bishops reacted to the latest atrocity by issuing a statement attacking 'this ghastly campaign of sectarian murders':

The religion of the victims is completely irrelevant to the heinousness of such crimes, but it throws some light on the nature of the campaign to point out that the great majority of the victims have been members of the minority community.

In our view altogether insufficient attention is being devoted to this ghastly campaign. We find it hard to understand why in so many assessments of the situation it is virtually ignored.

31 JULY 1975: THE MIAMI SHOWBAND MURDERS

On 31 July 1975 members of the Miami Showband were returning from a performance at the Castle Ballroom in Banbridge when their minibus was stopped at a fake roadblock set up by the UVF at Buskhill, near Newry. The UVF members loaded an explosive device on board the bus, with the intention of detonating it later and making it look like the band had been transporting it. The bomb exploded prematurely, however, killing two UVF members—Harris Boyle and Wesley Somerville; a dismembered arm found at the scene had the initials 'UVF' tattooed on it. Other UVF members then opened fire on the Showband, killing band members Tony Geraghty, Fran O'Toole and Brian McCoy and wounding Stephen Travers. Band member Des McAlea escaped because he had been blown through a hedge and then managed to lie unseen in a ditch. It later emerged that some of the UVF men who committed the murders had also been members of the UDR.

In a spurious—and largely fictitious—explanation for the murders, a spokesman for a recently formed UVF front organisation, the Ulster Central Intelligence Agency, claimed:

A UVF patrol led by Major Horace [sic] Boyle and Lieut. Wesley Somerville came across a minibus and car parked near the border about five miles from Newry. Major Boyle was suspicious of the two vehicles and ordered his patrol to apprehend the occupants of the vehicle for questioning. As they were being questioned, Major Boyle and Lieut. Somerville began to search the minibus. As they entered the vehicle a bomb was detonated and both men were killed outright.

At the precise moment of the explosion the patrol came under intense automatic fire from the occupants of the other vehicle. The patrol sergeant immediately ordered fire to be returned. Using self-loading rifles and sub-machine guns the patrol returned fire, killing three of their attackers and wounding another. The patrol later recovered two Armalite rifles and a pistol.

(*Daily Mail*, 1 August 1975)

Journalist Gary Gillespie reported:

No matter which story is accepted, the end result is the same— three young musicians killed and another seriously wounded. At the scene yesterday a few tattered pin-up pictures of the Miami members were caught in long grass—a symbol of the band that had been ripped apart. Other personal items such as hair brushes and instrument cases were scattered throughout the twisted remains of the minibus.

One member of the band escaped the attack altogether. He was 23-year-old drummer Ray Miller and he had made his own way home to Antrim after the dance. Yesterday he described the tragedy as being, "as if someone in England said the four Beatles were dead. These boys have given so much to Irish show business," he said.

(*News Letter*, 1 August 1975)

In an editorial entitled 'Beyond the Pale', the *Belfast Telegraph* commented:

The initial shock of the Miami showband killings has been over-taken by outrage. "For God and Ulster" is the motto of the Ulster Volunteer Force, which has admitted losing two of its officers in the incident. What, they should be asking themselves, did the deaths of five men achieve, for God or Ulster?

Whatever minimal support the UVF has had should die an instant death, after this. It has proved itself, since the first sectarian murder in 1966, a dangerously irrational and violent organisation, proud to admit to the most heinous crimes. Anyone who gets involved in its operations, or looks to it for support, now knows the possible rewards.

Because of the band's popularity, the ambush has left a deeper impact than almost any previous incident. If it helps to convince more people, on both sides of the fence, to reject paramilitary activity because of the tragedy and unhappiness it brings, some-thing may be salvaged from the wreckage of a pop group which only sought to entertain.

(*Belfast Telegraph*, 1 August 1975)

Despite its involvement in these and other murders, the UVF was not an illegal organisation at this time. Secretary of State Merlyn Rees had lifted the ban on both the UVF and Sinn Féin in April 1975 in an attempt to draw the organisations into exclusively political activity, but with little success. The UVF was again proscribed in October 1975. The *Irish News* noted that:

All the indications are that members of the UVF were responsible for these horrible killings. They are a further demonstration of the con-sequences which can flow from treating this sinister organisation with kid gloves. This stark tragedy has overtaken other similar tragedies and will, itself, be overtaken. Once again shattered bodies are mute witness to the insanity which can grip men's minds and which makes human life so expendable.

(*Irish News*, 1 August 1975)

In another attack later that day a minibus carrying a party of elderly people on a regular weekly run from Bleary to Banbridge was riddled with bullets by UVF gunmen as it slowed down to take a bend near Gilford, Co. Down. Seventy-eight-year-old Joseph Toland was killed and the driver, John Marks, was fatally wounded; five women were also injured.

In the wake of the attack on the Miami Showband there were fears that other bands might also become targets for terrorists. The *Belfast Telegraph* reported:

One top Ulster singer said this afternoon, "I am going to be very scared crossing the border, but I'm going to go. If some people in the South want to take revenge, they could well pick on a Northern band. But I think the murder of the Miami boys was an isolated incident, although we've heard of many bands being threatened. We don't want showbiz to be dragged into the gutter like this. Today I'm afraid of crossing the border."

Chart topping English pop group Kenny are fulfilling their engagements in Ballymena and Bangor tonight and tomorrow, despite the massacre … But top Eire showbands who play regularly in Northern Ireland have cancelled all their immediate dance dates here, "as a mark of respect." Meetings will be held on both sides of the border next week to decide the future of the whole dance band circuit throughout Ireland.

The Indians, who are managed by the same concern as the Miami, and who have never turned down a date in Northern Ireland, are staying away—at least for the time being. The Nevada is another band not coming.

(*Belfast Telegraph*, 1 August 1975)

On the morning after the funeral of Fran O'Toole, journalist John Moore wrote:

There is a rule among country people here that no one kills a song bird. Yesterday we buried one. And this island mourned.

It was so totally wrong. Pretty girls in summer dresses shouldn't have been weeping bitterly. And the cream of Ireland's musical talent should not have been sobbing around a graveside yesterday as the sun broke through an early morning mist.

They had come to bury Fran O'Toole, who was to pop fans in Ireland what Bay City Rollers singer Les McKeown is to England. Fran's bullet-shattered body had lain overnight in the church of Our Lady Queen of Peace in his home town of Bray, Co. Wicklow. It had been taken there from the ambush scene in Northern Ireland where life had been brutally driven from it.

For more than 1,000 people gathered in the church for yesterday's service the stark horror of the terror campaign had come to their doorstep at last. Shops, pubs and betting offices were closed as the funeral procession stretched from one end of Bray's main street to the other.

A town was mourning its favourite son. Irish cabaret star Dickie Rock never thought he would sing, "The Lord is My Shepherd", off-key due to emotion, from an organ loft as the body of Fran, the man who succeeded him as lead singer with the famous Miami Showband, lay in his coffin in the church beneath him.

(*Sunday People*, 3 August 1975)

In December 2007 a memorial to the Miami Showband members killed in 1975 was unveiled in Dublin. One of the surviving band members, Stephen Travers, welcomed the memorial as a fitting way to remember his colleagues. He added: 'We mustn't forget that during the '60s and '70s showbands were, without a doubt, the most effective fighting force against sectarianism on this island. They were a great antidote to the poison of the bigots and the evil of the people who tried to drive a wedge between the communities' (BBC News, 10 December 2007).

2 OCTOBER 1975: TWELVE DIE ON DAY OF UVF ATTACKS

Although largely overlooked in the list of the major atrocities of the Troubles, 2 October 1975 was a day on which a series of attacks by the UVF led to the deaths of twelve people, with forty-six more being

injured. The attacks came at a time when the UVF was a legal organisation and the IRA was nominally conducting a Truce. Despite this,
paramilitary bombings and killings continued.

A Catholic shop worker was shot dead by the UDA in a sectarian
attack on 18 September. On 22 September Catholic woman Margaret
Hale died nearly three weeks after a UVF attack on McCann's Bar,
3 miles from Loughgall. On 23 September the IRA claimed responsibility for a series of eighteen bombings across Northern Ireland the
previous day, which it claimed were carried out in retaliation for
Army house searches. The Provisionals also blew up three electricity
pylons near Crossmaglen, disrupting power supplies between
Northern Ireland and the Republic.

The extent of paramilitary activity increased dramatically on
2 October, however, with a series of UVF attacks. On the same day IRA
bombs exploded in Armagh city and in Sion Mills, Co. Tyrone. By the
end of that day eleven people had died: four UVF members killed by
their own bomb; three workers in a Belfast bottling plant (a fourth
would die later); a bar manager shot near an east Belfast bar; a
merchant seaman killed by a bomb in a bar in Aldergrove, Co.
Antrim; a photographer shot dead in a photographic studio in north
Belfast; and a woman hospital supervisor killed by a bomb in a bar in
Killyleagh, Co. Down. With weary predictability the *Irish Independent*
christened the day 'Bloody Thursday'.

The *Irish News* reported on the attack in Millfield:

> The worst incident of the day in Belfast was the murder of three
> Catholics at the bottling plant in Millfield, only a few hundred yards
> from the city centre. Gunmen burst into the premises of Sam Casey
> and Sons, and fired at point blank range at two male workers on the
> ground floor, killing one and seriously injuring the other.
>
> Then the gunmen ran upstairs and shot two married sisters, the
> manager's wife and secretary, in the head, again at point blank
> range. Both died on admission to hospital. As the assassins made
> their escape, the youth who had been seriously injured, ran out
> onto the street with blood pouring from his neck, and as he
> collapsed a motorist stopped and took him to hospital, where his
> condition is critical.
>
> When police arrived they described the scene inside as "horrific"
> and said it was obviously an attempt at mass murder. They added

that several hundred of pounds had been stolen by the murderers.

The two sisters who were killed were Mrs Irene McGrattan (47) of Thirlmere Street, the wife of the manager, and Mrs Frances Donnelly (35) of Strathmore Park North, his secretary. The employee who died was 18-year-old Gerard Grogan, of Carlisle Parade.

Mr Peter Grogan, brother of the dead youth, wept as he said: "I can't take it in—I just can't believe it. He was so happy working here. There was no earthly reason to kill him. He did no-one any harm."

(*Irish News*, 3 October 1975)

At the funeral of the two sisters two days later, Fr Peter Donnelly, Frances Donnelly's brother-in-law, asked: 'As human beings we can be excused for questioning how God can let this happen. This is not God's doing but the doing of evil men. May God influence them to see the pointlessness of their actions.'

The fourth victim of the Millfield attack, eighteen-year-old storeman Thomas Osborne, died on 23 October.

In the wake of the explosion in which four UVF members were killed by a bomb they were transporting, the *Belfast Telegraph* reported:

The first report of the explosion reached police in Coleraine when a caller phoned at 7.57. They were told it was on the Limavady side of Coleraine, but no exact location was given. A police patrol out searching then received a radio call, and exactly 28 minutes after the first report, arrived at the scene—a sliproad used frequently by courting couples.

There they were confronted by the day's most gruesome sight— the mutilated bodies of three men and the dismembered body of a fourth. Limbs were scattered everywhere, and during a torchlight search it was thought a fifth man may have been killed as well.

Parts of the car was scattered over a 100-yard radius. On an arm of one of the four men was the tattoo, "For God and Ulster", a UVF motto. …

Many motorists travelling between Coleraine and Limavady stopped, but were quickly ushered away from the immediate area, as detectives combed the scene. Today a mysterious laurel wreath was lying among the wreckage of the car.

(*Belfast Telegraph*, 3 October 1975)

Difficult as it was to believe, the death toll could have been even higher. Nearly forty people were having a lunchtime drink in the Bush Bar in Leeson Street, Belfast, when loyalist gunmen attacked. They opened fire with a machine-gun, but the mechanism jammed. Seconds later a bomb exploded in a side passage near the bar. Fortunately, there were no fatalities.

A statement from the UVF said it had carried out the attacks 'to register their utter disgust and displeasure at the failure of the civil and military authorities to take effective counter-terrorist action following recent IRA bombings ... The present policy of "detente" between the Government and the Provisional IRA is totally unacceptable to the vast majority of Ulster loyalists and cannot be tolerated any longer by the Ulster Volunteers.'

For the *Belfast Telegraph*:

The really shocking thing about yesterday's murder and mayhem is that many people are not shocked. They react to IRA and Protestant violence with the same shrugging of the shoulders and the same silent prayer: "Thank God it missed me." It's all too much to absorb or understand, so they switch to another channel.

That may be a natural response, after seven years of desensitisation, but it is not good enough, and never has been. This is everyone's war, in that everything they hold dear is under attack, and anyone who opts out of the struggle to contain and end it is helping the disintegration process.

Even though it hurts, Protestant and Catholic should take in every horrific detail about yesterday's killings, and try to imagine them happening to their own family. That is when people really come face to face with civil war—a term that rolls glibly off so many tongues—and they know that it is no solution to anything.

(*Belfast Telegraph*, 3 October 1975)

On 3 October the UVF was once again banned by the government. Little more than a month later, on 12 November, the NIO announced the closure of incident centres, effectively marking the end of the period of the IRA Truce.

6 DECEMBER 1975: BALCOMBE STREET SIEGE

Following a car chase and gun battle through the West End of London, an IRA gang burst into a flat in Balcombe Street, where they held married couple John (54) and Sheila Matthews (53) hostage. The four men barricaded themselves and their two hostages into one room. The area was evacuated and police marksmen surrounded the flat. A telephone link was set up and a series of negotiations began. The IRA men demanded an aeroplane to take them and their two hostages to Ireland. The police refused to allow food into the flat, but did allow water, which was lowered to them from the flat above. The siege received extensive television coverage.

One of the IRA members, Harry Duggan, was believed by police in the Republic to have been killed in Northern Ireland two years earlier. He was using the assumed name of Michael Wilson, but was identified by a set of fingerprints supplied to Scotland Yard by Gardaí. The other IRA men involved were Hugh Doherty, Eddie Butler and Joe O'Connell.

The siege ended six days later when the IRA men gave themselves up. They were questioned about the murders of Metropolitan Police officer Stephen Tibble in February (who, although murdered by the IRA, was not killed by those involved in the Balcombe Street siege) and television presenter Ross McWhirter in November, among others. In February 1977 the IRA members involved in the Balcombe Street siege were found guilty of six murders.

On the morning after the siege ended the *Irish News* reported:

Mr Matthews had not known whether he would see his wife—or the outside world again—as she walked to freedom along the balcony of their siege flat yesterday afternoon.

As she was rushed to hospital, he stayed behind, still held by the four IRA gunmen. But only two hours later he was at her side. The 138 hour siege of Balcombe Street was over. The softly, softly, drama ended quickly and quietly. No shots. No heroics. Just surrender.

The gunmen and their hostages came out one by one along the first floor balcony which had been the focus of attention for so long. For Mr and Mrs Matthews it was a short walk to freedom. For the four hooded men—covered every step of the way by an arsenal of police guns—it was the end of a gamble that failed. Last night the four were under police interrogation at Paddington Green police station, just a mile from Balcombe Street.

The sudden end to the siege surprised even the police chiefs on the spot. Contact was re-established between police and the gunmen over a new field telephone at 1.45 pm. Half an hour later the balcony door opened. A masked man climbed out and then gave Mrs Matthews a helping hand as she walked slowly towards the door of the adjoining flat. The man put his hands in the air and jumped back inside. A policeman with a rifle took aim at the siege flat window until Mrs Matthews reached safety.

(*Irish News*, 13 December 1975)

After eating a meal provided by the police the four IRA men emerged onto the flat's balcony, along with Mr Matthews, and then climbed onto the balcony of the next-door flat. Once inside, the IRA men were arrested.

On 14 December the *Sunday Mirror* carried a set of photographs showing the inside of the flat in the aftermath of the siege. The newspaper commented:

This is house-proud Sheila Matthews's living room—as she would hate to see it. It is strewn with the litter of six days of aching tension. Six days in which she and her husband, John, were the captives of 22b Balcombe Street, Marylebone, London. There are empty cigarette packets, cigarette ends and ash on the green fitted carpet. A pair of stockings and some string. Dirty plates caked with brown sauce. And a sofa shoved untidily against a door. All this dominated by a makeshift screen of pink nylon sheets draped over a clothes-horse in a bid to hide the chemical toilet.

Significantly, when the trial of the Balcombe Street gang began in January 1977 three of the accused refused to plead on the grounds that the charges did not include references to bombings at Guildford and Woolwich in October and November 1974, for which they claimed responsibility but for which others had been (wrongly) convicted.

Although not seriously physically injured, John and Sheila Matthews had clearly been traumatised by their experience. The morning after they left hospital the *Daily Mail* reported:

The pain was going from John Matthews and his face was keen to the questions that flew. But you could not take your eyes off Mrs Matthews. She fumbled for John's hand and held it tight.

Only the red of her eyes broke the paleness of her blank stares. A black fur coat hung loosely on her and she inhaled a cigarette so nervously the ash shook all over her green dress. There was nothing she wanted to remember.

"Was I frightened? I never thought I'd get out alive." The guns still pointed at her in her mind as she raised her head: "It was just those guns all the time, pointing and waving—' the sentence trailed off and she reached for her husband, "All the time, those guns—' She did remember how aloof the Irish gunman had been, "so aloof." "There was no rapport", John interrupted. "None at all," she recalled. Had she taken the Valium and tranquillisers? "On an empty stomach! I didn't have anything to eat until Thursday"—five days after the siege began.

Then the indignities came back to her. The caravan toilet behind a sheet, the foul language, the plots. Her head shook and tears reflected in the corners of her eyes.

"Were you tied up?" Mr Matthews was asked. "Yes, around here," he felt his ankles under the table. The gunmen had used his wife's tights as rope and the thought of this made her tears come back again.

Did you think you would ever get out alive? She dug her teeth into her lip. "No, no I didn't." A policeman helped her to her feet and she picked her way edgily towards the door.

(*Daily Mail*, 15 December 1975)

In April 1998 a number of IRA prisoners, including the Balcombe Street gang, were transferred from England to the Republic. The following month, as Sinn Féin leaders attempted to persuade their grassroots to support party candidates taking their seats in a Northern Assembly, twenty-seven republican prisoners were given temporary parole to attend the party Árd fheis. Members of the Balcombe Street gang were among those who attended and were greeted by Gerry Adams as 'our Nelson Mandelas'. They received a ten-minute standing ovation from the audience.

In another speech to the Árd fheis Michael O'Brien, the Officer Commanding republican prisoners in the South, remarked:

Comrades, we know we can move forward, never losing sight of our strategic objectives, never wavering and with the spirit of the experience I wish to share with you today. That experience was the return of six republican prisoners from England to Portlaoise prison last Tuesday, four of whom are known to you as the Balcombe Street men. Joe, Hugh, Eddie and Harry are here with us today.

You may ask what this has got to do with an assembly. It is this. After 23 years in British prisons: these men are our own Mandelas; fit, strong, unbowed, unbroken, humorous. They are politically astute and aware and full of honest opinion and integrity.

And all of that comes on the back of trust, belief and above all unity during those long 23 years in the belly of the beast. United we can do whatever we want just as those united POWs who have returned from England this week have endured and ultimately defeated the most barbaric prison system and conditions.

5 JANUARY 1976: THE KINGSMILL MASSACRE

While much of the violence of the Troubles may have been primarily politically motivated, there was also a clear sectarian dimension. On 4 January 1976 six Catholic men were killed or fatally wounded by the UVF in south Armagh. Fifteen minutes after John Martin, Brian and Anthony Reavey were fatally wounded by the UVF at Whitecross, the O'Dowd brothers, Barry and Declan, and their uncle Joseph were killed and their father injured at their home in Gilford. Seventeen-year-old Anthony Reavey survived for three weeks before dying from his wounds. After the shooting he described how the brothers had been watching television when:

… suddenly, the door opened and I saw men standing there with guns. I heard a shot and saw John Martin fall to the ground. Brian and I tried to make it out of the room but as Brian was getting out, he was shot.

I managed to get into the bedroom and got under the bed, but one of the gunmen shot at me as I lay there. He then left, probably thinking I was dead.

Wounded six times, Anthony crawled 200 yards to a neighbour's house. Terrible as the shooting of the Reavey brothers had been, their mother later revealed that the attack could have been even worse if most of the family had not been visiting her sister at the time but stayed at home, as they normally would have done (*Irish News*, 8 January 1986).

Anthony Reavey and Alan Black, the only Protestant to survive the Kingsmill massacre, would later share the same hospital ward.

On 5 January a minibus was driving workmen home from a textile factory in Glenanne. Five Catholic workers left the minibus at Whitecross. Further along the route the minibus was stopped by a man at Kingsmill crossroads. When the bus came to a halt a group of men, carrying assorted weapons, stepped out of the darkness and ordered the workers off the bus.

Alan Black later said that the workmen had had no sense that they were in danger. They were stopped by a red light and assumed it was an Army patrol. But when they were asked if there were any Catholics in the group, they began to feel uneasy.

The twelve workmen were lined up against the minibus with their backs to the gunmen. The gunmen asked if there any Catholics among them. Alan Black squeezed the arm of Richard Hughes (the only Catholic workman in the group) to try to warn him not to speak because he believed they had been stopped by loyalists intent on killing Catholics. Hughes was eventually singled out, however, and told to 'run up the road'. A few seconds later he heard gunfire.

Alan Black recalled that when the shooting ended he heard someone crying and saying prayers. He tried to call out, but was too weak. He had been shot eighteen times. Among the victims were brothers Walter and Reginald Chapman.

Ten years after the event Alan Black recalled the night of the Kingsmill massacre:

The talk on the minibus that night was no different than normal. There had been talk earlier in the factory that day about the killing of the young Reavey brothers from nearby Whitecross. It horrified us all, but we could not contemplate what was in store for us later that evening.

We passed through Whitecross village shortly after 5.30pm and when our minibus was stopped a short distance up the road past Kingsmill crossroads we thought it was the Army.

A group of about 12 armed men, unmasked but with their faces blackened and wearing combat jackets, surrounded the vehicle and ordered us all out on to the road. Even then few of us thought there was anything amiss.

One man, with a pronounced English accent, did all the talking and proceeded to ask each of us our religion. As the guns were pointed in our direction we were all ordered to put our hands on top of the minibus.

Our Roman Catholic works colleague was ordered to clear off and the shooting started. It was all over within a minute and after the initial screams there was a silence. I was semi-conscious and passed out several times with the deadly pain and the cold.

He recalled how a man appeared on the scene:

He was in a terrible state and was praying loudly as he passed along the row of bodies. He must have heard my groans and came across to comfort me.

Later I found out who he was and he asked me to maintain his anonymity. During those few terrible minutes he helped me remain alive until the ambulance arrived. I must have been lying on the roadside waiting on the ambulance for up to 30 minutes ... It was like an eternity and I can remember someone moving my body from one side to the other to help ease the pain.

('Kingsmill Massacre ... 10 years on', *News Letter*, 3 January 1986)

On 6 January the killings were claimed by 'the South Armagh Republican Action Force', but were widely attributed to the Provisional IRA.

The *Daily Mail* described the scene on the morning after the killings:

A wreath of plastic flowers in a lonely hedgerow yesterday marked the spot where ten men were massacred ... As dawn broke over the scene of the slaughter of Kingsmills [sic] it showed the few poignant reminders of the men who died.

On the narrow road, stained with blood, lay a set of false teeth, a tin luncheon box, four rain-soaked sandwiches, a blood sodden newspaper, an empty tea flask and eight pence. They had tumbled from the pockets of the Protestant factory workers as they were cut down outside their red minibus on their way home from work on Monday.

(*Daily Mail*, 7 January 1976)

The horrific attacks were condemned on all sides, with some of the strongest words coming from the head of the Catholic Church in Ireland, Cardinal Conway:

These foul murders stand condemned in the sight of God and men. I pray that all responsible for the killings of recent days may be brought to justice even in this life, as they certainly will be in the next. Those who take a life for a life are spitting in the face of Christ. If this vicious chain of murder and revenge is not broken soon, this community will sink even deeper into the mire.

(*Irish Independent*, 6 January 1976)

Added to the earlier killing of Catholics in the same area, the Kingsmill massacre heightened fears that an all-out sectarian conflict was approaching. In the *Irish Independent* James Kelly wrote that:

Northern Ireland was plunged last night into the depths of despair as the fearsome prospect, naked, all-out sectarian war, loomed after the horrific reprisal killing of 10 Protestant workmen in a bus ambush at Whitecross, near Newry. The slaughter, the worst single sectarian outrage since the North's troubles began, was staged clearly in revenge for the brutal murder of five innocent Catholics in two homes in the same area on Sunday night by extremist Protestants.

The sectarian assassinations and the Provisional IRA threat to launch a full-scale military campaign now threatens to orchestrate all the evil forces which have been thirsting for what they describe as a "fight to the finish".

(*Irish Independent*, 6 January 1976)

The *Irish Press* described the massacre as 'the worst deed': 'The North is on a bloody and inexorable slide towards a bloodbath, while the politicians dither and the soldiers stand aside. It is the ordinary people of Northern Ireland who must pay the terrible price of being unfortunate enough to be born and live in these times' (*Irish Press*, 6 January 1976).

In an effort to meet criticism of its security policy, on 7 January the government announced the first official deployment of the SAS in Northern Ireland. Six years later an Armalite rifle used by the IRA gang at Kingsmill was recovered by the Garda Síochána in Dublin. Ballistic tests suggested that the weapon had been used in sixteen killings and six attempted murders (*News Letter*, 9 February 1982).

2 JULY 1976: UVF ATTACK ON THE RAMBLE INN, NEAR ANTRIM

The UVF attack on the Ramble Inn in Co. Antrim on 2 July 1976 has become another of the almost forgotten atrocities of the Troubles. Two masked gunmen—one carrying a sub-machine gun, the other a pistol—stood at the doorway of the Ramble Inn and sprayed the bar with bullets. Four men died almost immediately and five others were injured. Two of the injured later died. Although the bar was owned by a Catholic, five of those who were murdered were Protestants. An anonymous phone call later claimed that the attack was in retaliation for an IRA attack on Walker's Bar in Templepatrick on 25 June, in which three had been killed (this, in turn, followed a loyalist attack on a Catholic pub, the Hunting Lodge, in west Belfast).

The Ramble Inn attack was only one in a series of attacks on bars, often conducted as part of a sectarian tit-for-tat murder campaign by loyalists and republicans. On 5 June 1976 alone eight men died in a five-hour period as a result of tit-for-tat killings, leading the *Daily Mirror* to dub the day 'Bloody Saturday'. Over the weekend as a whole, ten people were killed and seventy-five injured. The *Daily Mirror* reported that:

> The most horrific killings were at the Catholic-owned Chlorane Bar in Smithfield, Belfast. Four hooded men brandishing pistols and machine-guns burst into the lounge bar. They stood and sprayed until their magazines were empty. Four men died instantly including the owner, Mr Jim Coyle ...
>
> The killers, thought to be members of the outlawed Ulster Volunteer Force, arrived in a black taxi—which was found abandoned yesterday in the Shankill area. A senior police officer said, "Of all the pub shootings during the Troubles this was the worst. It

was an horrific sight." The raid was clearly a quick reprisal for the double killing at the nearby Protestant Times Bar in York Road two hours earlier.

(*Daily Mirror*, 7 June 1976)

The fifth victim of the Chlorane Bar attack, John Martin, died from his injuries eighteen days later. Although the intention of the UVF gang was clearly to kill Catholics, two of the five men killed in the Chlorane Bar were Protestants.

On 25 June an IRA attack on Walker's Bar, outside Templepatrick, left three Protestants dead: the owner's son and daughter, Frank Walker and Ruby Kidd, and salesman Joe McBride. The *News Letter* reported the attack as follows:

The bar was crowded with Friday night drinkers when three terrorists stepped into the hallway and opened up indiscriminately. At least one of them used an Armalite rifle, the Provisional IRA's favourite weapon. The brother and sister were killed instantly.

The killers turned their guns on the doorman outside and shot him dead. Another man, hit by the hail of bullets in the bar is very seriously ill in hospital.

There was chaos as customers dived for cover, "There seemed to be no end to it", a customer said later. "I was sitting having a quiet drink and the next minute bullets were crashing into the walls. It was a harrowing experience. I hope I'll not have another one like it," he said.

At first it was feared that the killers had hurled a bomb into the bar among the dead and injured. But later an Army expert found a live grenade from which the pin had not been pulled out.

(*News Letter*, 26 June 1976)

A week later what was intended as a revenge attack was carried out by the UVF on the Ramble Inn. Barrels filled with cement had been placed around the Ramble Inn in an attempt to prevent car bombs damaging it, but this did not deter the gunmen. The *News Letter* described what happened:

The Ramble Inn, which is Roman Catholic-owned, was filled with customers when the gunmen broke in. Immediately customers saw the sub-machine gun, some threw themselves to the floor. But the gunmen opened fire and soon three men, one of whom is believed to have been a 78-year-old Protestant who lived nearby, were killed. Five others were seriously injured by the hail of bullets.

The wounded were taken first to the nearby Massereene Hospital, Antrim, but owing to a shortage of staff there they had to be transferred to the Waveney Hospital, Ballymena, where doctors fought in vain to save the life of one of those who had been critically injured.

(*News Letter*, 3 July 1976)

A man who was in the lounge adjoining the bar at the time of the attack on the Ramble Inn told the *Belfast Telegraph*:

"All of a sudden I heard a rat-a-tat of gunfire. I shut the lounge door and would not let anybody out. When I went into the bar room a few moments later, there were people lying all over the place. The bar was crowded and the floor was covered in blood."

Inside the bar this morning there were blood stains on the wallpaper of the hallway leading from the bar into two adjoining lounges. Half-full spirit glasses and beer bottles sat on the tables unmoved from the moment of the shooting.

(*Belfast Telegraph*, 3 July 1976)

The *Irish News'* coverage of the incident, at a time when only four people had so far died, conveyed a weariness born of the fact that such atrocities had become almost commonplace.

It is confidently believed that the attack on the Catholic-owned Ramble Inn was aimed as a revenge attack for the triple shooting in a Protestant bar—Walkers of Templepatrick—a week before.

The outcome of the Ramble Inn shooting however, ironically demonstrated the sheer irresponsibility of such attacks. Three of the men who died were Protestants. It is well known in the area that the bar was supported by a mixed clientele and that the manager is a Protestant.

(*Irish News*, 5 July 1976)

Given that the tit-for-tat murder campaign seemed to be depressingly unending, it was hardly surprising that the media gave as much, or more, attention to a (comparatively) good news story. On 2 July a pregnant woman and a man were shot and wounded in a sectarian attack by a gunman firing on pedestrians from a car, which escaped along the Crumlin Road. The *Irish News* reported:

> A two-day-old baby girl, shot in the back before she was born, and her mother were "comfortable" in hospitals two miles apart in Belfast last night. The baby was delivered, a week premature, in the Mater Hospital late on Friday night. After her mother, Mrs Mary Gilmore, had been hit twice by bullets fired from a passing car on Crumlin Road.
>
> A bullet was removed from Mrs Gilmore's body at the same time that the baby, Catherine Anne, was delivered. Surgeons realised that the second bullet was lodged in the baby's body. The newly born infant was transferred to the Belfast Hospital for sick children, part of the Royal Victoria Hospital complex, where an operation was performed for the removal of the bullet.
>
> (*Irish News*, 5 July 1976)

On the same day the *News Letter* welcomed the fact that 'Ulster's miracle baby girl, shot while still in her mother's womb, was winning her fight for her life last night'.

10 AUGUST 1976: THE DEATHS OF THE MAGUIRE CHILDREN

On 10 August 1976 two of Anne Maguire's children were killed and a third fatally injured when a car driven by IRA member Danny Lennon, who had been shot dead at the wheel by the Army, careened out of control and crashed into the children. On 12 August more than 1,000 women held a demonstration for peace in the nationalist area of Andersonstown, in Belfast. Further rallies followed, eventually leading to the creation of the Women's Peace Movement, which later became the Peace People.

One response to the feeling that parts of Belfast were degenerating into anarchy came in Twinbrook on 11 August when a group of forty women chased off youngsters hijacking lorries and setting up barricades. One of the women involved said:

"They are only small boys and, in fact, there was an eight year old this morning who had his own barricade erected across the road. The youths went away and then they came back, because, apparently, they had been told to come back. But we told them to go away and they used some four letter words, but eventually went home."

The woman thought the Provisionals were responsible for sending the children out to set up roadblocks but added, "We just want peace and quiet ... This is a good estate and we want to keep it that way."

(*Irish Press*, 12 August 1976)

On the same day Belfast woman Betty Williams made an emotional appeal for the paramilitaries to end their violence. She said she had collected 6,000 signatures in the Andersonstown area calling for peace and stated that a peace rally would be held on Saturday outside the primary school where the three Maguire children had been fatally injured. She added: 'We would like to rally the support of the Protestant women of west Belfast as well as the Catholic mothers. We want all Christian women to go along with us in this venture' (*Belfast Telegraph*, 12 August 1976).

On the night of 12 August a memorial service was held for the Maguire children near where they had been injured and was attended by more than 1,000 women.

On the following day the *Daily Express* reported that:

Housewife power brought a quiet day in the Belfast streets. There were few reports of hijackings and little terrorist activity. A petition which states simply, "Provos out, peace, please", has already collected 6,000 signatures in the Andersonstown area and the organisers hope this will top 9,000 by tomorrow.

(*Daily Express*, 13 August 1976)

Many believed the women's actions could seriously undermine support for the paramilitaries. *Guardian* reporter Derek Brown wrote:

The growing peace movement and the general sense of revulsion which has followed the deaths of the Maguire children has largely snuffed out IRA-inspired street action in Belfast. The widespread rioting and hijacking, which started on Sunday and threatened to continue through the week, has all but ended.

Now there are signs that the peace crusade is growing beyond a simple emotional backlash. Protestant women in traditionally loyalist estates of west Belfast are starting to organise a parallel campaign and have said they will attend the rally being planned by Catholic women for today.

(The Guardian, 14 August 1976)

On 14 August the *Irish Independent* asked:

Could it be that "a collection of Belfast mothers" who could endure no more after the deaths of the three Maguire children, have started a fire of protest which will rid the city of the misery of violence?

A demonstration of 3,000 women began spontaneously without leaders, to clear Provisional IRA violence out of the West Belfast housing estates, has already gathered 6,000 signatures in a campaign for peace. A vast body of sympathisers attended the funeral of the children yesterday.

There is to be a rally today and the Catholic women have appealed for the support of Protestant mothers in "getting rid of the scum in our communities."

The surprise is that the peaceful men and women on all sides in Belfast have not long since been driven to confrontation with the thugs who have taken over the housing estates on both sides in Belfast and, through intimidation, have forced the people to endure with little open protest, killing and bombing and wrecking which has descended to sheer gangsterism.

(Irish Independent, 14 August 1976)

Mairead Corrigan, the Maguire children's aunt, was hopeful that the rally could help bring an end to the violence. She said that groups supporting peace would meet more regularly and added:

Peace starts in our own hearts, however, and if we are going to have a genuine peace, then we have got to say—"I forgive" and put old sores behind us. We will prove to the world that Catholic and Protestant people in Northern Ireland can live together.

(Belfast Telegraph, 14 August 1976)

The 15,000-strong rally on 14 August became a cross-community event in support of peace. The *Sunday Express* noted:

Together the huge crowd sang simple hymns common to both reli-
gions and with bowed heads recited the Lord's Prayer. Together
they shed tears at the spot where the three Maguire children died
violently, whose death pricked the conscience of Ulster. Then, as
quietly as they had come, they left. Not a single speech was made.
Later, rally organiser Betty Williams said:

We don't want speeches. There has been too much talk. This is
not a propaganda movement. It's a peace movement. We should
have done this four years ago. Too many people have died. It has
now got to the stage when you can't remember who died last week.

(*Sunday Express*, 15 August 1976)

Within days, however, graffiti appeared declaring Betty Williams a
'traitor' or announcing 'Death to Betty Williams', an attempt was
made to set fire to her home and a letter was distributed by the IRA
in Andersonstown warning that anyone found guilty of 'loose talking'
would be dealt with 'in a most severe manner'. The rallies were
severely criticised by republicans as being the creation of British
propagandists and also for ignoring the deaths of Danny Lennon and
twelve-year-old Majella O'Hare, who had been shot in the back by a
soldier on 14 August.

Nevertheless, on the day after the march the *Sunday News* reported
that:

Over 10,000 Catholic and Protestant women from all over Belfast
took part in the massive peace rally at Andersonstown yesterday.
After a short service of prayers and hymn singing a procession, led
by the Andersonstown housewife Mrs Betty Williams, made its way
down the Falls Road but was jeered by about 15 youths who waved
a tricolour.

The marchers, carrying placards calling for peace, walked to
Milltown Cemetery where the three Maguire children are buried.

But any hope of a sudden end to violence was shattered last
night when the Provisional IRA totally ruled out the possibility of a
peace initiative.

(*Sunday News*, 15 August 1976)

A statement from the Provisionals criticised the women's march for
peace as:

... the organised mobilisation of pre-confirmed anti-republican forces who have shown a willingness for collaboration. ... Mrs Williams and her tribe of impeccable whited sepulchres are easily inconsistent, and Majella has been ignored. ... this nauseating opportunism, this hypocrisy, this flagrantly political and one-sided stance, which ignores the root of the violence—British occupation of Ireland—and which excuses culpable collaboration.

(*Belfast Telegraph*, 20 August 1976)

The *Irish News* editorial took a different view:

At least no-one among the critics of last weekend's peace rally by the women of Andersonstown and district can deny the reality of it. The thousands of women who so spontaneously answered the call did not make a virtue of their presence; they yielded to a heart-felt desire for peace that overflowed after the tragic deaths of the Maguire children. They are calling for peace because they see clearly that violence has nothing to offer.

(*Irish News*, 20 August 1976)

The movement attracted support from both Protestants and Catholics and in late 1976 the Peace People organised a series of rallies throughout Northern Ireland and in Liverpool, Glasgow and Dublin. The leading figures in the organisation were Betty Williams, Mairead Corrigan and Ciaran McKeown. Williams and Corrigan were subsequently awarded the Nobel Peace Prize.

3 MAY 1977: THE UUAC STRIKE

The United Unionist Action Council (UUAC) strike came at an unusual time. Northern Ireland was going through a period of what was effectively Direct Rule with an Orange tinge. For unionists, Roy Mason was probably the most popular individual to hold the office of Secretary of State. The Labour government had agreed to the Ulster Unionist demand for an increase in the number of Northern Ireland seats at Westminster, the government was increasing spending on public services and improvements to the infrastructure. There were no plans for a high-profile political initiative and in February 1977 an Orange Order report dismissed the prospect of British withdrawal from

Northern Ireland as groundless. Significant, too, was that the number of those who were unemployed, around 60,000, was the highest in more than three decades, raising serious concerns about the safety of their jobs for those who might have considered supporting the strike.

Although the level of violence was decreasing at this time, it was still not certain that it would not return to the levels that had existed in the early 1970s. On the other hand, the security policy of 'Ulsterisation' had, at least partly, led to an increase in the number of security force deaths among locally recruited organisations—in 1975, seventeen of thirty-one members of the security forces killed were either RUC or UDR; in 1976, it was thirty-eight out of fifty-two.

In March 1976 the United Ulster Unionist Council steering committee had formed a United Unionist Action Council to oppose direct rule, and from May they organised vigilante patrols and roadblocks through the Ulster Service Corps (USC)—an organisation largely made up of former B Specials.

Unlike earlier instances of loyalist paramilitary roadblocks, the security forces now seemed more prepared to charge USC members with obstruction. On 19 April Ian Paisley, along with Ernest Baird and UDA chairman Andy Tyrie, addressed a crowd in Portadown, where USC members were being charged with obstruction, and announced the start of a campaign to bring back a majority rule parliament that would control security in Northern Ireland.

On 26 April the UUAC took out an advertisement in the *News Letter,* issuing an ultimatum to Mason that he had one week to start a new security offensive against the IRA and begin implementing the Constitutional Convention report or else the Council would commence an all-out strike.

Paisley was an unlikely candidate around whom to build a strike coalition. At the Democratic Unionist Party conference on 15 April he had harangued politicians who had considered a voluntary coalition with the SDLP. Paisley said that the DUP was 'seen as the effective resistance to republicans in any future government', later adding: 'We know why the UPNI, Alliance, SDLP and certain Official Unionists howl. We kept them from their goal—the surrender of Ulster for a few thousand a year, a government car and a government job' (*Belfast Telegraph,* 16 April 1977).

At the same time the government maintained its charm offensive with unionists. On 27 April Mason announced that a £70 million order had been received by Harland and Wolff, the first new order since 1974. This stood in contrast to a government decision, taken during the uwc strike, to delay £5 million support to the shipyard.

Divisions within loyalism remained a constant factor, however. On 30 April paramilitary groups said they were 'reluctantly' supporting the strike, but were critical of Paisley and Baird. They were determined that if the strike failed, they should not be left to carry the blame meted out by the politicians. Paisley, meanwhile, continued to drum up support for the strike and in Ballymena he declared: 'I am only remaining in political life to see the thing through and if it fails, then my voice will no longer be heard' (*Belfast Telegraph*, 30 April 1977).

On 1 May 1,200 extra troops were brought into Northern Ireland in advance of the proposed strike. As Mason indicated in his autobiography, however, this was more a case of window-dressing for unionists than any serious change in security policy. The following day Paisley and Baird met with Mason, but this came to nothing. Mason subsequently met Vanguard members, emphasised there would be no 'loyalist bashing' and said the number of Special Air Service soldiers in Northern Ireland had been increased.

Even more so than in 1974, the uuac strike was a battle to win the hearts and minds of unionists. Nowhere was this truer than in relation to power-station workers and petrol drivers. On 5 May Mason met shop stewards from power stations and, crucially, managed to convince them not to support the strike.

That the government was prepared to take a more aggressive stance against the strikers than in 1974 was apparent by the decision to remove more roadblocks and even to arrest Paisley and Baird, temporarily, on 10 May. Unlike 1974, however, this was taking place against a background in which most unionists were not unduly concerned at the threat to the constitutional position. As Mason well knew, most unionists were content to be reassured that the government was making an effort to improve security, and this was a point he emphasised in talks with unionist politicians, electricity workers and petrol-tanker drivers. The government's response was also more co-ordinated than in 1974, partly because decision-making was not split between the Northern Ireland Office and the Northern Ireland Executive.

The strike commenced on 3 May. As in May 1974, Larne port was closed and there was intimidation by loyalist paramilitary members to get workers out. A bomb damaged the Belfast–Bangor railway line in an attempt to prevent commuters going to work.

On 4 May the UUP withdrew from the UUUC in protest against the strike, claiming that some of those involved had plans to form a provisional government for Northern Ireland. UDA members later clashed with the RUC when the police tried to remove a barricade on the Newtownards Road in Belfast—a sign that things were already going badly wrong for the strike organisers, particularly when one of the objectives of the strike was to improve the safety of members of the security forces.

By 8 May many people were already going back to work amid signs that the strike was breaking down. In response to this, paramilitary intimidation increased in an attempt to enforce the strike. On Monday 9 May, 200 farm vehicles blocked roads into Ballymena. Other demonstrations took place in Belfast, Enniskillen, Larne, Portadown, Tandragee and Newtownards.

On 10 May a bus driver was shot dead by the UDA as part of an attempt to stop buses operating during the strike, but as with attacks on the police, this action also served only to undermine the strike's credibility. On 11 May sailings recommenced from Larne.

On 12 May a petrol-tanker driver was shot on Donegall Road, Belfast, leading tanker drivers in Belfast to stage a twenty-four-hour strike. The following day Mason and security representatives met tanker drivers' representatives to try to convince them not to support the strike, particularly as they knew it was on the point of collapsing. Mason kept the drivers' representatives talking and the UUAC strike was called off at midnight. Ian Paisley responded by stating that the strike had been a success in his constituency and he would not be leaving politics.

Despite the failure of the UUAC strike, the DUP did surprisingly well in the District Council elections held on 18 May. The party won 12.7 per cent of the vote and doubled its Council representation. The result suggested that while unionist voters may have had some sympathy for the strike's objectives, they were not prepared to join it.

17 FEBRUARY 1978: LA MON HOUSE BOMBING

On 17 February 1978 twelve people were killed (seven of them women) and twenty-three injured by an IRA incendiary bomb at the La Mon House Hotel in Castlereagh, on the outskirts of Belfast. The victims

included three married couples. Cans of petrol were attached to the
incendiary device, which exploded at 9.00pm and sent fire sweeping
through the dining room. An anonymous telephone warning was
given five minutes before the explosion; a second was received at the
time the incendiary exploded. Staff had begun clearing the hotel of
the nearly 500 people in the building when the bomb, attached to a
grille on a window outside the dining room, exploded. The bomb was
made of a mixture of chemicals and petrol, combined to create a
napalm-like liquid that would stick to any material with which it
came into contact. The explosion blew a shower of lighted petrol into
the room. Many of the hotel guests escaped out through windows
with their clothes on fire. Police later found most of the bodies against
a brick wall directly opposite the location of the bomb. Most of the
bodies were burned beyond recognition and dental charts, along with
scraps of clothing and jewellery, were used to identify the dead.

Several hundred people were attending two separate functions at
the hotel at the time, one for the Northern Ireland Junior Motorcycle
Club and the other for the Irish Collie Club. The motorcycle club's
function was being held in the hotel's ballroom, while the Collie
Club's event was in the Peacock Room, near where the device was
planted. All those killed were attending the Irish Collie Club dinner.

One witness told the *Belfast Telegraph*:

> My brother works there as a waiter and I went down to see if he was
> all right. When I arrived people were leaving in panic. I went into
> the main dining room but it didn't look too bad. But then people
> started being brought in without arms and legs and I knew it was far
> worse than I first thought. They were taken from the room where
> the dog club was holding its function. ... I also saw a number of
> charred bodies. It was terrible—there was nothing I could do.
>
> (*Belfast Telegraph*, 18 February 1978)

Still shocked by events, the hotel owner said: 'If they were so intent on
damage, they could have done this when the hotel was closed for the
night. These are people's lives we are talking about, not a building. People
who came here for a night out. I just cannot understand. I just can't.'

Mary Rainey, who had been in the Peacock Room, recalled: 'We
were just finishing our dinner. I remember a blast and remember my
plate jumping towards my head as the whole table fell. I felt some-

thing hit the back of me. The whole room was smoke and flames. I just couldn't see. Liquid seemed to flow down the centre of the room and then a sheet of flame shot up. We were at the top tables and were able to get out. The others were not' (*Belfast Telegraph*, 18 February 1978).

One police officer told the *Sunday Times*: 'The building went up like matchwood. People just got up and ran for their lives. There was a mass exodus with people running to their cars, jumping in and driving off as fast as they could' (*Sunday Times*, 19 February 1978).

As was often the case with such explosions, the extent of the casualties was unclear initially (the *Irish Times* and *Irish Press* reported that sixteen had died; the *Irish News* reported eighteen dead).

The *Irish Times* reported:

> As soon as the bomb went off the building was plunged into darkness as electrical services failed. In the panic, rescuers had great difficulty in finding the dead and injured and it was not until RUC and ambulance men arrived with their lighting equipment that the numbers of dead became known.
>
> (*The Irish Times*, 18 February 1978)

Eight fire-tenders arrived to fight the blaze, but by the time they arrived the fire, which had been fanned by a strong wind, was so well advanced that there was little they could do.

Joseph Morris survived the fire, but his wife Sandra did not. He recalled:

> Sandra and I were seated alongside Jim and Carol Mills and Mrs Sally Cooper. Mrs Cooper also died. We were just chatting after the main course and complimenting a lovely meal. Tommy Neeson— he was killed too—and his wife were also beside us. There was a bang and Sandra and I and Jim and Carol were engulfed in flames. The lights went out and the flames just stuck to everybody.
>
> Everybody was choking with the thick smoke and scrambled towards the doors. But the doors were locked and they only gave way when we broke down the hinges. My jacket was on fire and I threw it off. By the time the doors were broken down Jim [who survived] was semi-conscious and had, I think, given up the will to live. Then he was carried out. I think Sandra and Carol were already dead.

If only the lights had stayed on we would have known what was happening. The only light was the flames and you could not just shake them off. They just stuck to everything.

(*Belfast Telegraph*, 20 February 1978)

To add to the confusion scores of people from Belfast and Newtownards drove to the scene (the *News Letter* angrily described them as 'crowds of sightseeing ghouls'), which led to traffic congestion on the narrow roads leading to the hotel, making the emergency services job all the more difficult.

The response to the La Mon attack was universally scathing, with one of the strongest responses coming from the Church of Ireland Bishop of Down and Dromore George Quin, who said: 'If anyone had any doubts about the evil of these people they should have none now. Everyone must co-operate to bring these vicious murderers to justice.' Pope John Paul sent a message of sympathy in which he deplored the 'inhuman deed'.

SDLP leader Gerry Fitt asked anyone with information about the bombers to tell the police, 'Even if it is a father, mother, sister, brother, wife or children, their duty is to tell the police all they know. While such men are free no one is safe. This was the most brutal, cruel attack on innocent civilians that has taken place since the onset of the Troubles.'

The *Irish Times* called the La Mon attack 'the blackest deed in modern Irish times. It is more than killing—it has the apocalyptic stench of the pit' (*The Irish Times*, 18 February 1978).

In the wake of the attack the RUC detained twenty republicans from Belfast (including Gerry Adams) and distributed leaflets in west Belfast appealing for information about the incident. The leaflets featured a photograph of the charred remains of one of those killed. A police spokesman said: 'People in Ulster are hardened to violence, but this ghastly photograph has shocked everyone. Factory workers and shopkeepers have been calling in police stations for copies so they can display them in their works. We can only hope this will have the desired effect. We want to nail these killers' (*Daily Mail*, 20 February 1978).

On 19 February the Provisional IRA issued a statement accepting responsibility for the La Mon attack:

There is nothing we can offer in mitigation bar that our enquiries have established that a nine minute warning was given to the RUC.

This was proved totally inadequate, given the disastrous consequences.

We accept condemnation and criticism from only two sources— from the relatives and friends of those who were accidentally killed, and from our supporters, who have rightly and severely criticised us. ...

It has been the disastrous presence of the British interference in Ireland and that continuing presence in the Six Counties which is the root cause of unrest in our country.

All killings and tragedies stem from British interference and their denial of Irish sovereignty. The IRA will continue to resist the British with all the might we can muster.

27 AUGUST 1979: THE DEATHS OF LORD MOUNTBATTEN AND SOLDIERS AT WARRENPOINT

On 27 August 1979 the Queen's cousin, Earl Louis Mountbatten (79), Lady Brabourne and two children were killed when an IRA bomb exploded on Mountbatten's 30 ft boat at Mullaghmore, Co. Sligo. In world terms Mountbatten was arguably the most significant figure to die in the Troubles. He had been Supreme Commander of Allied Forces in South-East Asia during the Second World War and was later the last British Viceroy of India. In the wake of his death the Indian government announced a week of mourning. Ironically, it was later revealed that Mountbatten had been a supporter of Irish re-unification.

The *Irish News* reported on the international reaction to the death of Mountbatten including a message from the Pope:

Pope John Paul II yesterday condemned the killings on Monday and, calling the "tragic murder" of Earl Mountbatten of Burma "an act of shocking violence" paid tribute to the victim as "a courageous man whose death causes great suffering to the (British) Royal Family and to all the nation."

The Pope's message of condolence to Queen Elizabeth came at almost the same time as she was being told that another member of the Mountbatten family, the 82-year-old Dowager Lady Brabourne, who had spent the night in the intensive care unit at

Sligo general hospital, had died from the injuries suffered when a Provisional IRA bomb exploded on board their holiday yacht.

It brought the death toll on the ship to four including Lord Mountbatten, his 14-year-old grandson Nicholas and a 15-year-old crew member, Paul Maxwell of Enniskillen, who had joined the party for the trip.

The death tally in the worst day of violence in Ireland since the start of the unrest in the North was 22.

(*Irish News*, 29 August 1979)

Several hours after the Sligo explosion eighteen British Army soldiers were killed by IRA bomb blasts at Narrow Water, near Warrenpoint in Co. Down, close to the border with the Republic. A 500 lb bomb planted in a lorry loaded with hay was detonated by the IRA as an Army convoy drove past, killing six members of the Parachute Regiment. A second IRA explosion in the same area damaged a helicopter carrying members of a 'quick reaction force' from the Queen's Own Highlanders, killing twelve soldiers, including the Commanding Officer. Subsequent gunfire between soldiers and IRA men firing across the border from the Republic of Ireland led to the shooting of a civilian on the Republic's side of the border.

On the following day it became clear that the civilian killed near Warrenpoint had been shot by the British Army. William Hudson (29) was the son of one of Queen Elizabeth's coachmen. He had been working with his cousin, Barry, running Hudson's amusement arcade as part of Omeath's Gala Festivities. Barry Hudson, who had gone to the scene of the shooting at Ferry Wood Lane, 2 miles from Omeath, told the *Irish Press*:

When I first went down to the scene it was with my mother. At that time we heard no shooting from either side—only an explosion and saw lots of smoke. Later I returned to the amusement site, left my mother and picked up William and returned to the shore. After parking the car on the second occasion we went down to the water edge and the shooting started. I felt something hit my arm. I thought it was shrapnel at first. I said to Bill I better get out of here. But, when I turned to him I saw him lying down.

(*Irish Press*, 29 August 1979)

The Warrenpoint attack resulted in the largest number of British casualties in Northern Ireland on a single day. The killings were followed in turn by an upsurge in loyalist paramilitary attacks on Catholic civilians.

The first bomb, at Narrow Water, was hidden under straw bales in a trailer parked in a lay-by. The second bomb was 200 yards along the road, in a gate-lodge. The lay-by bomb exploded at 4.40pm as the last lorry in the convoy was passing. Sir Mike Jackson, later head of the British Army, who was serving in Bessbrook at the time, recalled:

> Bodies of the soldiers who had been riding inside the lorry were scattered across the road, many of them in flames. All this time the air was filled with the crackle of ammunition and blasts of explosive detonating in the ruined lorry, mixed with the screams of the wounded lying across the road. The surviving soldiers were very jittery. Convinced that they were being shot at from the other side of the water, they returned fire, killing an innocent tourist and wounding another. One soldier became aware of movement behind a roadside wall; pointing his gun, he shouted an order to come out with hands held high. Several shocked children appeared; they had been picnicking with their mother.
>
> (Sir Mike Jackson, *Soldier: the Autobiography*, pp 117–18)

Lieutenant Colonel David Blair arrived on the scene in a Gazelle helicopter and an eight-man quick reaction force arrived in two Land Rovers. They set up an incident centre at the gate-lodge, close to where the second bomb was hidden. Shortly before 5.00pm IRA members exploded the second bomb. Less than half-an-hour later Jackson himself arrived. He recalled:

> It was a horrifying scene. There was human debris everywhere, in the trees, on the grass verge and in the water: mostly unidentifiable lumps of red flesh, but among them torsos, limbs, heads, hands and ears. I had seen the effects of bombs before, of course, but never carnage on this scale.
>
> (Jackson, pp 120–22)

Part-time fireman Billy McKinley was one of the first to arrive on the scene:

The police were stopping everybody just outside Warrenpoint and at first refused to let us go through. They said they couldn't let us pass because of the shooting. I think the Army thought we had refused to go out but I remember one fellow shouting to us he was glad to see us when we did arrive.

It is hard to say just exactly what was happening. I know there were three or four bodies lying on the ground in flames. Everything else was covered by smoke. I remember pulling a leg and finding that that was all there was left of one of the bodies. I think it was one of the officers. The driver of the Army lorry was sitting in his cab with his hands on the wheel. His watch was still working.

The faces on some of those boys were terrible. You could see the terror in their expressions before they had died. The bodies were lying all over the place. It was so awful that we had to send for more plastic bags.

I don't remember very much about the shooting except that it seemed to start from the other side of the water. There was one body blown over 200 yards into a wood and I think another was found about the same distance away in the water. Straw from the lorry which contained the bomb could be seen on the far side of the river bank.

(*Belfast Telegraph*, 28 August 1979)

The 1980s

5 MAY 1981: THE DEATH OF BOBBY SANDS

As part of the campaign to regain Special Category Status, republican prisoners in the Maze Prison near Lisburn demanded the right to wear their own clothes rather than those issued by prison authorities. In October 1980 the prisoners rejected a NIO proposal that they be allowed to wear 'civilian-style' clothes provided by the authorities and, on 27 October, seven H-Block prisoners began a hunger strike in protest. On 18 December the protest was called off after fifty-three days following an appeal from Cardinal Tomás Ó Fiaich and hints from the government that there might be some movement towards granting political status. The republican prisoners claimed they received a document clarifying earlier proposals and, in effect, conceding to their demands. The NIO rejected this view and said the document merely summarised changes that had already been proposed.

After the inconclusive end to the 1980 hunger strike the relationship between the prisoners and the prison authorities broke down again quickly. On the fifth anniversary of the ending of Special Category Status—1 March 1981—the IRA leader in the Maze Prison, Bobby Sands, renewed the hunger strike. Other republican prisoners subsequently joined the protest on a staggered basis. In practical terms the campaign demanded recognition by the authorities of the prisoners' five demands: to wear their own clothing; not to undertake prison work; freedom of association; additional recreation facilities (including more visits and letters); and the restoration of remission of sentences lost as a result of the protest.

There was strong support for the campaign within the Catholic community, where many of the restrictions were viewed as unjust and the attitude of the prison authorities and government as unreasonable and oppressive. Attempts by representatives of the Catholic Church, including a papal envoy and Cardinal Ó Fiaich, to mediate in the dispute proved unsuccessful. During the course of the hunger strike ten prisoners died, beginning with Bobby Sands on 5 May and ending with Michael Devine on 20 August. Outside the prison a further sixty-four people died during the course of the campaign, including thirty members of the security forces.

Apart from the loss of life that took place during the campaign, the hunger strike also had a significant political impact with the announcement of Sands' election to the House of Commons in the Fermanagh-South Tyrone by-election on 11 April (and subsequently Owen Carron's in August), and the election of two hunger strikers to Dáil Éireann in June.

Just days after Sands' passing *An Phoblacht* reported on his dying and death:

Bobby Sands had, for over a week, been in a critical condition with death a possibility at any moment. Several times he had reported that he had felt himself slipping into unconsciousness but had managed to pull himself back.

His skin had become so thin that he was placed on a water bed to prevent his bones breaking through and by last Tuesday he was so weak that his conversation with the Pope's envoy, Father Magee, had left him completely exhausted.

By Thursday, he had lost all feeling in his mouth and gums and was having great difficulty in talking. He was also suffering great pain and medical staff indicated that he was on the point of death. By Saturday, Bobby had lost his eyesight completely and had no feeling in one side of his face, and then in the early hours of Sunday morning even his powerful determination could no longer keep him conscious and he slipped into a coma.

From this point on Bobby's death could have come at any moment and his family remained constantly at his bedside. His breathing became more laboured as his body struggled to stay alive but finally at 1.17 am on Tuesday 5th May, Bobby Sands died.

(*An Phoblacht*, 9 May 1981)

As news of Sands' death reached republican areas it was greeted by the sound of bin lids being banged on the roads and whistles being blown. After a time, rioting broke out. Lily Fitzsimons, a former member of the Relatives Action Group, later recalled:

We never dreamed they were going to let any of them [the hunger strikers] die. It was unbelievable. We carried on and we thought the British would listen but nine more fellows lost their lives. ...

It was the bin lids that wakened me in the middle of the night. The air was full of the noise from bin lids and whistles. One girl had a big bell and she went round ringing it, getting people up.

Then the knock came to my door. We all went onto the street but we didn't know what to do. We were saying: "Bobby is dead and what do we do now?"

We couldn't believe that a woman, a mother, would allow young men to die like that. But what else would you expect from Margaret Thatcher?

(*Daily Ireland*, 5 May 2006)

An Phoblacht also reported on the funeral:

On Thursday, the day of the funeral, over fifty thousand people marched in pouring rain from St Luke's chapel, after requiem mass, to the republican plot in Milltown cemetery. St Luke's was thronged and the congregation were uneasy when the parish priest, Fr Mullan, delivered a sermon on violence despite a consensus that the politics of the IRA had stopped at the church door with the removal of the tricolour from the coffin and the dismissing of the guard of honour so the politics of the church could, for the sake of harmony, have been foregone.

(*An Phoblacht*, 9 May 1981)

The funeral procession set out at 2.00pm amid what the newspaper described as a sea of people resembling scenes from the Iranian revolution. The Iranian representative in London had been due to attend the funeral, but his flight was delayed. However, a telegram from Tehran had been received by the Republican press centre, stating that a street near the British Embassy in Tehran was to be renamed after Bobby Sands, 'to honour the heroic death of the IRA freedom fighter.'

Many bystanders were in tears as the funeral cortege passed by:

People blessed themselves with the sign of the cross and some old men gave a military salute to the republican martyr. At Suffolk the procession turned up and around into Lenadoon to avoid the small Protestant enclave opposite Woodburn barracks. A piper played one of the H-Block songs, the words of which are:
"But I'll wear no convict's uniform,
Nor meekly serve my time,

That Britain might call Ireland's fight,
Eight hundred years of crime."

The funeral stopped close to the Busy Bee shopping centre and Bobby's coffin was removed from the hearse and placed on trestles. Then, from among the people emerged three IRA Volunteers armed with rifles who were called to attention in Gaelic by a fourth uniformed man. They delivered three sharp volleys over the coffin, removed their berets and bowed their heads in silence for a full minute. The impressive tribute captured the hearts of the huge numbers of people on the road and was eagerly filmed by the world media.

At the gates of Milltown cemetery those assembled on the pavement spontaneously burst out into a recitation of the rosary as the hearse, the guard of honour and the funeral cars carrying Mr and Mrs Sands, their daughter Marcella and son John and others of the family slowly passed through.

Gerry Adams officiated at the graveside ceremony which began with the playing of the Last Post. The Tricolour was then removed from the coffin and along with beret and gloves presented to Mrs Sands.

(*An Phoblacht*, 9 May 1981)

In September 1981 James Prior succeeded Humphrey Atkins as Secretary of State. By this time the relatives of some of those on hunger strike had already intervened in order to save the prisoners' lives and the campaign was beginning to lose momentum. On 3 October the six prisoners still involved in the protest ended their campaign. On 6 October James Prior announced that prisoners could wear their own clothing at all times and that half of remission on sentences that had been lost would be restored. Other demands made by the prisoners were not met.

20 JULY 1982: HYDE PARK AND REGENT'S PARK BOMBS

On 20 July 1982 two IRA bombs in Hyde Park and Regent's Park, London, killed eleven Army cavalry and bandsmen. A 25 lb IRA car bomb packed with nails exploded at 10.30am in Hyde Park, killing four members of the Blues and Royals and injuring twenty-three

Battle of the Bogside, Derry, 12 August 1969. (*Getty Images*)

British soldiers on patrol on the Falls Road, Belfast, 16 August 1969. (*Getty Images*)

Aftermath of the McGurk's Bar explosion, Belfast, 5 December 1971. (PA *Photos/Topfoto*)

Bloody Sunday, Derry. Father Edward Daly waves a blood-soaked handkerchief as one of the men shot by the British Army is carried away, 30 January 1972. (*Pacemaker*)

A British paratrooper comforts a woman injured in the Donegall Street bomb, Belfast, 20 March 1972. (*PA Photos/Topfoto*)

At Stormont, William Craig surveys a crowd protesting against the suspension of the Northern Ireland parliament, 28 March 1972. (*Victor Patterson*)

The aftermath of loyalist car bombs in Dublin, 17 May 1974. (*The Irish Times*)

Loyalists celebrate the end of the Executive, 28 May 1974. (*Victor Patterson*)

Security gates in Belfast city centre, December 1974. (*Getty Images*)

The morning after the Miami Showband massacre on 31 July 1975. (*Pacemaker*)

A Peace People rally in Belfast, September 1976. (*Topfoto*)

Warrenpoint bombs, 27 August 1979. (*Pacemaker*)

Bobby Sands' funeral cortège, Belfast, 7 May 1981. (*Pacemaker*)

The Droppin' Well bomb at Ballykelly, 6 December 1982. (*Pacemaker*)

Anti Anglo-Irish Agreement rally at Belfast City Hall, 23 November 1985. (*Pacemaker*)

The Brighton bomb, 12 October 1984. (*Bettmann/CORBIS*)

The Enniskillen bomb, 8 November 1987. (*Pacemaker*)

Loyalist Michael Stone attacks mourners at Milltown cemetery,
16 March 1988. (*Pacemaker*)

UFF attack on Sean Graham's Bookmaker's, Ormeau Road, Belfast, 5 February 1992. (*Pacemaker*)

The Shankill bomb, Belfast, 23 October 1993. (*Pacemaker*)

The Heights Bar, Loughinisland, after the UVF attack on 18 June 1994. (*Pacemaker*)

Celebrations in Andersonstown, Belfast, after the announcement of the IRA ceasefire, 31 August 1994. (*Pacemaker*)

Bertie Ahern, George Mitchell and Tony Blair after the signing of the Good Friday Agreement, 10 April 1998. (*PA Photos/Topfoto*)

The Omagh bomb, 15 August 1998. (*Pacemaker*)

Holy Cross protest, Belfast, September 2001. (*Reuters*)

Police officers arrive at Stormont before the raid on Sinn Féin offices, 4 October 2002. (*Pacemaker*)

Newspaper billboard on the Falls Road, Belfast, on the day the IRA announced the end of its campaign, 28 July 2005. (PA *Photos/Topfoto*)

Ian Paisley and Gerry Adams at Stormont, 26 March 2007. (PA *Photos/Topfoto*)

people. Just over two hours later a second explosion wrecked the bandstand in Regent's Park as the Royal Green Jackets band was playing, killing seven and injuring thirty. Seven horses also died as a result of the Hyde Park bomb. *The Guardian* reported:

> The Blues and Royals, 16 of whom were riding to take part in the Changing of the Guard at Horseguards Parade when the bomb went off, have now lost three men. Two died on Tuesday and a third early yesterday. Six men are still in hospital. One is critical and two serious. The seven who are not in hospital also received injuries. Colonel Andrew Parker-Bowles, commanding officer, said yesterday that the standard of the Blues and Royals had been blown out of the corporal-major's hand during the blast. The officer was still in hospital "very badly injured." The standard had been used again yesterday morning, after they had "washed the blood off," he said. It will be repaired later.
>
> For many soldiers, he added, more serious injury had been avoided because they were wearing ceremonial breastplates, armour and jackboots. The horses had taken the main force of the blast.
>
> Several hundredweight of sugar cubes, hundreds of cards and telegrams and five cases of whisky had been sent to Knightsbridge Barracks. Many of the cards are addressed to Sefton, the horse which was badly wounded by shrapnel and six inch nails from the bomb. Others are addressed to "Sefton and his mates."
>
> (*The Guardian*, 22 July 1982)

Despite the number of individuals who were killed or injured, much public attention focused on the fate of the horses injured in the Hyde Park bomb. One report noted the actions of insurance broker and former cavalry officer Richard Raynsford in events following the explosion:

> He was riding his motorcycle 150 yards behind the cavalcade when he was blown off the machine by the blast.
>
> "There was a wall of yellow flame and then cars, horses and people all in pieces," said Mr Raynsford, who spent a year on ceremonial duties at Knightsbridge Barracks. ...
>
> "I saw *Sefton*, I saw *Eclipse*—these are horse I know and love. A policeman who had been guarding the French Embassy came

running up and I told him, "Shoot those horses." He did his best but he loosed off into their bodies which did no good at all. So I took his revolver and shot the worst wounded in the ear. First one, then two others. It was the only thing to do. They were suffering in a terrible silence—that was the worst part. None of them could have recovered."

Mr Raynsford helped to free soldiers trapped under their horses and his prompt action saved the life of at least one trooper after the explosion on Tuesday. He called over a group of soldiers who had run from the barracks and together they shifted the horses. Underneath one lay the body of Lieutenant Anthony Daly, 23, the officer in charge of the guard, who had been married only a month.

(*Daily Express*, 23 July 1982)

The bomb at Regent's Park exploded at 12.55pm, halfway through a concert being given by the band of the Royal Green Jackets. The bomb exploded beneath the centre of the bandstand. The bandmaster of the Royal Green Jackets had checked the bandstand in Regent's Park, but had not found anything unusual. Major-General Desmond Langley, Army GOC of the London District, remarked:

He checked the bandstand as well as he could. He could see no evidence that it had been tampered with, like planks of wood out of place. That is an example that you can be very vigilant but it is not enough. I am very conscious that we have had IRA attacks in London before and we must do everything we can to stop it happening again.

It is difficult because ceremonial duties are by their very nature public, predictable, routine and totally non-tactical. If we attempt to vary times and routes it becomes counter-productive and we are not fulfilling our ceremonial function.

(*The Times*, 22 July 1982)

Many of the bandsmen injured by the Regent's Park bomb were treated at St Mary's Hospital, Paddington. The *Daily Telegraph* reported:

One surgeon, Mr Geoffrey Glazer, referred to "hideous" injuries. He said, "Most of the soldiers had shattered eardrums. Many needed surgery to remove shrapnel, debris and nails that were buried up to five inches deep in their flesh. Broken legs and arms were common among those who were flung through the air by the force of the blast."

Mr Glazer said the two worst injuries were a broken skull that required six hours of surgery and a fractured neck that, he believed, could lead to one soldier being permanently paralysed. "Not many remember the moment when the bomb went off. This is probably fortunate."

(*Daily Telegraph*, 22 July 1982)

One of the band members killed in Regent's Park was Robert Livingstone, who came from Bangor, Co. Down. His brother, Graham, was on duty with the Royal Green Jackets in Northern Ireland. Their father remarked:

The ironic thing is that he never worried about the Ulster troubles when he was stationed here. I would do the worrying but mainly for Graham on his anti-terrorist duties. I have nothing to say about his killers. What's the point of it? Life must go on for his family.

(*Belfast Telegraph*, 22 July 1982)

Outside Irish republican circles the attacks were again severely criticised. While on a tour of the USA, Secretary of State James Prior told the ABC TV 'Nightline' programme: 'any help, whether it is money, arms or moral support that is given to organisations like Noraid, organisations which support the IRA, is in fact aid given to terrorism and murder.' On the same programme Sinn Féin spokesman Joe Austin replied:

"The London bombings were conducted in the course of a war, as Britain had conducted bombings in the Falkland Islands and had awarded medals to participants in that operation. Those killed in London were British soldiers" ...

When his interviewer, Sam Donaldson, remarked that surely he would not compare the operations of combatant armies with what happened in London, Mr Austin mentioned that the British had bombed Berlin during the Second World War and the Americans had bombed Japan. As long as there is "a British presence in Ireland" such violence will continue, he added.

America should stop supporting British forces in Northern
Ireland, Mr Austin replied when told that President Reagan had
urged Americans not to help terrorism. He charged that the plastic
bullets, "which are directed against innocent civilians," are supplied
by the US.

"In the past year we have had 10 children killed by plastic bullets
that are produced in your country and that are shipped to the
British Army," he claimed.

(*The Irish Times*, 23 July 1982)

In the wake of the bombings there were fears that this was the beginning of another wave of IRA attacks in London. Again there were calls
for the use of internment and the re-introduction of the death penalty.
Some Conservatives also called for passport-free travel between Britain
and Ireland to be ended and a ban on Irish citizens voting in British
elections, but once again these suggestions gradually faded away.

6 DECEMBER 1982: THE BALLYKELLY BOMB

On 6 December 1982 an INLA bomb exploded at the Droppin' Well
public house at Ballykelly, Co. Londonderry. The explosion killed seventeen people, including eleven soldiers, mostly from the 22nd
Cheshire Regiment. The INLA targeted the bar because it was known
to be frequented by soldiers from a local British Army base. The pub
had been bombed twice before and had received numerous hoax
bomb warnings, including one just the previous week. Although the
bomb used in the attack was comparatively small, it was placed beside
a support pillar, which caused the roof to collapse on to the 150
people packed into the building.

The first rescuer at the Droppin' Well was nineteen-year-old John
White, who lived only 200 yards away from the bar. He arrived amid a
rain-soaked scene with dead and dying casualties and others screaming for help. With the help of his teenage friend Alan Thompson he
pulled a soldier, who had a foot blown off, from the rubble:

We carried him to a grassy bank and then went back and found
three other men, crushed under concrete beams from the roof. I
felt for their heartbeat but two of them were dead. The whole scene

was chaos. People were throwing rubble from one body onto another.

Among the dead was a girl who was a former school classmate of John White's and who he had seen hitching a lift an hour-and-a-half earlier:

> I shone the torch on her and saw that both her legs, one of her arms and half her face were gone. There were splinters of bone sticking out of the stumps of her legs. It was terrible. We carried her out and put her on a blanket and covered her over.
>
> Every time I went back it was worse. I found some men carrying out someone who had been totally blown apart. There was just nowhere solid I could put my hands. There was just his torso left. His stomach was blown out and there was a single shred of skin holding on one of his feet. Even his mother wouldn't have recognised him.
>
> I just couldn't stand it any longer, so I went and helped to get some planks and scaffolding. When I came back the area had been sealed off, so I went to bed after a while, but I couldn't sleep much.
>
> (*News Letter*, 8 December 1982)

Police, army and civilian rescuers continued to work through the night. Army bulldozers and forklift trucks were brought in to help in the operation and arc lights set up to provide light for the rescue operation. Engaged couple Peter Cooper and Michele Chapelle, both serving in the Army, were caught in the explosion. Michele Chapelle recalled:

> The music was playing and we were talking. I turned to face Peter and the next minute the whole place was filled with startling bright light. I was flung off my seat on to the floor and I couldn't find Peter. I was under rubble and I thought I was dead as I just lay there.
>
> I knew a bomb must have gone off. Everything was slowed down. It was just like a slow motion film. I heard people screaming and crying for help. It was horrific, but all I could do was just lie there.
>
> Then, I think about 10 minutes later, one of the lads who was in our group at the time started picking stuff off me. I didn't realise it was my own fiancé. He had survived thank God.
>
> I could smell the burning and the smoke was terrible. I saw bodies lying everywhere.

There was a live wire flicking around like a snake and one girl touched it by accident. She went flying I don't know whether she survived or not.

The whole place was in chaos. Then the lads grabbed me and I clambered out. There were still people screaming for help. The roof had come in on top of us. … There were injured people lying everywhere. I helped drag a few more people out because my burns were nothing compared to everyone else's injuries.

(*Belfast Telegraph*, 8 December 1982)

One of the first on the scene was local resident Hugo Guthrie, who described what confronted him when he reached the bar:

"The roof of the lounge had collapsed and quite a few people seemed to be trapped underneath. We managed to get several free and pull them clear of the wreckage." Among those Mr Guthrie helped rescue was a girl with leg injuries and burns, a man who had lost a foot, another trapped by a beer crate—rescuers used a saw to cut him free. Another girl had lost a leg in the blast.

"There was another woman, crushed by the falling rubble, who was obviously dead but a young man, I think he was a soldier, was holding onto her and screaming. Eventually one of his mates came along and pulled him away. He had to put an arm-lock on the youngster before he would move."

(*Belfast Telegraph*, 7 December 1982)

In the aftermath Richard Ford reported for *The Times*:

A few record covers lying among the muddy, jagged slabs of pre-stressed concrete piled on a grassy verge are the sad reminders of how an evening of laughter and dancing ended in tears and bloody carnage at the Droppin' Well public house in a small County Londonderry village.

The covers, along with twisted stereo equipment, were some of the records to which about 150 young people had been disco-dancing in a function room at the back of the pub in Ballykelly on Monday night. They included Stevie Wonder's Master Blaster, Survivor's American Heartbreak and My Boy Lollipop by Bad Manners.

Catholic and Protestant, soldier and civilian, had been enjoying the music and were preparing for the last 30 minutes of the regular Monday night Razzamataz disco with the inevitable smoochy records to end the evening. First there was a faint hissing sound and then a deadly explosion ripped through the single story room.

Whoever planted the bomb, believed to have been between 15 and 30lb of commercial explosive, had chosen his target and his positioning with precision. The pub was a well known haunt for soldiers from the Shackleton barracks nearby and the bomb was placed to cause maximum damage to property and injury to people.

(*The Times*, 8 December 1982)

In a statement claiming responsibility for the bombing, the South Derry Brigade of the Irish National Liberation Army (INLA) warned people not to mix with members of the security forces: 'the INLA is not prepared to tolerate them or let them live in this land in any form. We will pursue them for the enemies of the people that they are. ... It is now time to take the war to the English and their converts in their own areas.'

In the House of Commons on 7 December Margaret Thatcher said of the bombing: 'this slaughter of innocent people is the product of evil and depraved men, an act of callous and brutal men.'

Heated scenes in the Commons also surrounded Labour Greater London Council leader Ken Livingstone's invitation to Sinn Féin's Gerry Adams and Danny Morrison to visit London. When Labour leader Michael Foot attempted to ask Thatcher about the steel industry, Conservative MPs accused him of trying to avoid the issue and several chanted, 'Livingstone, Livingstone' or shouted, 'It's your party. They're your friends'. The GLC refused to withdraw the invitation, but on 8 December Home Secretary William Whitelaw banned Adams and Morrison from entering Britain under the Prevention of Terrorism Act.

9 JUNE 1983: GERRY ADAMS WINS THE WEST BELFAST SEAT AT WESTMINSTER

In the 1970s Sinn Féin was largely viewed as an adjunct of the Provisional IRA, but following the successes of Bobby Sands and then Owen Carron in the Fermanagh-South Tyrone by-elections and the

winning of two Dáil seats by republican prisoners in 1981, the republican movement made a strategic decision to contest future elections
throughout Ireland. The change in strategy was illustrated dramatically by leading Belfast republican Danny Morrison's speech at the
1981 Árd fheis when he famously stated: 'Who here really believes we
can win the war through the ballot box? But will anyone here object
if, with a ballot paper in one hand and the Armalite in the other, we
take power in Ireland?'

In 1982 Sinn Féin contested the Northern Ireland Assembly election
and won 10.1 per cent of first-preference votes, but failed to attract significant transfers from other parties and therefore took only five seats.

The June 1983 Westminster general election saw seventeen seats
being contested in Northern Ireland for the first time. Splits in the
nationalist vote led to unionists winning Mid-Ulster and the newly
created seat of Newry and Armagh. Most interest, however, centred
on the contest in West Belfast, where the sitting MP Gerry Fitt, now an
independent, faced a challenge from Joe Hendron of the SDLP and
Gerry Adams of Sinn Féin. In the run-up to the election journalist Ed
Moloney noted the change in Sinn Féin's attitude to electoral politics:

> The Sinn Féin headquarters on Belfast's Falls Road is neatly
> symbolic of the new mood. Once a run down, dilapidated building,
> it now sports an aggressive, brightly painted wall mural outside.
> Inside a fresh coat of paint has smartened up the once dirty walls
> and where prisoners' relatives used to wait amid bits of engines and
> bald tyres for a trip to Long Kesh there is now a waiting room fit to
> grace a doctor's surgery.
>
> Upstairs, where Gerry Adams has his office, is a bustle of activity.
> Sinn Féin activists, like junior executives in a fast growing corporation,
> answer phone calls from constituents looking to get re-housed or
> windows and roofs repaired. Their complaints are dutifully added
> to a register which eventually makes its way to Adams. They scurry
> around busily making sure the right calls have been made to the
> right people in the Housing Executive or the Department of the
> Environment. ...
>
> After half an hour of this it's time for a double-take: are these,
> one wonders, the same people who scorned electoral politics such
> a short time ago, who seemed to have embraced the revolution of
> Trotsky? Are these the same people who such a short time ago were

more interested in removing roof tiles with gelignite and blasting window panes into fragments? The answer is a very puzzled "yes".

(Fortnight, May 1983)

The SDLP was clearly the main target for Sinn Féin in the election as a whole. In the week before the election *An Phoblacht's* front page said that voters faced a plain choice between 'Pomp or principle':

> There can be no starker contrast between Sinn Féin and the SDLP than that revealed on Monday's [New Ireland] Forum meeting. In the marble splendour of Dublin Castle, a well-preserved imperialist relic, John Hume made his main election bid for the votes of the nationalist people—posing, as he likes to pose in Brussels and Washington (and would love to pose in Westminster), in what he believes to be a statesmanlike role, aloof from the common herd.
>
> In the palatial surroundings, Hume made not one mention of the sufferings of the nationalist people he claims to represent, but grovelled pathetically to British and loyalist opinion, before an audience of Free State politicians who had already made it clear that their own interests continue to rank a long way ahead of Irish unity or of the nationalist people of the North.
>
> But Sinn Féin, on the other hand, fights its election campaign on the stark streets of the North, among the people who suffer all the economic and social hardships of existing imperialist rule. And they experience from those people the direct harassment from the crown forces which is the ever present reminder of British oppression.
>
> Sinn Féin makes no apologies for supporting those nationalist people, nor for resisting that British oppression, but, as part of the people, offers a fearless and principled leadership.
>
> *(An Phoblacht,* 2 June 1983)

On a turnout of nearly 75 per cent Gerry Adams received 16,379 votes to Joe Hendron's 10,934 and Gerry Fitt's 10,326 (a majority of 5,445). In the election overall, Sinn Féin received nearly 103,000 votes, or 13.4 per cent of the poll.

Maeve Armstrong reported on the atmosphere after Adams' victory in West Belfast:

> Adams finally emerged from the City Hall and was given a jubilant welcome by elated supporters outside with shouts of "Easy, easy,

Gerry Adams, Sinn Féin, Sinn Féin" greeting him as a long line of cars sounding horns followed Adams' car along Adelaide Street and round into King Street.

Alongside his cavalcade ran scores of athletic youth, women and children keeping up as best they could. In Castle Street he was raised shoulder high by the youth, and people, young and old, cheered, cried and clapped his back. And all along the Falls, past Divis Flats where a Tricolour flew, cars and taxis sounded their horns and people joined in the victory march up to the Republican Press Centre at Sevastopol Street.

Bin lids, traditionally a warning of the enemy's presence, were instead rattled in triumph by women as again local people raised Adams onto their shoulders. Addressing the crowd from an upstairs window, it took several attempts by Adams to make himself heard before the singing, whistling and clapping died down. But even throughout his short speech he was affectionately heckled by the people, whom he told:

"I didn't win the election, you people won the election, every one of the 16-odd thousand who voted Sinn Féin; all the people who worked for the past three weeks; all the prisoners' families who have suffered over the years; all the widows of the republican Volunteers; and of all the people who have died—they won the election today."

(*An Phoblacht*, 16 June 1983)

Former MP Gerry Fitt attributed his defeat to his opposition to the hunger strike campaign, which he believed encouraged tribalism. He later said:

Even though I appear to have been rejected by the nationalist population, I still have the feeling that in their innermost hearts, most would say, "What did Gerry ever do that was wrong, apart from criticise tribalism?" I was middle of the road, and the middle of the road is where you get knocked down, and I was. But nobody ever yet said that Gerry Fitt was a bad MP.

(*The Times*, Lord Fitt obituary, 27 August 2005)

Adams retained the West Belfast seat in 1987, but in the April 1992 general election narrowly lost out to Joe Hendron, whose success was at least partly due to a significant number of Protestants in the area voting for him as the candidate most likely to oust Adams. In May 1997 Adams won back the seat for Sinn Féin, however, and retained it at subsequent elections.

25 SEPTEMBER 1983: THE MAZE ESCAPE

On 25 September 1983 thirty-eight IRA inmates at the Maze Prison used guns, knives and hammers and chisels taken from the hobbies room to threaten warders and then seized a lorry that was delivering prison meals inside the compound in an attempt to escape from the prison. One prison officer died and another was seriously wounded during the escape. Nineteen of the prisoners were recaptured afterwards, but the rest escaped. By August 1992 five of the escapees, including Gerry Kelly and Brendan McFarlane, had been recaptured, three had been killed by the Army and the remaining eleven were still on the run. In June 1991 Belfast High Court awarded £47,500 compensation to twelve prisoners who were assaulted by warders after they were recaptured. The Maze escape proved to be a major propaganda coup for the IRA and a source of severe embarrassment for the British government.

The IRA prisoners' escape committee in the Maze was led by Lawrence (Larry) Marley. He had escaped from Newry Courthouse in 1975, had been recaptured in 1976 and then transferred from the Cages at the Maze (Long Kesh) to the H-Blocks after an escape attempt in 1978. It was Marley who initiated the idea of using a food lorry that entered the prison as the means of making a mass escape.

After republican prisoners presented themselves for prison work in November 1982 they were given greater access to facilities in the prison and greater freedom of movement within the prison grounds, allowing them to gain knowledge of the shape and size of the prison. Importantly, the greater freedom of movement given to prisoners within the prison meant that up to thirty prisoners could be moving on a wing at any given time, under the supervision of only three wardens.

In the summer of 1983 the IRA prisoners' escape committee presented a plan to the camp leadership, which was subsequently cleared by the Army Council. Bobby Storey was put in charge of the operation, with Brendan McFarlane as his lieutenant. Initially it was planned to

make the escape on Sunday 18 September, but this was put back a
week to avoid coinciding with the All-Ireland Gaelic Football Final,
when there would be increased traffic and security checks.

On the appointed day republican prisoners overpowered prison
officers in block H7 and thirty-eight prisoners attempted to escape.
Two days after the escape twenty-one were still on the run; thirteen
wore uniforms taken from prison officers, while others had earlier
shaved off moustaches in an attempt to disguise themselves. In the
course of the escape prison officer James Ferris was stabbed as he tried
to sound the alarm button. He subsequently died of a heart attack.

Harry Murray was one of several escapees who tried to get away by
using a prison officer's car. However, in the confusion he found he had
been left behind and instead headed towards the wire fence. He later
recounted what happened next:

> Bobby Storey and Billy Gorman were trying to climb over but
> Billy's coat was snagged. Twenty screws were charging towards us.
> Bobby managed to get over, while I was trying to free Billy. I turned
> around and a screw was aiming a gun at my head. I raised my gun
> and told him to drop his. He told me to drop mine first—so I did
> and shot him in the thigh.
>
> I then swung the weapon round to the rest of the screws and the
> scene was like something from a Charlie Chaplin film—they were
> covering their heads with their arms, trying to duck and running
> into each other. ...
>
> I ran up the hill, turned and saw that Billy was lying at the wire,
> covered by a screw with a gun. I ran on and about five yards from
> the top I felt a dull thump in my thigh. The next thing I knew I was
> looking up at the sky and my gun was lying a few feet away. I didn't
> realise what had happened until I turned and saw my foot lying on
> my shoulder. I knew then I had been shot, although I hadn't felt
> much pain.
>
> (quoted in *Iris*, Autumn 1993)

On 27 September the *Irish News* gave background details of those who
had escaped, including two of the most high-profile prisoners:

> An IRA man who took part in a bombing blitz on London 10 years
> ago is among the 21 prisoners still at large following the Maze

breakout. Gerard Kelly (30) was one of eight people jailed for life at Winchester Crown Court for causing explosions at the Old Bailey and Great Scotland Yard. More than 100 people were injured in the car bomb blasts, Kelly, from Belfast, was transferred to the Maze in 1975, at the same time as fellow bombers Marion and Delours Price were returned to serve the remainder of their sentences in Armagh. The sisters have since been released.

Another escaper who has not been captured is Brendan McFarlane (31), described as the IRA's officer commanding in the Maze during the hunger strikes of 1981.

McFarlane, of Ardoyne, Belfast, was jailed for life for his part in a gun and bomb attack on the Bayardo Bar on the Shankill Road in which five Protestants were killed. In 1978 he attempted to escape from the Maze dressed as a prison officer, but was swiftly re-captured.

(*Irish News*, 27 September 1983)

Dermot McNally was one of eight escapees who walked to south Armagh and then spent time in a series of safe houses. He later recalled:

There were a few times I was so nearly caught. One time, I'd just arrived at a house I was staying in. I'd taken off my shoes and coat and sat down to smoke a cigarette. My bag was lying on the floor. There was a big bang on the door. The wee girl was in the house, she was only about 13. She went to the door and opened it. I heard her coming to the door of the room where I was. She shouted in, "Mammy, it's the Guards, they want to search the house." I jumped out the window, no shoes on me, but I got away. That kid was so quick-thinking, she saved me.

(Quoted in *Iris*, Autumn 1993)

On 26 January 1984 the governor of the Maze resigned following the publication of the Hennessy report into the breakout, which laid most of the blame on the prison staff. Both the Prison Officers' Association and the Northern Ireland Prison Governors' Association argued that political restraints imposed by the NIO after the hunger strikes were the main cause for the escape. In its editorial *The Sun* looked else-where for those responsible for the escape, noting:

The Maze jail-break is a massive blow to hopes of an end to the reign of terror in Ulster. It has unleashed vicious men on society and given a moral victory to the IRA just when it seemed on the point of crumbling. Now there will be the usual enquiry into what went wrong. But do we not need a more immediate gesture?

Nicholas Scott is the minister responsible for the prisons in Ulster. Why doesn't he submit his resignation? That may be seen as harsh, and even unfair. But if politicians were prepared sometimes to pay the price of failure, maybe there might be less failure in future.

(*The Sun*, 27 September 1983)

Despite being the Minister responsible for one of the greatest security failures of the Troubles, NIO Minister Nicholas Scott did not resign; he remained at the NIO until 1987.

20 NOVEMBER 1983: THE DARKLEY MASSACRE

Three church elders were killed and seven other people wounded on 20 November 1983 when republican terrorists burst into the Mountain Lodge Pentecostal Hall in Darkley, Co. Armagh, during a Sunday service and began firing at random with automatic weapons. The shooting was claimed by the 'Catholic Reaction Force'. An immediate political consequence of the incident was the decision of the Ulster Unionist Party to withdraw from the Northern Ireland Assembly in protest when the government refused to change its security policy.

Only a week earlier Charles Armstrong, the Ulster Unionist chairman of Armagh District Council (who was also a part-time Major in the UDR), had been killed when an IRA bomb exploded under his car. Secretary of State Jim Prior also faced a furious response from the DUP in the House of Commons. Prior's call for people to 'leave the security situation to security forces. Do not take the law into your own hands' led Ian Paisley to reply that 'if there is no protection by the security forces, people are entitled to defend themselves.' The Rev. William McCrea asked Prior if he had 'any information or evidence that the well-known mass murderer from my locality, Dominic McGlinchey, has been involved in this devilish deed or that any of those who escaped recently from the Maze were involved.' In his maiden speech in the House of Lords, Gerry Fitt spoke of the 'brutal and callous' murders in Darkley and said they had defiled the very soil of the island of Ireland.

The RUC later stated that one of the weapons used in the attack had previously been used by the INLA. On 27 November INLA leader Dominic McGlinchey admitted that his organisation had been indirectly involved in the Darkley Massacre, in that it had supplied a Ruger semi-automatic rifle that was used in the attack.

There was much speculation that the murders were committed in retaliation for the killing of Adrian Carroll in Armagh city on 8 November by a group calling itself the Protestant Action Force (PAF) (a cover name for the UVF). On 21 November the Catholic Reaction Force said the attack at Darkley was in retaliation for the killing of Catholics over the previous two years by the PAF, 'under the protective umbrella of the Ulster Defence Regiment and receiving moral support from the two main Unionist parties'. The statement concluded: 'By this token retaliation—in which we could easily have taken the lives of at least 20 more innocent Protestants—we serve notice on the sectarian PAF-UDR to call an immediate halt to their vicious indiscriminate campaign against innocent Catholics, or we will make the Darkley killings look like a picnic' (*The Irish Times*, 22 November 1983).

The attackers had hijacked a taxi in Dundalk, blindfolded the driver and held him hostage in the back of the car during the course of the shooting in Darkley. He was later released and contacted the police, despite warnings from the terrorists not to do so.

At Darkley, the congregation of around seventy people was singing hymns at 6.15pm when the gunmen burst in. One of the inner doors of the gospel hall was closed to keep the cold out and this gave some protection to the worshippers when the shooting started.

Church Elders Harold Brown, Victor Cunningham and David Wilson were killed. The men who died were shot inside the doorway where they were standing to welcome other members of the congregation. Fatally wounded, David Wilson ran up the centre of the hall, then collapsed and died in a room beside the main hall. The gunmen sprayed the hall with bullets and fired more shots at the building as they left.

Journalist Michael McCarthy described the scene the day after the attack:

In the frosty morning sunshine you could see immediately that the Mountain Lodge Pentecostal Assembly Hall was no cathedral. And

somehow that made it worse. It was more of a Portacabin, a big
brown wooden hut about 500 feet long plonked down incongru-
ously on the top of its country hill.

No towering granite walls. No marble pillars. No stone buttresses.
All the congregation had to protect them was planks.

Yesterday morning police were methodically drawing chalk circles
on these planks, marking the places where the bullets, sprayed in
hate, had ripped through to smash an elbow here, tear open a face
there and snuff out three lives forever. In the House of God. ...

Inside, the domestic bricabrac of the church lay savaged.
Benches were upturned. Blood stained a prayer book. A bullet hole
scorched through a hymn sheet. In the porch where the three
church elders, Mr Wilson, Mr Brown and Mr Cunningham, had
been shot dead a calendar on the wall read, "He is able to save them
to the uttermost that come by Him." And the blood of the three
men He had not been able to save lay on a pool on the floor underneath, still wet.

(*Daily Mirror*, 22 November 1983)

A report by Charles Mallon was equally harrowing:

Inside the church, where gospel meetings have been held for thirty
years, the two rows of plastic covered benches were in disarray.
Flowers which had adorned the organs were trampled on the floor
and a blue carry cot blanket was left behind in the obvious panic
which followed.

The RUC man could not understand who would carry out such
a deed. "Only devils from Hell could have," he insisted. He lifted up
a gospel song sheet to show the piercing bullet hole. Whoever held
that on Sunday night was one of the injured.

He lifted up forgotten bottles of orange and lemonade, a
"Monster Munch" bag of crisps to keep the children quiet during
hymn singing. One sheet escaped his notice. On it a child had
scribbled almost illegibly "Jesus Saves".

But the porch of the Mountain Lodge Hall on the remote hill-
side showed a real horror of the slaughter. "I washed part of one
man off the wall there. But I had nothing to clear it up," said the
RUC man pointing at the pool of blood and water on the floor.

(*Irish Independent*, 22 November 1983)

The head of the Catholic Church in Ireland, Cardinal Tomás Ó Fiaich, was unstinting in his criticism of the gunmen:

> Words cannot express my horror at this foul deed. The slaughter of three innocent people and the serious wounding of several others is an unspeakable crime. But to carry out this deed when they were at prayer in their local place of worship adds the guilt of sacrilege and blasphemy to that of murder. It is a direct attack on the God whom they were worshipping.
>
> To those who perpetrated this atrocity I say: "Don't dare to claim the name Catholic for your band of evil doers." The Catholics of this area abhor your crime and never want to hear of you again.

The head of the Church of Ireland, Archbishop John Armstrong, described the Darkley attack as 'the worst incident ever in Northern Ireland's 14 years of troubles'.

In a sign of public opposition to the attack, on 22 November the leaders of the Catholic, Church of Ireland, Presbyterian and Methodist Churches in Ireland jointly visited Darkley, met the families of the victims and prayed with them.

17 DECEMBER 1983: THE HARRODS BOMB

Six people were killed and ninety-one injured when a 20 lb IRA bomb exploded outside Harrods department store in London. At 12.45pm the police received a bomb warning via the Samaritans, followed by a second warning to Scotland Yard ten minutes before the explosion. The explosion occurred at approximately 1.20pm and could be heard across several miles of central London. It set more than a dozen cars on fire and shattered windows in nearby buildings. Three of the six people killed were police officers. On 18 December the Provisionals issued a statement, claiming that 'Steps will be taken to ensure there will be no repetition of this type of operation. We regret the civilian casualties, even though our expressions of sympathy will be dismissed.'

The bombing took place on the busiest Saturday for shopping in the period leading up to Christmas. In the week leading up to the Harrods attack, a bomb had exploded outside the Army barracks at Woolwich and police had detonated another bomb in Kensington. A

number of commentators believed that the upsurge in IRA activity
was a response by the more militarist 'hawks' within the IRA to those
who were promoting the 'ballot box and armalite' approach outlined
by Danny Morrison in 1981.

The car bomb had been parked after police had checked the street
subsequent to receiving a warning that there was a bomb inside
Harrods store and two more outside. The car bomb was double-
parked, therefore soon drew the attention of police. As police officers
examined the car it was detonated by remote control. An Inspector
was found dead under a car. The *News of the World* reported:

> The [police] dog handler was lying face down across his animal,
> which had two of its legs blown off and had to be put down by a
> police marksman. Forensic experts took nearly two hours to find
> the remains of the police woman.
>
> (*News of the World*, 18 December 1983)

Munna Malik, who worked in a tailor's shop near Harrods, was one of
those who covered the dead and injured with sheets and blankets. He
recalled:

> I saw three men lying dead. One police man had very badly shat-
> tered legs. I remember his wallet was sticking out of his pocket.
> There was an Alsatian dog, I suppose it was a police Alsatian, which
> had its hind legs blown away. It was just lying there with its eyes
> and mouth open.

Police Constable John Gordon was less than five yards from the bomb
when it exploded and lost both legs as a result of the blast, while his
dog Queenie was put down because of the injuries it suffered. A year
later he told the inquest: 'Queenie was not trained to sniff out explosives but she was very uneasy and I had great difficulty in controlling
her. She had never behaved like that before. She was pulling very
strongly and I couldn't understand it.' After giving evidence he added:
'It was as if Queenie could sense that something was about to happen.
Animals can be like that. The hair on the back of her neck was standing up. I couldn't figure out then what she was trying to tell me, but I
do now. She was trying to save my life' (*Daily Mail*, 15 November 1984).

Another eyewitness, Douglas Free, said:

I could see bodies lying on the pavement, people stumbling around so completely shocked they didn't know what was happening. I saw one little girl clinging to her mother, who was trying to hold her stomach, where blood was gushing from a wound. The woman was hit by flying glass.

(*Sunday Times*, 18 December 1983)

His girlfriend, Annie Eyston, said:

We were remarking on how many police were in the area—we thought there might be a bomb scare. Suddenly the whole place just erupted. All the shop windows seemed to fall out.

Douglas was flung across the road. I found myself the only one standing. There were bodies everywhere. Someone screamed, "Get down, get down". I saw a policewoman, obviously dead. She didn't look much like a human being any more. Two other policemen were lying nearby. There was blood everywhere, I saw a woman with her legs bright red. Douglas ripped open her clothes and she had a huge lump of glass in her stomach. Her young daughter was screaming hysterically. She kept saying, "Why have they done this to us? We haven't done anything to them." ...

All I could think of was what lousy bastards they were. The only thing that kept me going was this little girl. Her mother was obviously dying. I took hold of her, and some people took us into their house.

(*Sunday Express*, 18 December 1983)

One of those who narrowly escaped being caught in the explosion was the actress Diana Rigg. She told reporters:

I had been shopping in Harrods for about 45 minutes and I had just left when the bomb went off. I was in a shoe shop a few doors along when we heard the explosion. People started streaming past. Some were covered in blood and I saw children being carried into an ambulance. It was ghastly, just ghastly.

The police, fire and ambulances were there within seconds. If there was a ten minute warning, the general public were completely unaware of it. The odd thing is I don't feel lucky, I just grieve for all those who were killed and injured. So many of them appeared to be children.

(*Sunday People*, 18 December 1983)

Searches were carried out in other shopping areas of London and a number of stores in Oxford Street were evacuated. A warning that a bomb would explode in Littlewoods at 2.30pm proved to be a hoax. Streets around Oxford Street were blocked off and nearby tube stations closed. Roadblocks were set up by the police at Sloane Square, Hyde Park corner and Knightsbridge Barracks.

The attack was widely condemned across Britain and Ireland. The *Sunday Express* reported:

> Shoppers in the main stores in Dublin's O'Connell Street listened in stunned silence as TV monitors told them the news. Hundreds headed for home, too sickened to continue their search for Christmas gifts. "How can they do this?" asked a young housewife. "Families shopping for toys—children going to see Father Christmas—mothers taking little ones for a day out in London. These are the victims.
>
> Surely to God they must know that. Haven't they got mothers and children of their own? ... If they say they have done this in the name of Ireland, please don't believe them."
>
> (*Sunday Express*, 18 December 1983)

By the following day staff at Harrods had already begun clearing up bomb damage and the shop was open to customers on Monday. Initially trade was slow, but within months Harrods became the first European store to achieve a turnover of more than £200 million in a financial year.

Twenty-two-year-old Jane Arbuthnot was one of three police officers from Chelsea Police Station killed in the explosion. A year after the event her mother spoke of trying to come to terms with her daughter's death:

> It hurts, it physically hurts to think about that afternoon. You can't believe this thing has happened to your daughter. It was a night-marish time and it's absolutely true that as time goes by and you throw yourself into other things the nightmare lifts, but the pain is still there.
>
> Events like the Brighton bomb can trigger off your emotions. Or when I see pretty things in a shop window. Janey was very fond of pretty clothes.
>
> (*The Times*, 14 December 1984)

12 OCTOBER 1984: THE BRIGHTON BOMB

On 12 October 1984 the Provisional IRA exploded a bomb in a room on the fifth floor of the Grand Hotel, Brighton, which was being used by many senior Conservative party members during the party's annual conference. The 20 lb bomb exploded at 2.54am, sliced four floors out of the middle of the building and killed five people, including Sir Anthony Berry MP and Roberta Wakeham, wife of the government chief whip. Norman Tebbitt, a close political ally of Margaret Thatcher and Secretary of State for Trade and Industry, was one of more than thirty people injured in the explosion. The Prime Minister, Mrs Thatcher, narrowly escaped injury. The *Financial Times* (13 October 1984) described the attack as 'the most violent challenge to constitutional authority in modern British political history'. An IRA statement released shortly after the explosion said: 'Today, we were unlucky ... but remember, we only have to be lucky once—you will have to be lucky always.' IRA member Patrick Magee was later convicted of the bombing and given eight life sentences, while two of his five accomplices were also given life sentences. Magee was among those given early release from prison under the terms of the Good Friday Agreement.

Several hours before the explosion the hotel had been busy, with many of those present discussing the events of the conference. Aidan Hennigan described the scene:

> The bar was packed with people in carnival mood and the atmosphere was relaxed after some fairly tense arguments about unemployment in the conference hall and at fringe meetings during the day.
>
> Approximately four hours later, the bomb on the fifth floor of the Grand ripped a gaping hole in its façade, sending masonry and shattered rooms crashing down almost to floor level. Our first news was that an attempt had been made to wipe out the entire Cabinet, including the Prime Minister, Mrs Thatcher.
>
> Many young people and elderly people had retired from the [Conservative party] ball and were chatting amiably in the foyer, retiring to bed or having a nightcap. What followed were scenes of incredible confusion and dismay.
>
> Outside the Grand, with colleagues, I watched ferries of ambulances arrive with doctors, nurses, police and voluntary helpers

seeking to assist the injured. I saw the Education Minister, Sir Keith Joseph, covered in dust, in his pyjamas, being led from the Grand to the next door Metropole Hotel which was being used as a temporary hospital.

(*Irish Press*, 13 October 1984)

Conservative councillor Ron Farley was in a bar on the hotel's ground floor when the bomb went off:

There was a small explosion and then a bigger one. Everyone was showered with glass and I shouted at them to get down. I shouted to the people to join hands. There were about thirty or forty of us who linked up and we slowly made our way out through the back. Some of the people were crying or sobbing.

There was one policeman lying on the floor covered in rubble. We pulled away all the dust and rubbish, he was injured, I don't know how badly. Then I found this poor old dear, a 70-year-old lady. She had one eye missing, it was terrible.

(*The Guardian*, 13 October 1984)

The *Sunday Times* 'Insight' team reported on the impact of the explosion on the hotel:

The force of the upward blast did the most visible damage to the Grand's elegant façade. It blew out the front wall of the centre bedrooms on the fifth, sixth and seventh floors, wrecked their adjoining bathrooms and took off the roof ... But it was the downward blast that was more devastating, and deadly. From top to bottom of the hotel, the floors of the centre seaview bedrooms collapsed; it was as though some monstrous drill had bored a vertical shaft from the roof to the basement.

(*Sunday Times*, 14 October 1984)

Barry Perkins of the East Sussex Fire Brigade spoke of the immediate rescue operation:

To discover where the victims lay rescuers had to shout into the rubble and wait for a response. One fireman, Station Officer Fred Bishop, became on first name terms with Mr Tebbit. Our first visible sign of the minister was his nose appearing through the rubble. ...

There was a partial collapse of the building, with further collapses very possible at each stage of the rescue. This was never more likely than at the last stage when firemen were working on the exposed face of the building facing the sea. I was standing on compacted floors which were literally balancing there, where they had wedged themselves.

(*Daily Telegraph*, 15 October 1984)

One of those trapped in the explosion was the conference organiser, Harvey Thomas. His room had been directly above the bomb and the explosion left him trapped and hanging over a drop of five floors. The *Evening Argus* reported:

Mr Thomas, a devout Christian and former crusade director with Billy Graham, thinks: "Right, if I am going to die, first John, chapter one, verse nine: If we confess our sins, He is faithful and just to forgive our sins and to cleanse us from all unrighteousness"—if not from the rubble of the Grand Hotel. "Lord if I have anything unconfessed, take it as read."

He lies there on his back, masonry pouring on top of him, burying his head, blinding his eyes and filling his nose and mouth. Thinking quickly, he holds his hands over his mouth to make a vital pocket of air, but it is a struggle to breathe. Water from a burst tank cascades down on to him.

He has crashed through two floors, and he is lying with a bath full of shattered stone bearing down on his chest, and a girder across his ribs. His life hangs in the balance over that gaping void as he silently says his second prayer: "Lord please give me spiritual strength and the physical strength to hold off the crushing weight." ...

But it was to be a long, agonising wait before he would hear that his prayers had been answered.

(*To Kill the Cabinet*, an *Evening Argus* publication)

Some commentators viewed the bombing as an attempt by the IRA to bring about a repressive security reaction from the British government, which in turn might increase international support for a united Ireland. Within the Conservative Party, Thatcher was facing pressure over her economic policies, record unemployment figures and a possible leadership challenge. As with the Falklands War, however, the

Brighton bomb saw Thatcher at her unshakeable best. As Maeve
Binchy wrote from London:

> All day long was heard the sound of praise for Mrs Thatcher, praise
> that was either grudging or generous, depending on the politics of
> who gave it. For someone who was writing a speech at 3 o'clock in
> the morning, whose bathroom was blown up and whose Cabinet of
> Ministers might well have been blown up too, she had a calm that
> was enviable and for a great many people highly reassuring. She
> could have had no sleep whatsoever they told each other totting up
> the hours. She was an example to everyone.
>
> Two men came into a bar which said that people should not come
> in wearing working clothes. They were dressed in paint-splattered
> overalls and looked up at the television. With such serious news
> nobody was likely to refer to their clothes. One said, "I don't know
> that's what the IRA wanted, but they've just made sure that she's
> with us for the duration."
>
> (*The Irish Times*, 13 October 1984)

28 FEBRUARY 1985: NEWRY RUC STATION ATTACK

The incident in which the RUC suffered its greatest loss of life came
during a period in which there was a general upsurge in violence. In
the two weeks leading up to the attack on Newry police station a
prison officer, a police officer, a man accused by the IRA of being an
informer, a former UDR member and three IRA men were killed. On
the same day as the Newry attack a part-time UDR member was killed
near Pomeroy.

Just after 6.30pm IRA mortars struck the canteen in Newry RUC
station, killing nine police officers and injuring nearly forty other
people, including a number of civilians. The canteen was packed as
many officers were on an evening tea break.

The IRA rockets had been fired from the back of a lorry—hijacked
earlier from near Crossmaglen—that was parked on waste ground
200 yards away from the station. The IRA attackers mounted a 6 ft by
3 ft steel support on to the back of the lorry and bolted it to the floor.
Nine steel tubes were placed on the support and the security forces
believed that a mortar was fired from each of the pipes. Each mortar

was estimated to be the size of a fire extinguisher and held 40 lb of explosives (*Belfast Telegraph*, 1 March 1985). The mortars flew over a housing estate and struck the police station in quick succession, causing severe damage. All of those who were killed were in a wooden portable building used as a canteen, which was completely destroyed when it received a direct hit from one of the rockets. Another mortar hit an observation post at the front of the station, destroying cars in the street outside.

In the aftermath of the attack rescue workers searched through the night to find those who were unaccounted for. As the explosions had knocked out powerlines, the search was carried out in darkness. A RUC spokesman said that they were not able to remove the dead for some time because the damage made it difficult to tell the bodies apart. Casualties were taken to Newry's Daisy Hill Hospital and off-duty staff were called in to help in operating theatres.

The mortar attack killed nine police officers, including two police women, Rosemary McGookin and Ivy Kelly. The most senior officer killed in the incident was Chief Inspector Alexander Donaldson.

A local nurse, Brenda Finnegan, who lived close to the station, recalled the moment the attack took place: 'I was just leaving the house when suddenly there was a blue flash and a big explosion. I was blown off my feet and forward on to the ground. I was screaming uncontrollably. Then there were more explosions and blue flashes—each time they were coming nearer to me. I could hear other people screaming. I thought I was going to die' (*Belfast Telegraph*, 1 March 1985).

One police woman described the area as 'a scene of utter devastation. I have lost God knows how many friends and colleagues tonight. I just cannot believe what has happened. It is sheer bloody slaughter.'

Another police officer commented on the aftermath of the attack: 'Part of the police station is totally devastated. The fire brigade and ambulance service did an incredible job in digging out the casualties and nursing their wounds. The rescuers had to wade knee-deep in rubble to reach the injured. These people were our colleagues … but some of the bodies are so badly mutilated we cannot even begin to guess at identities of all of the victims at this stage' (*Daily Mail*, 1 March 1985).

Belfast Telegraph reporter Ken Devlin described the terrible vista:

The scene of the RUC's worst tragedy since the Troubles began was nothing more than a small row of bricks which had supported the portable building. The portable structure itself was not just destroyed. Quite simply, it was not there.

An adjoining portable building which was used as a kitchen was virtually intact but nothing remained of the dining area in the station yard which had taken the full force of a mortar.

Twisted tables and chairs were piled in a heap beside pieces of splintered timber and what remained of the flimsy walls of the structure. A mangled fruit machine lay on its side. Some broken crockery could be seen in between the rows of bricks. A policeman's car and an RUC Land Rover were parked in the small yard strewn with glass and debris. Windows in the station itself were smashed and some curtains fluttered limply in the wind.

(*Belfast Telegraph*, 1 March 1985)

Three women who provided catering in the canteen avoided serious injury because they were shielded by heavy kitchen equipment, which took most of the force of the explosion. They then scrambled through the debris to try to help the injured.

This was not the IRA's first attempt to land mortars in Newry police station. In April 1980 an attempt to fire mortars at the station from the back of a lorry parked 100 yards away failed because of a faulty firing mechanism. On that occasion only two of the ten mortars exploded— one fell short of the station and blew a hole in its wall and the other exploded in mid-air. Nonetheless shrapnel from the mortar injured more than twenty-five people (*The Irish Times*, 1 March 1985).

Claiming responsibility for the attack, an IRA statement said it was 'a major and well planned operation. It indicates our ability to strike when and where we decide.' A number of newspapers interpreted the attack as the IRA exacting revenge for the SAS killing of three IRA members five days earlier.

In the wake of the attack the government faced criticism for its security policy, particularly from unionists, although calls for the reintroduction of the death penalty were rejected by NIO security minister Nick Scott. The minister's argument, that 'we can never stop this sort of one-off attack', was scathingly rejected by Ulster Unionist leader James Molyneaux, who responded: 'How can he describe Newry as a one-off attack with nine people dead and more than 30 injured? At best his attitude can be described as complacent' (*News Letter*, 2 March 1985).

Among those who narrowly avoided being caught up in the blast was Fr Denis Faul, who had been due to meet Chief Inspector Donaldson at 7.00pm. He told RTÉ: 'I was engaged in bringing a young man to the police station to make a complaint ... half an hour later I would have been in the police station' (*The Irish Times*, 1 March 1985). The *Belfast Telegraph* commented: 'February 28, 1985 adds a Bloody Thursday to go with all the other bloody days of the week.' The *News Letter* believed that 'February 28, 1985 must mark an indelible water-shed in the affairs of Northern Ireland and in the banishment of terrorism and murder from our land.' The *Irish News* stated: 'This morning there are more bodies in the morgue, more people struggling for life in hospital, more families bereaved. They and all the other victims who went before them make at least one point glaringly obvious. Northern Ireland should be the number one priority— no, the only priority for the governments in Dublin and London. A solution, an end to the conflict can be found. It must be found.'

15 NOVEMBER 1985: THE ANGLO-IRISH AGREEMENT

On 15 November 1985, after months of negotiation between British and Irish civil servants, the Anglo-Irish Agreement (AIA) was signed by Prime Minister Margaret Thatcher and Taoiseach Garret FitzGerald at Hillsborough Castle in Co. Down. The AIA established an Inter-Governmental Conference (IGC), which would meet regularly to deal with political matters, security and related matters, legal matters and the promotion of cross-border co-operation. Under the terms of the Agreement the British government was committed to make determined efforts to resolve any differences arising with the Irish government within the IGC.

The Irish government, along with nationalists and unionists in Northern Ireland, interpreted the AIA as giving the Irish a major input into the running of Northern Ireland—in effect, something approaching joint British–Irish authority. For the British, however, the Republic of Ireland's role was to be merely consultative and one of its main contributions, especially as far as Margaret Thatcher was concerned, would be to improve security co-operation.

While the AIA failed to appeal to republican paramilitaries, who believed it copper-fastened partition, the greatest degree of opposition

came from unionists. Within days unionist-controlled District
Councils began adjourning in protest against the Agreement, forcing
the NIO to set council rates. Secretary of State Tom King was attacked
by loyalist demonstrators outside Belfast City Hall, and on 23
November a massive anti-AIA rally was held outside Belfast City Hall.
Protests continued in the subsequent months, including attacks on
the site of the Anglo-Irish secretariat at Maryfield, near Belfast.

James Naughtie reported on the atmosphere at Hillsborough on
the morning the Agreement was signed:

> Walking up to Hillsborough yesterday morning, along a frosty lane
> piled with autumn leaves and shining under a clear blue sky, every-
> thing seemed at peace, for a moment. Then, through the air there
> came a raucous, megaphoned voice: "Ulster is British. No sell out
> to FitzGerald and Haughey. No sell out to the IRA. No surrender."
> The shouting was going on as ever in a last pointless appeal to a
> Conservative Prime Minister. As she landed away behind
> Hillsborough House in her helicopter, she will have heard hardly a
> word of it, save perhaps the occasional echo of an angry yell carried
> on the breeze.
>
> Inside the House, the English nationalist sat down with the Irish
> nationalists and did a deal, probably the most important for
> Ireland since 1921. It was a hard, hard bargain for Mrs Thatcher (as
> well as for Dr FitzGerald) but from the moment she decided that it
> had to be so the diehard Unionists were lost. It's a resolute
> approach, certainly, and it shows that there is no way back.
>
> (*The Guardian*, 16 November 1985)

The chasm between the perceptions of unionists and nationalists as to
what the Agreement meant was obvious from the beginning. The
News Letter commented:

> Betrayal, sell-out, disaster. These are epithets that will undoubtedly
> jar the ear of the Prime Minister, Mrs Thatcher. Of their crudeness
> there can be no doubt. Of their accuracy or otherwise time will tell.
> At the Hillsborough Press conference Mrs Thatcher went to great
> lengths to convince the world of her government's good faith in its
> dealings with the Ulster people.
>
> It may be that she will have a measure of success in this respect,
> especially with those far removed from the centre of affairs. But the

people who have been at the sharp end of 16 years of republican violence and nationalist propaganda will certainly question the Government's good sense, even if they were to accept it in good faith.

It matters little to loyalists whether they have been betrayed accidentally because of stupidity, or deliberately through duplicity: the effect is the same.

(*News Letter*, 16 November 1985)

The *Irish News*, on the other hand, welcomed the Agreement:

No one would claim that the document is in itself a solution, but it is a brave and commendable attempt to begin the healing process. Its historic significance can be gauged by the fact that from the establishment of the Northern State in 1921 until the late 1960s, it was not even possible for British MPs to raise discussion of Northern Ireland matters at Westminster. And, as recently as 1971 the then British Prime Minister, Edward Heath, delivered a stern rebuff to the Irish government for daring to interfere in "the internal affairs of the United Kingdom." ...

Moreover, for the first time the Irish Government has been given a direct say in the internal administration of the north and, specifically, a role as the advocate of the minority at the highest levels.

(*Irish News*, 16 November 1985)

The Agreement also received a wide welcome in Britain and internationally. *The Sun* commented:

No Prime Minister since the days of Churchill has stood up so well for Britain. She would never enter into any deal that would sell British citizens in Ulster down the Liffey. In fact, the agreement is a sensible step to getting the two communities in the North to live peacefully together after 700 years of bitterness and bloodshed. And it should now be easier for the security forces on both sides to work together to isolate the evil men of violence. That's why the deal must be given a chance.

(*The Sun*, 16 November 1985)

There were signs that the Agreement would not be widely accepted in Northern Ireland, however, such as the strongly critical comment from the *Belfast Telegraph*:

Consent is a recurring theme, but is it consent to the right to say "no", if it fails an electoral test? The sentiments are fine—peace and reconciliation—but insufficient attention has been paid to the mistrust engendered by 16 years of conflict.

If this is the price for Nationalist consent to participation in Northern Ireland, it has been fixed at an unrealistically high level. The Nationalist minority would have input into government, while unionists would be excluded. That will not work.

(*Belfast Telegraph*, 16 November 1985)

On 23 November unionists held a massive protest rally against the Anglo-Irish Agreement. In his autobiography Richard Needham, the longest-serving NIO Minister, described the unionist mood at the time:

The signing of the Anglo-Irish Agreement on 15 November 1985 appeared to be the first step down the path to British withdrawal. To unionists, it showed that nationalist politicians North and South would use IRA violence as a way of extorting constitutional advantage to the detriment of the Union. In protest 250,000 people crammed the centre of Belfast on the following Saturday. The NIO claimed it was 30,000. It was not. It was the biggest rally of the Protestant people since the signing of the Edward Carson-inspired covenant in 1912.

(Richard Needham, *Battling for Peace*, pp 76–7)

Lorna Donlon reported on the rally for the *Sunday Tribune*:

The loyalist marchers had converged on the City Hall from five points around the city, starting to assemble from early morning. Each of the parades was led by numerous bands and Lambeg drummers.

"Iron Lady be warned. Your iron will melt from the heat of Ulster," screamed one banner in a sea of Union Jacks, "If you want Republican rule, go live down South," proclaimed another. "The Pope is an anti-Christ. We need no Popies to help us on our way," said a third. An effigy of Mrs Thatcher and an Irish tricolour were burned.

There were no protesters in paramilitary uniform. Official Unionist Party spokesman Frank Millar had made it clear earlier in the day that they would not be welcome. But a number of youths were arrested by the RUC after they occupied a building opposite Belfast City Hall during the demonstration. ...

Over 300 buses and a number of trains carried protesters from all over the province, to what one man described as, "the greatest show of loyalist strength since Carson's day."

(*Sunday Tribune*, 24 November 1985)

For the rest of the 1980s and the 1990s the replacement of the AIA continued to be a key unionist objective; this was highlighted subsequently by David Trimble as one of the main achievements of the Good Friday Agreement negotiations in 1998.

2 NOVEMBER 1986: SINN FÉIN VOTES TO TAKE SEATS IN THE DÁIL

On 4 October 1986 Sinn Féin announced that a motion would be put forward by the party executive at its next Árd fheis to allow candidates to contest the forthcoming election in the Republic, and to take their seats in the Dáil if elected. A similar motion had been defeated the previous year, but those in favour of taking seats in the Dáil (many from the North) had worked to change opinion in the South. David McKittrick noted in *The Independent*:

Republican sources argue that dropping abstention would represent "removing the handcuffs" which have prevented Sinn Féin developing beyond a fringe party in the Republic. They believe up to five Dáil seats could be won through votes coming from republican elements, left-wingers and the disaffected young.

Irish politicians view these moves with something akin to dread. Small parties and independents hold a number of Dáil seats and Sinn Féin could mop up some of these.

(*The Independent*, 9 October 1986)

In advance of the Árd fheis the IRA held a general army convention and voted by more than a two-thirds majority to remove the ban on taking Dáil seats. On 14 October an IRA statement said that it was not against Sinn Féin members contesting Dáil elections and taking seats, if elected.

However, former IRA leader Seán MacStiofáin responded by saying: 'As one who has served the republican cause for almost thirty years, I challenge the right and authority of the IRA to make such compromising decisions. ... It will have the same devastating effect as the Official-Provisional split of the early '70s' (*Belfast Telegraph*, 15 October 1986).

The *Irish Times* responded by stating:

> Sinn Féin seems set to enter Leinster House. Barring unforeseen upsets, it now seems certain that the party's upcoming Árd fheis will endorse the strategy devised and promulgated by the Northern leadership—notably Messrs Adams, Morrison and McGuinness.
>
> It might be a good omen. Talking—of any kind—is better than killing. But there should be no flights of optimism at this stage. This is a strategic decision, not a conversion. The twin policies of the Armalite and the ballot paper remain. This merely seeks to utilise the ballot paper route more effectively than heretofore. The "armed struggle" will go on. People will continue to be murdered.
>
> (*The Irish Times*, 16 October 1986)

By 26 October the media were predicting a walk-out at the Árd fheis if the proposal was passed. In *The Times* Richard Ford commented:

> By ensuring that the Provisional IRA backs the proposal the leaders believe that anyone who walks out would not have the ability to set up a rival organisation with the support of military men.
>
> The leadership insists that taking seats in the Dáil would not diminish the "armed struggle" in the North or lead inevitably to reformism and the abandonment of military operations. It is precisely that which Mr Ruairí Ó Brádaigh, the former party president, fears, saying that it is impossible to remain a revolutionary organisation while sitting in the Dáil.
>
> "Going into Leinster House means accepting the Army, the political police, the special courts, the internment camps and all the apparatus of repression and collaboration with the British. We didn't survive the centuries to be beaten now."
>
> (*The Times*, 28 October 1986)

Although opposition to the change came from older republican leaders in the South, there was also some criticism in the North. One Belfast republican who had been close to Gerry Adams wrote:

Leaders can be wrong and they very often are. Four years ago I remember Gerry Adams saying, "when you talk about constitutional politics in an Irish context, it is British constitutionalism to which you refer." What happened Gerry, where did it go wrong? What changed? Where and when did it change, or had the decisions already been taken, even then, as your oration at Bodenstown in '83 would suggest?

(*Irish Press*, 28 October 1986)

Letters from prominent republican activists supporting the proposed change appeared in *An Phoblacht* in the weeks leading up to the Árd fheis, although Thomas Maguire, the only surviving member of the Second Dáil of 1921–22, came out against the proposal, as did Cumann na mBan and leading Noraid member Michael Flannery.

On the eve of the vote Adams called for party unity, but warned that 'anyone who leaves us over this issue will regret their decision in the years ahead.'

Of the debate itself John Foley reported:

Sinn Féin's historic debate on whether it should change its abstentionist policy was barely 15 minutes old when one activist remarked to another: "I think the day is ours." He was correct—but neither he nor the thousand or so others in the Round Room of the Mansion House could have imagined the drama and tension of the following five hours.

In the end, the debate and the Árd fheis was a resounding success for the organisational skills and pragmatism of the leadership, who see the abstentionist policy as a political cul de sac. But between 11.30 am and 5 pm when the vote result was declared by the chairman of the Árd fheis steering committee there took place a discussion of compelling interest conducted with palpable sincerity.

(*Irish Independent*, 3 November 1986)

In the *Irish News* William Graham wrote:

Only a few minutes after the historic vote 429 for abandoning abstentionism, 161 against, Mr Ó Brádaigh led out between 30 and 50 delegates but was joined by more supporters who were not

delegates. The vote to end abstentionism of Leinster House required
a two-thirds majority and this was achieved by a narrow margin.

However, the passing of the vote was still a considerable victory
for Sinn Féin President Gerry Adams who did his homework and
had the majority of delegates on his side.

(*Irish News*, 3 November 1986)

Almost inevitably the vote precipitated a split and the formation of a
new organisation—Republican Sinn Féin. Michael Devine reported:

Despite a last minute plea by President Mr Gerry Adams who
warned of the danger of a split, a walk-out was led by former IRA
Chief of Staff Mr David O'Connell and former president Mr Ruairí
Ó Brádaigh. They were followed from the conference in the
Mansion House by a group of about 100 supporters, some of them
singing the Republican song, "Take it down from the mast, Irish
Traitors".

They immediately headed for an hotel on the western outskirts
of Dublin where a room had been pre-booked for a meeting. After
about an hour behind closed doors Mr Ó Brádaigh called a press
conference at which he announced the formation of the new party.

He claimed the decision to end the abstentionist policy went
against the fundamental principles of Sinn Féin. He said the object
of the new organisation would be, "to organise the Irish people, at
home and abroad, in opposition to British interference in the
affairs of the historic Irish nation."

(*Belfast Telegraph*, 3 November 1986)

On 5 November an IRA statement welcomed the decision, but assured
its supporters that the armed struggle would continue. The following
day Dick Walsh commented in the *Irish Times*:

Mr Adams must face the logic of the decision taken at the weekend—a logic which was underlined by speakers who supported
abstention, among them the former president of the organisation,
Mr Ruairí Ó Brádaigh. Taking seats in the Dáil, if and when that
happens, is not simply a matter of convenience. It is a recognition
of the institutions of the State, of which the Dáil is one and the
Army, our Army, is another.

No-one who accepts the authority of the Oireachtas, as defined by the Constitution, can claim the right on behalf of the Irish people, to wage war. That right belongs to the Government and the Army; and those who deny it are the usurpers.

(*The Irish Times*, 6 November 1986)

A general election in the Republic, held on 19 February 1987, led to the formation of a Fianna Fáil minority government in March, led by Charles Haughey. On this occasion Sinn Féin took 1.9 per cent of first-preference votes, but failed to win any seats.

8 MAY 1987: LOUGHGALL

On 8 May 1987 eight IRA members were shot dead by the SAS in the Co. Armagh village of Loughgall when they attacked the local RUC station. Anthony Hughes, a civilian caught up in the ambush, was also killed and his brother, who was a passenger in the car he was driving, was wounded. British intelligence agents had discovered that the IRA was planning a bomb attack on the local police station and an operation involving forty SAS members was set up to ambush the IRA active service unit. SAS members were positioned inside the station and in a nearby wood, while others were assigned to cut off the IRA attackers if they tried to escape.

The IRA unit attacked the station with a mechanical digger carrying a 200 lb bomb, which was detonated and destroyed part of the police station. The SAS fired over 100 rounds of ammunition into the digger and into a van carrying other members of the unit. The civilian was killed when he drove through one of the SAS groups. The ambush effectively destroyed the IRA's East Tyrone unit and was the highest death toll suffered by the organisation in any single incident. The ambush came less than two weeks after the IRA killed seventy-three-year-old Maurice Gibson, one of the most senior judges in Northern Ireland, along with his wife, Cecily.

The *Irish Independent* reported of the Loughgall ambush:

The shooting began when a heavily armed Provo active service unit drove a bomb, concealed in the bucket of a mechanical digger, through Loughgall on Friday night to the police station.

The JCB crashed through the perimeter fence at the station and almost immediately shots were fired. Moments later the bomb exploded wrecking the barracks. The firing continued for some time, and when it stopped the scene resembled a battlefield with corpses strewn around.

Three of the IRA men, including the driver of their Toyota van, died before they were able to get out of the vehicle. Two IRA men died by the side of the van and another near the smouldering wreckage of the digger.

Two members of the gang had attempted to escape by running up a nearby laneway, but were shot dead. One lay on the pavement and the other fell in the lane.

(*Irish Independent*, 11 May 1987)

In the wake of the attack one Loughgall resident recalled that 'the explosion was just massive—it shook the whole village. … Then the shooting went on and on, automatic gunfire, for at least 20 minutes. About five minutes after it finished, the police had the whole place closed off. It was like that for the rest of the night, helicopters, search-lights, the works. We only found out from the television what had been going on' (*Belfast Telegraph*, 9 May 1987).

A number of newspapers quoted the local Church of Ireland rector as saying: 'The IRA came to kill, they did not care who they killed, and they were killed themselves; what can they expect? … I think it is terribly sad that this motorist could be driving past, going about his business, and be killed in this way. As regards the other dead men, well, I pity their unfortunate families.'

One of the IRA men killed, Patrick McKearney, had been on the run since escaping from the Maze Prison in 1983. Pat Kelly, the officer commanding the East Tyrone Brigade, was another of those killed. Helen Shaw described his family background:

Kelly grew up in Dungannon town, the only boy in a close-knit family of five. His parents, Vincent and Anne Kelly, both locals, still live near their son's home in the small republican Lisnahull estate, just outside the town. The parents of Kelly's wife Kathleen, live just across the road from her home.

On Saturday, as news of the men's identities spread through Dungannon, black flags were hung from windows throughout the town. Kathleen, who is expecting the couple's fourth child within days, was taken to a relative's house along with the three young children, while Kelly's parents and family faced the wave of reporters and cameramen which descended on the doorstep.

At Kathleen's parents' house Kelly's father, Vincent, spoke of the "long, proud tradition of republicanism" in the family and said it was a tradition "any Irishman or Irishwoman" should be proud of.

When asked of his son's IRA involvement, he said he knew he was "a republican"—but knew nothing of the role he played. He said all he knew was that his son and the other "volunteers" had been "vastly outnumbered", and that it seems several of the men had been pursued and shot dead in ditches.

He said: "They had no cause to shoot them dead—they could have captured them if they had wanted—The question is, if they knew about this attack in advance, why did they not apprehend them?"

(*The Irish Times*, 11 May 1987)

Most British newspapers showed little sympathy for the fate of the IRA members at Loughgall, with *The Star* commenting:

Only the weak-willed and the warped will shed a single tear over the killing of eight of the IRA's nastiest hit men this weekend. The SAS ambush was a job ruthlessly done, and it was all the better for it. In fact, it is a pity that it took the authorities so long to summon up the courage to sanction such an operation.

For too long there has been too much pandering to Republican opinion both north and south of the border in an attempt to keep the Anglo-Irish Agreement alive. The folly of this pussy-footing is seen in the reaction of the Irish Foreign Minister, who whole-heartedly approved of the ambush and the new super-tough policy.

The only whines of "murder" came from the IRA's mouthpiece, the sinister Sinn Féin leader Gerry Adams, and sympathisers like Dublin's *Sunday Tribune* newspaper. Mr Adams and his evil henchmen are forever bragging that they are at war with Britain. The gunmen and the bombers, they say, are legitimate soldiers. So be it. But if they take on the REAL soldiers of the SAS, they shouldn't cry if they get hurt.

(*The Star*, 11 May 1987)

John Devine assessed the security situation in the wake of Loughgall:

> Provisional IRA invincibility, projected in the aftermath of the
> murder of Lord Justice Gibson and his wife [on 25 April], was no
> more accurate than the image suggested now of an organisation on
> the ropes because one of its major fighting units was wiped out in
> the Loughgall ambush.
>
> What Loughgall proved was that, acting on good intelligence,
> state fire-power can be as murderous as anything that the IRA can
> throw against it. Anyone with reservations about the morality, or
> legality, of the state emulating the IRA, in lying in wait to deal out
> death, are reduced to merely deploring the wanton loss of life,
> rather than dealing up front with the wider questions posed. ...
>
> The IRA's ruthless murder of the Gibsons and callous disregard
> for the safety of anyone who, even innocently, might have come
> between them and their targets set the scene for the public reaction
> to the Loughgall massacre.
>
> They have single-mindedly brought about a public opinion
> climate in which a state policy of an-eye-for-an-eye is not only
> demanded but found generally acceptable—if only by silence. A
> population inured to murder of men, women and children seems
> able to accept, without difficulty, a dangerous escalation of a state
> policy towards terrorism—where multiple death is an acceptable
> measured response; and if not acceptable is neither objected to nor
> questioned.
>
> (*Irish Independent*, 11 May 1987)

8 NOVEMBER 1987: THE ENNISKILLEN BOMB

On 8 November 1987 eleven people were killed and sixty-three injured
when an IRA bomb exploded 20 yards from the town's war memorial
at 10.45am, just before the annual Remembrance Sunday ceremony
was due to commence. The building in which the bomb was hidden
had not been checked by the police because it was furthest away from
where members of the security forces were likely to be and the civilians who were standing there were not considered likely targets for a
terrorist attack. The blast brought a three-storey gable-end wall down

on the group of about fifteen people, who had lined up against the railings outside St Michael's reading rooms. At the time the explosion occurred ex-servicemen and women of the Royal British Legion, UDR members and the regimental band were 200 yards away, preparing for the parade. The attack was widely viewed as the IRA's response to a series of recent setbacks it had suffered, including Loughgall.

The bombing was widely condemned and the IRA subsequently expressed its regret for the event, but suggested that the bomb could have been triggered by a security forces' electronic scanning device. Prime Minister Margaret Thatcher later attended the rescheduled memorial service in Enniskillen.

Unlike many of the atrocities of the Troubles, the Enniskillen bombing acted to bring the community together and a number of schemes were established to this end, including The Spirit of Enniskillen Trust, Enniskillen Together and the Marie Wilson Voyage of Hope, a scheme for teenagers that was named after the daughter of Gordon Wilson, who was killed in the explosion.

The *Belfast Telegraph* described what happened that day:

> The victims had gathered as usual beside an old school in Belmore Street, known locally as St Michael's reading rooms, to watch the colourful annual parade to the town's Cenotaph. Seconds later ten lay dead and dozens of others were seriously injured when the building collapsed under the force of a 30lb bomb. A 20-year-old trainee nurse died five hours later from her injuries.
>
> The gable wall of the school disintegrated in the blast, burying men, women and children under a heap of rubble. Many of them were trapped between fallen masonry and metal railings mangled in the explosion. Among the dead were three married couples and a retired policeman. Some were prominent members of Enniskillen Presbyterian Church and last night special prayers were said in churches throughout the country.
>
> (*Belfast Telegraph*, 9 November 1987)

Local resident Pat O'Doherty felt the effects of the blast in his home:

> I rushed to the window; there were people rushing around in panic trying to find their relatives and dust was covering everyone and everything.

I was clawing around with a member of the UDR who realised that the woman we were digging out was his mother, but by the time we got to her she was dead.

(*The Guardian*, 9 November 1987)

A Boy's Brigade member, who was to lay a wreath, lost both his parents in the explosion; the fathers of two other Boy's Brigade members were also killed. Another member of the Boy's Brigade recalled:

We were standing ready to lay a wreath when we heard an almighty explosion. We dropped our wreaths and ran over to where the people had been buried. There were people with their arms and legs sticking out of the rubble, crying for help. It was a horrifying sight. At 11am we should have been remembering the dead not digging them out.

(*Daily Telegraph*, 9 November 1987)

Many of the injured were taken to Enniskillen Hospital. The chief administrative medical officer Dr Bill McConnell said:

Nurses, some in tears, bravely carried on even though they knew those being brought in. The injuries were horrific and there were many children among those so cruelly hurt. ... We saw the injured coming in with cuts, bruises and shock, as well as those more gravely wounded who had severed limbs and shrapnel wounds to the stomach.

It's harrowing enough for all our staff and particularly for the bereaved relatives and friends who are still here waiting for news. But for those who escaped it will be the weeks afterwards in which the suffering will continue to be felt. It will be the psychological trauma of seeing the horror, the appalling horror and savagery of what happened.

(*Daily Mail*, 9 November 1987)

Even with the perspective of two decades of violence, the Enniskillen bombing—soon dubbed the Remembrance Day Massacre or Poppy Day Massacre—was viewed as being perhaps the worst atrocity committed during the Troubles because of the circumstances in which it took place.

John Hume condemned the bombing as 'an appalling atrocity, an act of sheer savagery in that respect for the dead and commemoration of the dead is something which is respected in all civilised societies. Whoever carried out this atrocity did so ruthlessly and in a completely calculated fashion, because this is the single most provocative act committed against the Unionist people in the last 17 years' (*Belfast Telegraph*, 9 November 1987).

The visceral reaction to the bombing was captured by *The Star*, which commented:

> There is no possible name for the sick people who did this. There is no word in the English language to describe the bombers whose act of cowardice, of barbarity, of perverted patriotism was perpetrated yesterday—Remembrance Sunday.
>
> In every true, decent heart in this land we know what scum these people are. They struck as men, women and children gathered to pay silent tribute to the fallen of two World Wars.
>
> Not for the IRA the mud and blood of a real battlefield where brave men and women gave their own lives. Just a secret bomb designed to destroy those who wished to remember lost relatives and comrades. Millions died in the fight for freedom all over the world. These cynical terrorists spit on their monumental sacrifice.
>
> (*The Star*, 9 November 1987)

The newspaper was one of a number of sources that called for the introduction of hanging for those convicted of terrorist actions. The *Irish News* was equally scathing of the Provisionals. In its editorial, 'Beyond the pale', it stated:

> The slaughter of 11 people in Enniskillen yesterday was a heinous, revolting and indefensible crime. Already condemnation has come from across the political spectrum and one can be certain that will not be the end of it.
>
> At the time of writing, responsibility for this gruesome massacre has not been admitted by any organisation. However, the finger of suspicion points to the IRA, a suspicion hardened by the Provisionals' claim of another cenotaph bomb in Fermanagh, this time in Pettigo.
>
> What can possibly be achieved by murdering 11 people, including six pensioners and a young nurse? That must be the question

which is exercising the minds of those who will have to explain what they hope to accomplish with this outrageous barbarism.

At this year's Sinn Féin Árd fheis, President Gerry Adams told his colleagues that the armed struggle had become "a war of attrition". Given that yesterday's horror was most probably carried out by the IRA, there is no longer any doubt what kind of "attrition" he was referring to. Innocents beware! ...

Yesterday's criminal act of carnage was the biggest mistake ever by the IRA. No one has the stomach for such pointless bloodletting anymore; no one with an ounce of self-respect would want to be associated with it. The IRA and its political mentors have proven, conclusively, that they are not fit to have any role in deciding our future. They have surely, finally put themselves beyond the pale.

(*Irish News*, 9 November 1987)

Ronnie Hill, the principal of Enniskillen High School, was among those injured in the bombing. He received a fractured skull and internal injuries in the explosion and fell into a coma from which he never recovered. Ronnie Hill died in December 2000. His wife, Noreen, had not been with him at the time of the explosion because she had just completed a course of chemotherapy treatment for cancer. Twenty years after the Enniskillen bombing she remarked: 'The older I get, the more I miss him. I'm in my 70s now. Losing a partner is never easy but, when you're younger, you've more things to fill your life. My cancer has returned. If Ronnie was here he'd be going to the hospital with me. But life goes on, you just have to cope' (*Sunday Tribune*, 28 October 2007). Noreen Hill died five months later.

6 MARCH 1988: GIBRALTAR

On 6 March 1988 three unarmed IRA members on active service were shot dead by the SAS in Gibraltar. The IRA members—Sean Savage, Daniel McCann and Mairead Farrell—did not have immediate access to a bomb when they were killed. A car containing 140 lb of semtex plastic explosives and 200 AK-47 rounds was found two days later in Marbella. It was widely believed that the IRA's intention was to explode a car bomb during the Changing of the Guard ceremony at the official residence of the Governor of Gibraltar, due to take place on 8 March. The sas members shot Mairead Farrell first, then Sean Savage. Danny McCann was walking some distance behind his two colleagues and was shot 100 yards away as he tried to avoid the ambush.

Many early reports of events in Gibraltar were inaccurate, particularly on the question of whether the ira members had been challenged by police before they were shot, and especially on the question of whether they had left a car bomb. (On 7 March a number of newspapers said that a 500 lb car bomb had been planted, while *The Sun* reported that 'explosives experts were battling to defuse a powerful bomb left in a car in Gibraltar's main shopping street'.) Controversy also surrounded the accuracy of the statement of events given by the British government and the question of whether the ira members could have been arrested rather than killed.

A week after the events the *Sunday Times* reported:

It had, until the shooting started, been a sleepy Sunday afternoon with Gibraltar basking in the spring sunshine after two weeks of rain. The vast council housing estate, intersected by Winston Churchill Avenue, where the first two shootings had occurred, had appeared almost deserted. Many of the 4,000 residents were across the border at a children's fair in La Linea.

The avenue down which the shooting occurred—the main thoroughfare to the border—was still busy with motorists heading towards Spain, although the petrol station had closed some hours earlier. When the sas men went into action, the traffic was stopped at lights further up the road.

As the echoes of the shots died away among the dozen blocks of flats overlooking the scene, the sas men vanished in police cars as rapidly as they had arrived. A crowd quickly formed: terrified parents and their children from an adventure playground yards from where McCann was gunned down, a group of boys who had been playing football beside the petrol station and tenants from the estate.

By then all that was left was the bodies on the pavement, bullet marks on two of the forecourt pumps and another bullet embedded in the tree under which McCann died.

(*Sunday Times*, 13 March 1988)

Eyewitness Pepi Celecia told the press:

> I saw a smartly dressed couple walking past the petrol station. They
> were both carrying motor-cycle crash helmets. The woman was
> wearing a navy blue skirt and white blouse, with black stockings and
> high-heeled shoes. She had a heavy black bag over her shoulder. The
> man was in a white outfit with sports shoes.
>
> I then saw a well-built blond-haired man in a light blue jacket
> and jeans walk up behind them. The couple were heading towards
> the frontier. That's when I heard the shooting.
>
> The woman fell onto the pavement and the man fell over a low
> wall into the garage forecourt and remained propped up against
> the wall, half sitting with his head dropping.
>
> The man who was doing the shooting came within four yards of
> them and fired four or five shots into their bodies. The man had
> been hit in the heart. Blood was pumping from him. The man who
> did the shooting got into a Gibraltar police car which did a U-turn
> and sped away towards the town centre.
>
> (*Daily Mirror*, 8 March 1988)

While the Irish media tended to be critical of the action, there was
more support for it in Britain, albeit coupled with calls for the
government to be more open about exactly what had happened. The
Daily Telegraph commented:

> The Government must tell us why it gave a succession of contra-
> dictory accounts to the world about Sunday's events. Unless it
> wishes Britain's enemies to enjoy a propaganda bonanza, it should
> explain why it was necessary to shoot dead all three terrorists on the
> street, rather than apprehend them with the considerable force of
> police and sas which appears to have been deployed in the locality.
>
> (*Daily Telegraph*, 8 March 1988)

The *Irish News* was particularly critical, comparing the killing of the
ira members to 'strains of the Mafia':

> On the admission of the British Foreign Secretary in the House of
> Commons, the ira volunteers were unarmed and the car did not
> contain explosives. The suspects were not escaping in a fast moving
> vehicle. They were not even running. They were actually walking.

It is glaringly obvious that they could have been apprehended and taken into custody. Instead, they were assassinated in cold-blooded ruthlessness that one associates with the Mafia on the streets of Palermo.

The approval of a civilised society for counter-terrorist activity must always be based on the premise that the forces of law and order are in truth what they are proclaimed to be—agents of law and order. If they act outside the law their conduct is no less criminal than that of the terrorists they are combating; in fact, it could, depending on the circumstances, be more criminal.

(*Irish News*, 8 March 1988)

News of the deaths of the IRA members sparked a wave of rioting in nationalist areas of Belfast, particularly in the New Lodge Road and Ardoyne areas. There was more rioting the following night when it was revealed that no car bomb had been found in Gibraltar.

The death of Mairead Farrell also sparked arguments at Queen's University, Belfast (where Farrell was an under-graduate), both among students and between the Students' Union and university authorities as to how her death should be commemorated.

There was further controversy involved in flying home the bodies of the IRA members, as the *Daily Mirror* reported:

The bodies of the three IRA terrorists shot dead in Gibraltar were finally flown home yesterday—shunned to the last by the people of the Rock. Airport staff refused to load the coffins onto the charter jet hired by Sinn Féin, and it was left to the RAF to put them on board and refuel the aircraft. Hundreds of locals stood around the airport and cheered as the plane left.

(*Daily Mirror*, 15 March 1988)

When the coffins of the IRA members, which had been flown into Dublin, headed North they were welcomed by republicans. However, as the funeral cortege reached the border the RUC demanded that the Tricolours on the coffins be removed:

After a short time a compromise was reached in which the flags were folded up and placed on the top of each coffin concealed by floral wreaths.

Sinn Féin president Gerry Adams agreed to the fold up of the flags and the cortege then passed into the North shortly before 11 pm.

The cortege then moved on briefly before halting again at RUC lines where Martin McGuinness and Gerry Adams spoke to senior RUC officers.

Said Gerry Adams: "They asked us to take the national flag off the coffins and we said, They are staying on."

Mr Adams added that Sinn Féin agreed to cover the Tricolours with wreaths. Further lengthy delays followed at Newry as RUC Land Rovers attempted to head off local people trying to join the cortege.

There were scuffles and a number of people were struck by Land Rovers when they tried to form a line behind the leading hearse. In their efforts to thwart this move an RUC Land Rover patrol smashed into the back of an *Irish News* [reporter's] car in a bid to shunt it out of the way.

In Belfast, the IRA said a three-volley rifle salute had been fired at a shrine specially erected at Rodney Drive in West Belfast. ... A uniformed IRA colour party is understood to have consisted of four members—one giving orders in Irish and three firing their rifles over large photographs and wreaths of the dead.

(*Irish News*, 15 March 1988)

The European Commission of Human Rights would later rule that the SAS had not used excessive force in killing the IRA members, but in 1995 the European Court of Human Rights ruled, by a ten to nine majority, that the killings were unnecessary.

16 MARCH 1988: MILLTOWN CEMETERY AND THE CORPORALS

The Gibraltar killings sparked a series of events that led to further deaths in the same month. On 16 March three mourners were killed by loyalist paramilitary Michael Stone during the funerals of the three IRA members killed in Gibraltar at Milltown Cemetery, in Belfast. On 19 March British Army corporals Derek Wood and David Howes, wearing civilian clothes, were murdered by the IRA after their car was surrounded near the funeral cortege of Kevin Brady.

Funerals had often provided a focus of conflict between republicans and the security forces. On 5 March 1988 the funeral of IRA member Brendan Burns led to clashes between republicans and the police. The *Sunday Tribune* reported:

> Fighting broke out between police and mourners in a South Armagh graveyard yesterday during the funeral of Brendan Burns, one of two IRA men killed by their own bomb last Monday.
>
> Riot police rushed into the crowd with batons when an IRA colour party in khaki jackets and balaclavas appeared, and started carrying the coffin from St Patrick's Church to the graveyard in Crossmaglen. The IRA men escaped into the crowd in the confusion. A man and a woman were injured.
>
> Hundreds of police surrounded the graveyard and extra troops in riot gear were flown in to back them up. The huge security operation was mounted in South Armagh to prevent the IRA putting on a paramilitary display at the funeral. Extra police and troops were sent to the area and roadblocks set up in cross-border routes.
>
> The RUC said its sincere wish was for the Burns funeral to be peaceful, dignified and law-abiding. But they were not prepared to stand back and watch when the IRA men shouldered the coffin.
>
> (*Sunday Tribune*, 6 March 1988)

Mourners also complained that RUC members had jeered and taunted them. SDLP Deputy Leader Seamus Mallon asserted that he had received assurances from the RUC that they would maintain a 'discreet presence' during the funerals, but that they had, in fact, been confrontational. Mallon described the behaviour of the RUC as 'a stark and frightening example of policing at its worst' (*Irish News*, 7 March 1988).

At Milltown Cemetery little more than a week later loyalist Michael Stone threw grenades and fired into the crowd of mourners, killing Thomas McErlean, John Murray and IRA member Kevin Brady. On this occasion the police had stayed back from the funeral in an attempt to reduce tension, although this decision later led to claims that the RUC had colluded with Stone to leave the funerals more vulnerable to attack. As the coffins were being lowered into the graves, Stone began shooting and throwing grenades at mourners. Retreating towards the motorway he continued to fire and throw grenades while being pursued by a group of mourners. He was eventually caught and beaten by some of the crowd before the RUC arrived and took him into custody. Stone later claimed that his objective had been to kill Sinn Féin leaders Gerry Adams and Martin McGuinness.

Mini-cab driver John Jordan described how a bullet fired by Stone had narrowly missed him:

> I felt sure they were shooting over the coffins and the next thing I heard was a blast. This big fellow ran past and fired straight into my vehicle, hitting the front windscreen. He kept throwing blast bombs as he was going along. The bombs were bouncing and exploding. Everyone fell to the ground. He ran off down the grave-yard firing hand grenades like eggs.
>
> I helped two men who were seriously injured, and one of them was obviously dying. One of them had been shot in the back of the head, and the other in the neck. I couldn't understand how he missed me. I just threw myself to one side.

In all, nearly sixty people were injured in the Milltown cemetery attack, including a pregnant woman and a seventy-two-year-old grandmother. In March 1989 Stone was convicted of six murders, five attempted murders, three counts of conspiracy to murder, six of wounding with intent to kill and fifteen other offences. He was released in 2000, but in November 2006 Stone was arrested at the doors of Parliament Buildings at Stormont carrying weapons and explosives.

During the funeral procession of Kevin Brady, Army corporals Derek Wood and David Howes of the Signals Regiment were beaten by a mob and then driven away to be killed by the IRA. The two corporals drove towards the funeral cortege at high speed and then tried to reverse, but had their exit blocked by a black taxi. Many of those present undoubtedly feared another attack was taking place, similar to that at Milltown cemetery. The windows of the soldiers' car were smashed and they were dragged out. One of the soldiers fired a warning shot before they were overpowered, beaten, stripped and then dragged to Casement Park sports ground, where they were again beaten before being taken to waste ground and shot. Derek Wood was shot four times in the chest and twice in the head. He also had four stab wounds in the back of his neck and numerous injuries over the rest of his body. His body was found wearing only a T-shirt, underpants and socks. David Howes was shot five times—once in the head, through the eye, and four times in the chest. He also had multiple injuries to his body.

Many of the media personnel who had covered the event also found themselves coming under pressure. Cal McCrystal reported for the *Sunday Times*:

> Much of what happened was video recorded by an army helicopter crew and by local and foreign media cameramen. The journalists were approached by men from the funeral procession introducing themselves as IRA personnel and demanding that video cassettes be handed over. Many felt they had no alternative but to oblige; others were able to smuggle their cassettes to safety.
>
> But these newsreels, which allowed the world to view the killings in detail, were also sought by the Royal Ulster Constabulary as potential evidence. When the journalists involved protested, on the grounds that to hand over the newsreels could endanger their safety at future IRA-sponsored public events, the material was seized by police. ... The BBC's Northern Ireland Controller, Colin Morris, feels these opposing pressures strongly. Broadcasters, he says, have been accused of putting themselves above the law because they have refused to hand over voluntarily the television tapes. The fact that they eventually did so, under threat of arrest, did not appease those critics who argued that journalists and camera crews are ordinary citizens.
>
> (*Sunday Times*, 9 April 1989)

On 23 March a memorial service for the two corporals was held at the cenotaph at Belfast City Hall. Gareth Gordon reported:

> More than an hour after the lunchtime service had ended women, many crying, still came with their simple floral tributes. None had ever known Cpl David Howes or Cpl Derek Wood but yesterday they were the only names in anyone's thoughts. "God bless you both," said one inscription on a posey placed high on the cenotaph because the steps were too full to take any more.
>
> The city centre ground to a halt as the hastily arranged service became a magnet for people who knew of no other way to express their disgust at what had happened in Andersonstown. Employees

from Shorts, the shipyard and other factories left work to attend after first holding a short act of remembrance at the Royal Avenue security gates for the two UDR men murdered there last month.

Members of the city's brass bands, still wearing their day-time clothes, brought their instruments to provide the sombre tunes. Others, unable to get anywhere near the centre strained in vain for a glimpse from the back.

(*News Letter*, 24 March 1988)

After the murders the RUC announced that it would return to policing funerals more closely in future.

15 JUNE 1988: THE LISBURN 'FUN RUN' BOMB

On 15 June 1988 an IRA bomb killed six soldiers in Lisburn, the location of Army Headquarters in Northern Ireland, after they had taken part in a charity 'fun run'. The bomb exploded at approximately 9.00pm as spectators and competitors were leaving at the end of the fun run event. Ten bystanders were injured. The bomb exploded under the soldiers' unmarked Ford Transit van when they stopped at traffic lights on their way back to their barracks. It was believed that IRA members had attached the 7 lb Semtex bomb to the underside of the van, parked in Lisburn leisure centre car park, while the soldiers were taking part in the run. The soldiers had driven off in the van without checking to see if a bomb had been planted underneath. Off-duty soldiers had been banned from taking part in the Belfast marathon two months earlier.

One of those killed, Corporal Ian Metcalfe, had been wounded in a previous IRA sniper attack and was due to leave Northern Ireland the following week. Another casualty, Lance-Corporal Graham Lambie, had married only three months earlier and had decided to run in the race even though he was not registered. Lance-Corporal William Paterson had replaced another runner who had pulled out of the race six hours before it started.

The *News Letter* reported:

Any sense of accomplishment for the fun runners quickly evaporated following the no warning IRA bomb blast. More than 4,000 people, including husbands and wives, families and children took part in the event which started out with a festive atmosphere. As the runners paced themselves around the streets, hundreds of others turned out in the sunshine to watch the happy event.

Not long after the participants crossed the finishing line a loud blast broke the peace and there was panic everywhere. People started screaming and running around in confusion, not knowing what was happening. Traffic flowing along the one-way system towards Market Place, the scene of the blast, came to a standstill.

(*News Letter*, 16 June 1988)

A lorry driver who witnessed the explosion described the scene:

I saw two soldiers lying on the road. One had both his legs blown off, but his hands were still moving. He was trying to crawl. The driver was stuck to the wheel. He had no legs and his face was gone—but he was moving too. There was something on the ground. I thought it was a bit of the van—then it moves as well. I realised it was a man. He put his hand up to his mouth—then he died.

Somebody got a fire extinguisher for all those poor men. They were all burning. A policeman put three of them out. I've never seen anything so dreadful in all my life.

(*The Sun*, 17 June 1988)

In the wake of the attack the street was cordoned off to allow detectives to search the debris for evidence. During the course of the day women and children left flowers in the middle of the road as tributes. Ann Blake, who lived near the scene of the explosion, remarked, 'I am ashamed of what happened. The terrorists knew the fun run was on. There could have been hundreds of people killed. It could have been worse than Enniskillen and the worst thing about it is, in another week it will all be forgotten about' (*News Letter*, 17 June 1988).

As with other attacks where there had been significant security forces casualties, there was speculation as to whether it had been planned well in advance based on information passed to the IRA or had been more opportunistic. The loyalist paramilitary 'Protestant Action Force' (a cover name used by the UVF) threatened to kill Catholic staff at Lisburn Leisure Centre, claiming it was they who had set up the soldiers for assassination. Staff at the centre immediately walked out of the leisure centre in protest and refused to return until the threat was withdrawn.

An IRA statement referring to the bombing said that, 'Every care was exercised by our volunteers to ensure minimum risk to the local civilian population.' However, the statement also warned people to avoid contact with Crown force personnel.

The *Irish News* responded to the bombing by stating:

> Last night in Lisburn, what should have been a night of enjoyment for many thousands of people, many of them children, was turned into a hell-hole of brutal carnage. The memory of the awful scene of destruction will be imprinted on their souls for the rest of their lives. That is the real legacy of the Provisional IRA. Last night it achieved absolutely nothing but add to sorrow which has surrounded Ireland and its political problems for the past 20 years.
>
> The result of their savagery will only be to harden hearts and block progress towards an eventual solution.
>
> (*Irish News*, 16 June 1988)

The *Belfast Telegraph* was also critical:

> There have been few acts of terrorism in Northern Ireland's recent history more coldly and callously carried out than last night's bombing in Lisburn. Six soldiers died in the carnage, but what a miracle it was that many more civilians were not killed or injured. To place a bomb on a van, in the certain knowledge that it will explode somewhere in a crowded town, takes a special kind of ruthlessness which is the hallmark of the IRA. The anguished apologies after Enniskillen can be seen for what they were—lying propaganda—in the pictures of mangled wreckage and bodies in Lisburn. When the IRA spots a target, civilians are expendable.
>
> (*Belfast Telegraph*, 16 June 1988)

A week after the bombing a memorial service for the soldiers was held in Lisburn's Market Place and attended by 8,000 people. The *Belfast Telegraph* gave a sombre account of the service:

> Old age pensioners, teenagers, mothers with babies in their arms, disabled people in wheelchairs, businessmen, youth groups and the

Salvation Army, were among the gathering. Faces crowded shop windows which had been shattered just seven days ago by the van bomb blast.

A tight police security cordon was thrown around the area, while Army marksmen perched on buildings and a military helicopter hovered. As a solemn procession of dignitaries, led by the Mayor, wended towards the makeshift platform, all eyes were drawn to the exact location of the tragedy. But that spot, by coincidence the only part of the street to catch the evening sunshine, had disappeared beneath a knee-deep carpet of flowers.

The prayers, hymns and Biblical passages, relayed by a scratchy tannoy, were closely followed by the hushed and almost motionless crowd. … Queuing alongside clean-cut young men in suits, waiting to sign a Book of Condolences, were leather-clad bikers in torn jeans and Motorhead t-shirts.

At 8.45 the haunting notes of The Last Post echoed round the streets as wreaths were laid by the Mayor, Army and British Legion, followed by two minutes' silence.

As the memorial service drew to an end, however, there was not the usual stampede towards the car parks. Most people made their way, in almost an act of pilgrimage, towards the flower strewn pavement in front of the Market Place traffic lights. While they remembered six young men who ran a race, but lost their lives, the last rays of the evening sun faded away.

(*Belfast Telegraph*, 23 June 1988)

20 AUGUST 1988: THE BALLYGAWLEY BUS BOMB

Eight soldiers of the 1st Battalion Light Infantry were killed and twenty-eight others injured when their unmarked bus was blown up by a 200 lb IRA landmine in a drainage culvert outside Ballygawley, Co. Tyrone. The soldiers were returning to barracks in Omagh after a period at home on leave. Unusually, the IRA used a Semtex bomb rather than one based primarily on home-made explosives and this added to the devastating effect of the explosion. The Ballygawley bomb highlighted the upsurge in IRA attacks on military personnel: in 1988 twenty-six had been killed after the bus bomb alone—more than had been killed in all of the previous four years. Some commentators

saw this as an attempt by the IRA to regain credibility after a number
of bungled operations (most significantly at Enniskillen) in which
civilians had been killed.

The morning after the Ballygawley explosion the *News of the World*
reported:

> The blazing bus careered along the road for 100 yards after the
> explosion then skewed into a hedge. ... Seconds later two more
> buses, carrying local band members, arrived at the scene of carnage
> near the village of Ballygawley, County Tyrone. The musicians,
> many of them young girls, were horrified to see one soldier's
> body—minus head and arms—wrapped round a signpost. But the
> youngsters fought back their revulsion to help the victims. They
> flung off their band uniforms to cover the wounded and dying.
> Local farmers dashed out with sheets to provide makeshift
> bandages.
>
> (*News of the World*, 21 August 1988)

The *Belfast Telegraph* also reported that after the explosion loyalist
bandsmen and their supporters, who were in two coaches returning
from a parade in Portadown, stopped to give help. Once of those
present, Barbara Dundas, recalled:

> The scene was horrific—screaming and bodies lying in the ditch,
> the field, across the road and everywhere. ... I knelt beside a
> soldier. He was badly injured and kept asking were his legs blown
> off. I assured him that he was all right and told him not to go to
> sleep. I kept telling him I wouldn't leave him and asked him what
> he was thinking about. He answered "My daughter ... my wife". I
> stayed with him until he was lifted into the ambulance.
>
> (*Belfast Telegraph*, 22 August 1988)

A local doctor arrived on the scene half-an-hour after the explosion
and was faced with utter devastation:

> The doors of the house shook at about 12.20am. A quarter of an
> hour later the phone rang and a farmer's wife told me what had
> happened. When I got there, there were bodies scattered all over the
> place. They were lying in the ditches, in the fields. There were some

hanging out of the bus. They seemed to be in two lots. The first lot had been blown out of the bus, the second group were lying 20 yards up the road.

The local people and the people from the bus behind were giving them what aid they could. One lady was giving cardiac massage to a dead soldier and trying to resuscitate him.

The locals took the walking wounded in their cars up to the hospital and the other ladies sat beside the soldiers and gave them what comfort they could. I went round and sorted out those I could do something for and those that were dead.

(*The Guardian*, 22 August 1988)

Ken Maginnis, Ulster Unionist MP for Fermanagh-South Tyrone, was one of the first to arrive on the scene and he saw one of the soldiers as he died in a cow shed: 'Four of us went in. The young man was gasping his last—just dying. He had crawled through six inches of mud into the most available cover and died over a bale of hay' (*News of the World*, 21 August 1988).

Maginnis was among the many voices who called for internment to be used against certain individuals (although others, including former Prime Minister Edward Heath, saw it as likely to be counter-productive), saying: 'I and the people in this area know who detonated that bomb. The police know who detonated that bomb and they have been allowed the freedom to do it. That is not good enough after 20 years of death and destruction' (*Belfast Telegraph*, 20 August 1988).

Some sections of the British press called for even stronger measures. The *Sunday Mirror* restated its political preference for 'the Irish to govern themselves', but continued, 'as that long term political solution is sought, the short term military problem must be tackled with utter ruthlessness. We do not have to stoop to the barbarous methods used by the IRA. But our determination to wipe them out must match THEIR determination to destroy life and democracy' (*Sunday Mirror*, 21 August 1988).

In June, Gerry Adams was reported as saying there were two reasons why attacks on British soldiers were 'vastly preferable' from Sinn Féin's point of view to the killing of UDR and RUC members. The first reason was the propaganda impact in Britain and the second, he was quoted as saying, was that 'when British soldiers die it removes the worst of the agony from Ireland' (*News Letter*, 22 August 1988). After the bus bomb the *Mail on Sunday* called for Sinn Féin to be banned: 'Sinn Féin is as much a part of the IRA as any military unit. Sinn Féin has blood on its hands. And to pretend otherwise is to acquiesce in what is a cynical and hollow sham' (*Mail on Sunday*, 21 August 1988).

The *Sunday Times* suggested that it would have been comparatively easy for the IRA to watch for the arrival of the soldiers:

> Careless talk by a soldier to an acquaintance outside the base, or a civilian worker inside, would have been all that was necessary to tell the IRA when the soldiers were due back from leave.
>
> The soldiers then flew in to Aldergrove airport on flights including the regular 9.35 pm BA shuttle on Friday night. Although people entering the airport are frisked, it would be easy for an unarmed terrorist simply to hang around to check on arrivals.
>
> From the airport there are only two routes to Omagh which a coach can take, either northwards past Londonderry or southwards past Dungannon. The decision about which route to take has to be made almost immediately on leaving the airport, as the roads go in opposite directions. Having seen the coach turn southwards, it would have been an easy matter for an IRA watcher to alert a terrorist group.
>
> (*Sunday Times*, 'Insight', 21 August 1988)

Prime Minister Margaret Thatcher and Secretary of State Tom King both broke off holidays and returned to London to review the security situation in the wake of the attack. The bombing was claimed by the East Tyrone Brigade of the IRA, which had suffered heavy casualties at Loughgall the previous year.

12 FEBRUARY 1989: PAT FINUCANE MURDERED BY THE UFF

In February 1989 solicitor Pat Finucane was killed by the UFF at his home in north Belfast, in front of his family. UFF members smashed down the front door of the house with sledgehammers and shot Pat Finucane dead. The organisation claimed it had killed Finucane because he was an IRA officer, but this accusation was strenuously denied by his family. It was also rejected by the IRA and by the RUC. The Finucane family questioned the fact that police checkpoints had been in place in the area less than an hour earlier, but by the time the murder took place these had been removed.

More than a decade later Pat Finucane's son, Michael, recalled:

On Sunday February 12 1989, armed gunmen broke into my family home, ran to the kitchen where we were eating dinner, and shot my dad 14 times in front of my mother, my sister and brother. I can still remember it clearly. It is an image seared into my mind. The thing I remember most vividly is the noise; the reports of each bullet reverberating in the kitchen, how my grip on my younger brother and sister tightened with every shot. It's not a memory I care to visit very often, but it's there. I expect it always will be.

Throughout his career, my father was the subject of intimidation and harassment from RUC officers. Detectives made threats, communicated to him by clients he represented. They began as snide comments about his legal ability or general personal insults, but escalated before long into death threats.

(*The Guardian*, 13 February 2001)

The issue of collusion, i.e. the extent to which state forces assisted, or participated in, the murder of individuals for political reasons, remains a source of great controversy. It is a subject that touches on the grey areas of intelligence-gathering and counter-terrorism and the question of whether agents of the state could operate on the fringes of the law in order to defeat terrorism.

In August 1989 this issue received even more attention when the UFF handed leaked official documents to a BBC reporter and claimed that the British Army, the UDR and the RUC all gave information to them because no official action was being taken against republican suspects. After allegations that UFF murder victim Loughlin Maginn, shot dead at his home in Rathfriland, Co. Down, had been killed as a result of leaked information, nationalists called for a full investigation. On 5 September Bishop Cahal Daly, among others, called for an investigation, saying:

It is not a case of mere internal discipline within the forces, it is not a case of breach of police or Army regulations, it is a question about whether police or Army personnel have been colluding with terrorists.

Until these suspicions have been allayed or those found guilty have been duly dealt with by the law, the awful presumption will remain that some serving policemen or soldiers may have been knowing accessories to intended murders.

Another case in which leaked security information was alleged to have led to a loyalist murder was that of Gerard Slane, who was killed at his home in Belfast in September 1988. A month after his murder the loyalist paramilitary magazine *Ulster* carried a photograph of Slane that his family said had been taken in Castlereagh Holding Centre five years previously.

Joe Hendron of the SDLP said that Gerard Slane was interrogated and had his photograph taken by the RUC on only one occasion in his lifetime. His widow, Teresa, and his family are adamant that the clothes Slane was wearing during his detention in Castlereagh could be identified in the *Ulster* photograph (*Irish News*, 3 October 1989).

On 14 September 1989 the Deputy Chief Constable of Cambridgeshire, John Stevens, was appointed by RUC Chief Constable Hugh Annesley to investigate the theft and leaking of intelligence documents. The Stevens Inquiry subsequently found that there was no institutional collusion between loyalists and the RUC. Nonetheless, the issue was again given renewed significance by the murder of solicitor Rosemary Nelson in March 1999. She was killed when a loyalist bomb exploded under her car at her home in Lurgan, Co. Armagh.

In 2001 former Canadian judge Peter Cory was appointed to examine several high-profile cases where collusion was alleged to have taken place, including those of Pat Finucane, Billy Wright and Rosemary Nelson. The Cory reports led to a number of inquiries being established. Even then, there were disputes as to the nature and powers of the inquiries. In April 2005 the BBC's Ireland correspondent, Kevin Connelly, noted:

The government has legislated to create a new type of tribunal which would be very firmly under the control of government ministers and would fall very far short of the sort of independent, public investigation which the Finucane family is demanding. The Finucane family will not accept that sort of limitation and so the argument over the nature of the institution continues, 16 years after Pat Finucane's murder.

It is worth remembering too, that there are plenty of grieving families in Northern Ireland for whom there will be no inquiry. They are cases where there was no obvious political dimension beyond the fact that a murder happened to suit the sinister purpose of one paramilitary group or another at some moment in the Troubles; the killings of many members of the security forces, for example, fall into that category—a source of resentment to Unionists.

The Nelson inquiry and the others like it might run on for years, as the Bloody Sunday tribunal has, and at least to individual families they offer hope of closure. But in general terms Northern Ireland's troubled relationship with the pain of the past is very far from being resolved.

(BBC News, 19 April 2005)

In November 2006 an independent report was published by a group headed by American academic Douglass Cassel (who had been approached by the Pat Finucane Centre of Derry to undertake the inquiry). It examined twenty-five cases involving seventy-six killings between 1972 and 1977, and claimed that members of the security forces had colluded with loyalist paramilitaries in all but two of the deaths. Among its findings the report noted:

In meeting with victims and family members in the 25 cases it reviewed, the panel was deeply moved by how acutely they continue to feel their loss, and how severely they still suffer the effects of the injustices today, some three decades after the murders.

What happened long ago has not been forgotten or relegated to the past. Their wounds have not been healed. Their suffering has not been alleviated.

(*Report of the Independent International Panel on Alleged Collusion in Sectarian Killings in Northern Ireland*, pp 83–4).

In the same month a report from a committee of the Dáil also claimed that there had been significant collusion between loyalist paramilitaries and the security forces.

In January 2007 a report from the Police Ombudsman for Northern Ireland stated that members of the RUC's Special Branch protected a UVF member, who was a police informant, from prosecution despite his involvement in up to sixteen murders. The Ombudsman said that there was insufficient evidence to prosecute police officers involved in the incident because evidence was either missing or had been destroyed. In March the Ombudsman's report was criticised in turn by the Police Federation, the body representing the views of police officers.

22 SEPTEMBER 1989: ROYAL MARINES SCHOOL OF MUSIC BOMB

Ten soldiers were killed and more than 20 injured when an IRA bomb exploded at the Royal Marines School of Music in Deal, Kent. One of the injured soldiers died from his injuries almost a month later.

Early reports suggested that eight soldiers had been killed and seventeen or eighteen people were trapped in the rubble. Ten doctors were taken to the scene of the explosion and provided emergency treatment to the injured. Ambulance crews in the county immediately lifted a ban on over-time work, which they had been conducting as part of a pay dispute.

Although it was initially believed that many of the casualties would be teenagers, most of those killed were in fact aged in their twenties and thirties. Christopher Nolan, aged twenty-one, died on 18 October and was the youngest victim of the bombing. Corporal Trevor Davis was the oldest bandsman to die, the lead trombonist had turned forty two weeks earlier. He had five children aged between ten and nineteen years old. His father said: 'Trevor joined the Marines straight from school, and simply loved it. He never knew anything but his music and never talked about the possibility of violence. I don't think the idea even occurred to him' (*News Letter*, 25 September 1989).

The *News Letter* reported on the explosion:

A huge bomb, up to 50 lb of explosives, blew up their Royal Marine School of Music barracks as 250 trainee musicians, aged 16–20, prepared for their day ahead at Walmer, near Deal in Kent.

One band was already playing outside the recreation area. Inside, youngsters grabbed a drink in the coffee room, others pulled on their uniforms. It was 8.26 am. Then, as one survivor put it, there was a bang and the music stopped.

The roof of the two-storey north barracks was lifted into the air and the building collapsed like a pack of cards. A marine screamed out, "The band is under there." Colleagues and firemen desperately dug with their bare hands to get to those trapped. Ambulancemen dropped their overtime ban to help in the major rescue operation. When the dust had cleared, 10 people were dead and 22 were injured, 19 of them seriously enough to be detained in hospital. They were young men who yearned only to improve their musicianship, to show their prowess around the world, often for charity causes.

(*News Letter*, 23 September 1989)

Later that day the IRA claimed responsibility for the bomb. Referring to a visit by Margaret Thatcher the previous week, the statement said: 'Mrs Thatcher visited occupied Ireland with a message of war at a time when we want peace. Now we, in turn, have visited the Royal Marines in Kent, but we still want peace and we want the British government to leave our country.'

The *News Letter* editorial took a cynical stance on the government's public response to the latest IRA attack:

How, after all this time and so many previous incidents of a similar nature, is it not possible to provide better protection for both military and civilian targets? In Belfast yesterday Law and Order Minister John Cope said the latest outrage would make the authorities even more determined to resist the terrorists. They must be pretty determined now for they have had plenty of occasion to stiffen their sinews over the years. Either that or they were singularly lacking in determination at the start. We have heard it all before, John.

(*News Letter*, 23 September 1989)

If anything, the *Irish News* was even more critical of the IRA attack at Deal, as well as of the murder of Heidi Hazell, the wife of a British soldier, in West Germany on 7 September:

If it takes English blood to make the day for the Provisionals, then we can be sure that they rate death above all other things. Dead bodies mean more to them than the collective outrage felt by all

Irish people, more than the shame felt by most in this country at such an act carried out supposedly in the name of Ireland. ...

Cowardice is the motive which prompted IRA members to creep into the barracks and plant a device which they knew would render horrible deaths to off-guard soldiers. Cowardice is the reason why they then ran off into hiding—the same motive which prompted them to shoot an army wife 14 times in West Germany.

There are other victims in the aftermath of the Deal blast. What now for the growing Irish community in Britain? What hostility will they endure as ordinary English people vent their anger? What of the Birmingham Six and Guildford Four? How can their cases be advanced in the present climate?

What of those who work tirelessly to advocate the benevolent face of Ireland abroad. How can they be taken seriously when unseen people drown out their efforts with murderous explosions?

(*Irish News*, 23 September 1989)

The mother of one of the bandsmen killed in the explosion called for the bombers to be shot. She added, 'How can I describe how we feel? Our lives will be empty forever.'

In a break with Royal protocol Prince Philip, who held the position of Captain General of the Royal Marines, commented on the incident after visiting the School of Music and talking to the injured in hospital: 'It is senseless. One simply wonders what sort of mentality can even contemplate such meaningless acts. It is appalling.' Asked how he felt about those responsible for the bombing he replied, 'Not very charitable, to put it mildly.'

In the wake of the bombing there was some criticism of the fact that the base had been guarded by a private security firm. Among the critics was the Ministry of Defence Police Federation Chairman Mick Jones. He said that he had warned the Ministry of the dangers of using civilian security firms in these circumstances:

We have been pushing the ministry hard about the dangers of not providing professional, adequate policing of places where there are large numbers of lives at risk or where they have attempted to reduce our members for economy grounds.

The forces are in a difficult position these days with manpower but when they do privatise you are in a dangerous position because you are talking about profit margins. How can you put a price on lives? Unfortunately that is an element these days. Account book manpower policy is almost obscene.

(*Irish News*, 23 September 1989)

Somewhat ironically, the Royal Marines band was in Northern Ireland carrying out a number of engagements in military bases. Two days after the attack on the Deal base a Royal Marine band played at a thanksgiving and memorial service for 80,000 seamen who died during the Second World War, which was held at St Anne's Cathedral, Belfast.

Despite the extent of the death toll, one of the greatest in the course of the Troubles, it received less coverage by the press in Northern Ireland than perhaps might have been expected. For most of the period after the Deal explosion the headline stories of many newspapers continued to focus on the recent revelations of security leaks from the security forces to loyalist paramilitaries, which had led to the appointment, on 14 September, of John Stevens to investigate the theft and leaking of intelligence documents from the RUC.

The 1990s

24 OCTOBER 1990: SEVEN KILLED IN PROXY BOMB ATTACKS

Five soldiers and a civilian were killed in an IRA 'proxy bomb' attack on an Army checkpoint near Derry on 24 October 1990. A member of the Royal Irish Rangers was killed by another IRA proxy bomb at a checkpoint at Killeen, near Newry.

The *Irish News* reported on 'the day terror struck on four fronts':

> In eight hours as many people died violently in Northern Ireland yesterday. Proxy bombs were used in separate attacks by the IRA to kill six soldiers and a civilian. In a third IRA proxy bomb drama the driver was tied to the seat of a van containing more than 200 lbs of explosives. The eighth victim was a Catholic taxi-driver from Dungannon who went missing on Tuesday evening after going to pick up a fare.
>
> (*Irish News*, 25 October 1990)

The greatest loss of life was in Derry, where Patsy Gillespie, a kitchen worker at a local Army base, was kidnapped and his family held hostage. He was then forced to drive a van carrying a bomb to a permanent vehicle checkpoint at Coshquin, close to the Donegal border. The van was stopped for searching shortly after 4.00am, whereupon the IRA detonated the bomb while Mr Gillespie was still on board, killing him and five soldiers of the King's Regiment. Six other soldiers were injured in the blast, as were a number of people in nearby houses and a driver who had been approaching the checkpoint. The size of the bomb was estimated at 1,000 lb.

Henry McDonald and Seamus Kelters reported on the ordeal of another of the men forced to drive bombs to the security checkpoints while their families were held hostage:

> A gang of up to eight masked men forced their way into the home of Mr Gerry Kelly, three miles from Gortin, just hours after attacks at Derry and Newry and tied him to the seat of his camper van

which they had loaded with explosive. Speaking at his home yesterday he spoke of the "terrible ordeal."

He said, "I just kept thinking about my family and what would happen to them. The sweat was dribbling down my face. All sorts of things were going through my mind and I thought this was it."

As he drove to Lisanelly barracks in Omagh, tied to the seat, the gang tailed him. "They told me that the rope was there to make sure I didn't jump out and that when I arrived at the camp the Brits would loose it and let me out. I was tied round my waist. I didn't really know why they did it but I was absolutely terrified. They told me they had fitted a 50-minute timer on the bomb. When I got to the camp I managed to free myself and started running. Somebody caught me and I was able to tell them there was a bomb in the camper."

Mr Kelly, who worked as a mechanic at the army base for 14 years but has now left his job said: "It was a ghastly ordeal and frankly I don't think I'll ever get over it. I'm now thinking of quitting Ireland completely."

(*Irish News*, 26 October 1990)

Unlike at Derry and Newry, only the detonator of the bomb exploded and severe damage was avoided.

Cyril Smith of the Royal Irish Rangers, who came from Carrickfergus, was killed when an IRA proxy bomb was detonated at Killeen, near Newry. The sixty-five-year-old driver had been kidnapped and eight members of his family held hostage. The driver managed to escape from the van and shout a warning before the bomb exploded. He was hit by debris and sustained a broken leg in the blast.

Brian Bethell, the step-father of Paul Worral, one of the soldiers killed near Derry, said:

Bombs and bullets can only ever kill the body, never the memory, never the personality, never the hope. Bombs and bullets get you nothing except a dead body and an equally dead cause. You have killed a name only, for you did not know him. What do you think you have achieved? I shall tell you—simply that you have killed our son, that is all, and in doing so I hope you have strengthened the resolve of all decent people to see you and those of a like mind defeated forever.

Our son will live forever, as will our memories. Paul lived for the Army and in the end he died for it.

(Belfast Telegraph, 25 October 1990)

The *Irish News* criticised Martin McGuinness' comment that the attacks were the consequence of Britain's refusal to accept the Irish people's right to self-determination. An editorial argued instead that the attacks were the consequence of the IRA's refusal to accept the Irish people's right to live in peace:

The IRA makes much of its long tradition. UFF and UVF killers too draw their justification from the pages of history. Most of us were born long after those history books were written. We cannot be treated as the prisoners of the past. We have our lives to lead, we have our aspirations and can fight for them using democratic means and the force of argument, we have the future.

The cause of Irish unity is not the preserve of the IRA; it is the aspiration of many good and decent people. But the rewards of unity—a nation united by a sense of identity and community—cannot be bought with the lives of others who cannot share those rewards.

(Irish News, 25 October 1990)

The *Belfast Telegraph* referred to the deaths at the security checkpoints and to the sectarian murder of taxi-driver Frank Hughes by the UVF and the murder of William Skey by the UFF (who claimed the victim was 'an informer') when it commented:

Words have been failing to describe Ulster's atrocities for 20 years, but they are even more inadequate today. The deadly cycle has taken a most vicious turn for the worse, with two cowardly murders adding to the toll of seven dead in the checkpoint bombings of Londonderry and Newry. In all, 18 have been killed in the last 19 days, making this month one of the most costly in lives and human suffering since the troubles began. After sentencing people to carry bombs to a place of execution for themselves and others, what more has the IRA to offer? Do they intend to kill us all?

They might shrug off such a charge, but it is the only logical conclusion that can be drawn from their present campaign, directed against soldiers, policemen, unionists, nationalists, Protestants, Catholics, the lame, the halt and the blind. Everyone is in their firing line, to be tied down—as their bomb-carrier in Omagh was— and used as human ammunition against whatever target they choose. Yet their Sinn Féin apologists can still turn a blind eye to the barbarity, choosing to complain about "the Irish people's right to self-determination", as if they have paid the slightest notice to the crystal clear message of the ballot box on either side of the border in recent years.

(*Belfast Telegraph*, 25 October 1990)

14 MARCH 1991: THE RELEASE OF THE BIRMINGHAM SIX

After sixteen years in jail the Birmingham Six were freed. Hugh Callaghan, Paddy Hill, Gerry Hunter, Richard McIlkenny, Billy Power and Johnny Walker were wrongly convicted in 1975 for what was then the worst incident of mass murder in British peacetime history. They had been found guilty on the basis of forensic evidence, but it was claimed that confessions had been beaten out of them by the police. In July 1975 the forty-five-day trial ended with each of the men being given twenty-one life sentences. Hugh Callaghan later recalled how he came to sign a confession after being intimidated by police interrogators:

> I was in a state of shock. I do not know what I said. They said things to me, I agreed and they wrote it down. This must have gone on for about three-quarters of an hour. At the end, one of the officers put a pen in my right hand, placed it over the paper and guided my hand as I signed.
>
> (Quoted in Chris Mullin, *Error of Judgement: The Truth about the Birmingham Bombs*, p. 102)

In March 1991 the six men were released after their second appeal in three years. British Home Secretary Kenneth Baker acknowledged that this was the third case in eighteen months involving Irish people (including the Guildford Four) where there had been a miscarriage of justice. The decision to release the Birmingham Six came after new tests on West Midlands Police documents suggested that officers might have forged notes and given false evidence. Forensic tests purporting to show that two of the men had handled explosives were also shown to be unreliable.

At a preliminary appeal hearing against the convictions on 25 February 1991 a representative from the Department of Public Prosecutions conceded that the Department would no longer rely on the evidence of the police officers who had conducted interviews of the Birmingham Six in 1974, and that it would no longer argue that the convictions were safe and satisfactory. Scientific evidence used in the convictions had already been discredited, opening the way for the men to be released.

One of those who had campaigned for the men to be freed, Labour MP Chris Mullin, commented: 'The judge at the original trial, Lord Bridge, said if the defendants were telling the truth then the greatest conspiracy in the annals of criminal history had occurred. Those words will have to be remembered.'

The announcement that the men were to be freed came on 14 March. On the following day Seamus Kelters reported:

The Birmingham Six arrived at the Old Bailey yesterday in prison vans and left in limousines. According to the little steel clock in Court 8, it was 3.32 pm precisely when Lord Justice Lloyd told the men they were free to go.

A huge roar of naked relief erupted from relatives and supporters in the public gallery. The men reached over the dock, embracing lawyers and Chris Mullin, the Labour MP who had campaigned so long for their release.

Observers were close to tears. Some wept openly. Bishop Edward Daly was one of those who clasped the men's hands through a crush of well wishers around the dock. Some reporters, in the main Irish, clapped and waved. ...

Finally at 4.10 pm out flooded the men to cheers louder than the Old Bailey Street has ever heard. A mass whirr of motor-drives went up from a wall of camera men perched on steps. Billy Power seemed to come out first. It was difficult to be certain. Best vantage points were taken by television crews who had chained and bolted their ladders in place last week.

Then came Richard McIlkenny, Paddy Hill, Hugh Callaghan, Gerry Hunter and John Walker—holding each other as they took their first steps into free air.

(*Irish News*, 15 March 1991)

At a press conference held immediately after their release, Paddy Hill said that the police had known of evidence proving their innocence from the beginning. He added: 'We were made scapegoats to please the public and it was connived up to the very highest level. I feel very bitter it took sixteen and a half years. I feel very bitter people didn't want to listen. If anyone who had an ounce of common sense looked into our background, they would have seen we had nothing to do with this.'

The *Irish News* blamed the lengthy imprisonment of the Birmingham Six on the police who had secured the men's 'confessions', the British judiciary and also blamed the British tabloid press for whipping up anti-Irish feeling. It concluded:

> The best we can hope for out of this disgraceful affair is that in future Irish people can expect justice in English courts and that the judiciary will discharge its duties to uphold the rights and privileges of the citizen regardless of where they come from and the magnitude of the crime of which they are accused.
>
> (*Irish News*, 15 March 1991)

The *News Letter* also welcomed the release of the Birmingham Six, but noted that it had 'come just under 16 years too late to permit of justice being done in its entirety.' The report added:

> The rock that British justice perished on (temporarily it is to be earnestly hoped) was the presumption on the part of the Crown and the judiciary that prosecution witnesses were incapable of telling lies and defence witnesses were unlikely to be telling the truth.
>
> The absurdity of this position becomes manifest when it is considered that if it were true then there would be no need for all the costly paraphernalia of the law; justice would at all times be served by taking evidence from police witnesses and ignoring anything that might be said to the contrary.
>
> (*News Letter*, 15 March 1991)

The *Belfast Telegraph* commented:

> For 16 years justice had failed them. The whole judicial system had turned a blind eye to what was increasingly apparent to many

people on the outside—and what was officially accepted by the Court of Appeal yesterday afternoon—that they were innocent. ...

There are other implications arising from the men's release. What will happen to the police officers whose evidence was discredited? Will the real bombers be pursued vigorously as promised? Is it practical for investigations to be re-opened 16 years after the terrible night of November 23, 1974, when 21 people were murdered in Birmingham? The nightmare for the Birmingham Six may be over, but the trauma for the relatives of those killed and the injured has not been allowed to heal. It may never be erased. They and the Birmingham Six equally are victims of the IRA.

(*Belfast Telegraph*, 15 March 1991)

17 JANUARY 1992: TEEBANE CROSSROADS

Eight civilian workers (all of whom were Protestants) were killed when the IRA exploded a bomb near their minibus van at Teebane crossroads near Carrickmore, Co. Tyrone. The IRA used a 100-yard-long command wire to detonate a bomb, estimated at anywhere between 400 lb and 1,500 lb, as the minibus drove past at 5.20pm. The blast tore open the minibus and threw the dead and injured onto the road and into nearby fields.

The men were returning from work at Lisanelly barracks in Omagh when the bomb exploded. Seven workers were killed by the blast, the eighth victim, Oswald Gilchrist, died four days later. An IRA statement described the men they had killed as 'Crown forces collaborators'.

In June 1991 the IRA had attempted to kill construction workers from the same company by planting a bomb in a hut timed to explode when the men gathered for lunch. However, on that occasion the men had moved to another site when the bomb exploded. Including those who died at Teebane, since 1985 the IRA had killed twenty-four people carrying out contract work for the security forces in Northern Ireland.

Gary Grattan reported on the aftermath of the bomb:

The van had just overtaken an Ulsterbus moments before the explosion. Teenage schoolgirls travelling home to Cookstown were among the passengers. They were said to be hysterical at seeing the extent of the carnage and several needed to be sedated later by local doctors.

One man who was quickly on the scene said passengers on the bus had thrown coats over the injured and were trying their best to comfort them. Another local man, who did not wish to be named, said: "I could see the flashing blue lights of ambulances and could hear the sirens. I pulled the car out and went to the scene. I could see the van was completely wrecked and there were four bodies lying on the verge. I knew they were dead because canvas covers had been thrown over them," he said.

(*Belfast Telegraph*, 20 January 1992)

A local farmer, who was one of the first on the scene, phoned for an ambulance from a nearby house. The daughter of the house-owner said:

Once he had done that, he and my father went to the scene to see what they could do. My father said the scene was just terrible, unbelievable. He said there was not much they could do, but try to make the injured comfortable. The fire brigades and ambulances got there very quickly, within about 15 or 20 minutes. He said the police got there slightly later. My father and the other man left after the police got there. Both my parents have been badly shocked by this, and my father is getting worse as the night goes by.

(*Irish News*, 18 January 1992)

There was widespread condemnation of the attack, as well as of the government's security policy. Dr Rodney Sterritt, Moderator of the Presbyterian Church in Ireland, commented that the IRA seemed to be able to commit evil deeds when and where it chose.

As details of the attack emerged, Secretary of State Peter Brooke was in Dublin appearing on RTÉ's 'The Late, Late Show', which began at 9.30pm. Brooke was encouraged by presenter Gay Byrne to sing 'Oh My Darling Clementine', accompanied by a pianist. He remained in Dublin the following day and attended a rugby match between Ireland and Wales.

Brooke's decision to sing on the television programme caused grave offence in Northern Ireland and he subsequently offered John Major his resignation; the Prime Minister refused his offer.

Despite this, Ulster Unionist MP Willie Ross predicted that Brooke's 'days in his present office must surely be numbered'. Ian Paisley said that the hurt had been boiling over at the funerals of the men he had attended: 'People were coming out of church saying, "Big man, you are going to meet the Prime Minister, you tell him how we feel—the Secretary of State might as well have danced on the graves of our loved ones as what he did."'

The Prime Minister received a warmer welcome when he visited Belfast on 20 January, as reported in the *News Letter*:

> As Mr Major went walkabout in Belfast, there were full marks for his bravery, but black marks for his Ulster Secretary. "Why don't you take Mr Brooke home with you when you're going—because he's not welcome here?" asked one little old lady as she shook hands with the Prime Minister in the middle of Chichester Street. "Action, not party songs," shouted a younger woman, in another thinly veiled reference to the Secretary of State's brief musical slot on Friday night's Gay Byrne Show.
>
> The hecklers were, however, in the minority as many shoppers marvelled at Mr Major's courage to wander the streets of the city so freely. "He's a lovely man, a brave man and he's got lovely lips," said Bangor mother Kelly McMahon after planting a surprise kiss on the Tory leader's unsuspecting cheek.
>
> (*News Letter*, 21 January 1992)

Another report in the same newspaper highlighted some of the long-term effects of Teebane and other incidents:

> *News Letter* readers agreed with one thing John Major said yesterday on his visit to Northern Ireland—the effects of the Teebane massacre on the lives of the injured and the relatives would never go away. ... Mr Major promised that the killers of the seven would be, "hunted for the rest of their days until we find them," but a relative of one of the 10 Bessbrook workers murdered by the IRA in 1976 said no one had been made amenable for that slaughter. The callers asked not to be named "because of the present situation"—emphasising their lack of faith in security policy.
>
> (*News Letter*, 21 January 1992)

The *Belfast Telegraph* also conveyed the view that Ministers seemed to have lost sight of some of the responsibilities of their positions:

> Seven men lie dead and seven more injured—one critically—bringing grief and misery to so many households. In the circumstances, the only reaction of the Government and its Ministers should have been to express their horror and then immediately buckle down to the task of reassuring the public that all possible measures would be taken to apprehend the murderers. No doubt the Secretary of State, Mr Brooke, thought he was doing the right thing by seizing the opportunity to address viewers in the Republic—and many in Northern Ireland—in "The Late Late Show." But whatever gains he may have made, in his interview, he tossed away by agreeing to sing a song—on such a tragic evening. It was a gross error of judgment, from which he may never recover, and was even compounded by his decision to stay on to attend an international rugby match, instead of returning post haste to oversee the security response to Friday night's atrocity.
>
> (*Belfast Telegraph*, 20 January 1992)

5 FEBRUARY 1992: UFF MURDERS AT SEAN GRAHAM'S BOOKMAKER'S

Five Catholic men were shot dead on 5 February 1992 by the UFF at Sean Graham's bookmaker's shop on the Ormeau Road, Belfast. The UFF claimed that the murders were in response to the Teebane massacre, which had taken place less than three weeks earlier.

Two sectarian murders were carried out by the UFF in the weeks after Teebane and were seen by some as retaliation for the IRA attack. On 30 January the UFF murdered Catholic man Paul Moran and made the spurious claim that he was a member of the IRA. Moran's widow said: 'After the Teebane bomb in which eight people died, I remember him saying how awful it was and he wondered how many Catholics would die in retaliation—he never thought he would be one' (*Irish News*, 31 January 1992). On 2 February the UFF murdered Paddy Clarke in front of his wife and son at his home in north Belfast.

The attacks were followed by the murder of Protestant delivery driver Gordon Hamill by the IRA in Co. Tyrone and then, on 4 February, the killing of three men at Sinn Féin's party office on the Falls Road by an off-duty RUC officer. The policeman, Allen Moore, drove off and later shot himself. The view that the attack was the result of a single RUC officer who had cracked under stress was rejected by Gerry Adams as 'an insult to the families bereaved today and to the intelligence of other citizens'.

As was often the case in the course of the Troubles, one incident of mass murder was followed by another. At 2.25pm on 5 February two UFF gunmen entered Sean Graham's betting shop on the lower Ormeau Road and opened fire on staff and customers. Staff were afforded some protection by the shop counter, but there was little or no protection for the customers. Nearly all the customers were either killed or wounded.

One eyewitness, who arrived shortly after the shooting, was interviewed by Stephen O'Reilly:

I was working at my car just round the corner when I heard the banging. At first I thought it was just a car back-firing, but when it carried on I ran round the corner. A woman shouted at me to stop because someone was shooting.

I ran on around and into the bookies. By the time I got there the gunmen had left. When I opened the door I saw bodies lying all over the place. It was terrible. There was smoke and blood everywhere. I didn't see anyone in there who hadn't been shot.

There were three or four people huddled on top of each other in a corner as if they had been trying to protect themselves. It was hard to see where people had been wounded there was so much blood.

Most of the people were lying still, some were definitely dead. One old man was lying under the counter with blood on his face. I saw two of the staff behind the counter. They looked as if they were phoning, probably for ambulances.

There was one wee lad, lying just inside the door. His eyes were flickering open and closed. I kept telling him to hang on, that help was on the way. By that time there were lots of people inside trying to help. Then the police and ambulancemen arrived and the police started to cordon off the area.

(*Irish News*, 6 February 1992)

The journalist added that as they talked a man came over and whispered that his friend had died on the way to hospital.

One of the survivors of the attack was sixty-eight-year-old Paddy Loughran, who had been standing in the corner of the betting shop office filling in a betting slip when the loyalist gunmen opened fire. He recalled: 'I didn't realise what was happening. When I looked round the corner, everybody was on the ground. I was the only person left standing. At first I thought there had been a hold-up, then I saw the blood everywhere. My best friends are dead now.'

The youngest victim of the UFF attack was fifteen-year-old schoolboy James Kennedy. His mother said that she had always been concerned about the safety of James and her other sons. She told the *Belfast Telegraph*:

> "I prayed that it would never happen to us. When the boys came in at night the door was closed and they never went out again. They could never understand why we were so protective of them, but now they know. My poor child was only 15. He was only starting out in life," she said.
>
> Mrs Kennedy said she did not want any other mother to go through what she was having to experience. "Everyone has the same feelings, no matter who they are. I want whoever did this to be caught."
>
> Mr Kennedy said his son had been killed because he had happened to go into the bookies to place "a wee bet."
>
> "This is just the devil coming in to human beings. He will reclaim them some day. They say God forgives everyone, but we will never forgive them for that," said Mr Kennedy.
>
> (*Belfast Telegraph*, 6 February 1992)

In its editorial on the day after the bookmaker's shop murders, the *Irish News* commented:

> It has become fashionable in some media circles to talk of "tit for tat" killings. This analysis of what is happening on our streets today is completely bogus and constitutes an insult to the dead. The use of the phrase "tit for tat" implies that one group or organisation is taking revenge for the actions of another. After yesterday's killings the UFF admitted responsibility and said that the attack was carried out in revenge for Teebane Cross.

But how could it have been? The people killed on the Ormeau Road yesterday were placing bets in a bookie's shop. None of them was connected in any way with any paramilitary organisation. They were killed because the shop was in a Catholic area and so therefore there was every chance that the people inside it were Catholics. ...

After Teebane there was, quite rightly, a loud and unanimous outcry. The people who committed the massacre were roundly condemned on all sides. In contrast, the policeman responsible for the Falls Road killing is being portrayed as a hero who went over the top.

Politicians and journalists have a responsibility to be absolutely consistent in all matters pertaining to paramilitary and sectarian murder. You should never wait to see who the victim is before deciding whether an assassination should be condoned or condemned.

(*Irish News*, 6 February 1992)

In its editorial the *Belfast Telegraph* referred to the recent case in which UDA intelligence officer, and British Army agent, Brian Nelson had pleaded guilty to five charges of conspiracy to murder and fourteen charges of possessing information useful to terrorists:

It is also an affront that an organisation like the UDA, many of whose members masquerading under the banner of the UFF are actively engaged in murder, continues to be legal. Army agent Brian Nelson proved it to be a nefarious organisation intolerable in any civilised society. There is never an acceptable level of violence, but the current spate of murders has left even this battle-hardened province numb.

(*Belfast Telegraph*, 6 February 1992)

The UDA was eventually declared an illegal organisation in August 1992.

20 MARCH 1993: BOMBS IN WARRINGTON

Three-year-old Johnathan Ball was killed and fifty-six people were injured when two IRA bombs placed in litter bins exploded at a shopping centre in Warrington, Cheshire, on Saturday 20 March 1993. Twelve-year-old Tim Parry, an enthusiastic Everton football supporter, had been out shopping for a pair of Everton football shorts when he was caught in the explosion and received critical injuries to the head. His father, Colin Parry, said: 'I have a son who is not going to live, a 12-year-old boy pulled apart—for what?' On 25 March Timothy Parry died from the injuries he received in the explosion.

An IRA statement issued on the day after the explosions claimed 'Responsibility for the tragic and regrettable death and injuries caused in Warrington yesterday lies squarely at the door of those in the British authorities who deliberately failed to act on precise and adequate warnings.' The police claimed that only one warning had been received, via the Samaritans in Liverpool, and that the message said there was a bomb in an unspecified Boots chemist store in Liverpool.

In the chaotic aftermath of the explosions, when it was thought that two people had already died, Ian McTear reported:

A child is believed to be one of two people killed in a no warning bomb blast in a crowded Warrington shopping centre today. A spokesman for the Merseyside Ambulance Service said there appeared to have been two explosions in a litter bin. He added at least two victims were known to have died, one of whom was possibly a child, and 20 others were injured.

"The scene is appalling. It is a terrible, shameful disaster. We are picking up casualties far and wide who were running away from the scene in fright," he said.

A fleet of 17 ambulances was at the incident, including a number from Greater Manchester Ambulance Service. There were reports of an unexploded third device in the area. Police were unable to confirm what caused the explosions.

Shopkeeper Bob Wild said the area of the blasts was a scene of devastation. He went on: "People wondering what had gone off, terrific noise, glass outside the Halifax Building Society. One young lady was badly injured and her boyfriend was holding her tightly, screaming," he told Sky News.

(*Belfast Telegraph*, 20 March 1993)

The murder of the two children by the IRA sparked a wave of public anger across Britain. The *Star* scathingly commented that, 'By blowing up children and young families the IRA have disgusted the world. ... Seeing these scum swing would raise the biggest cheer since

Hitler was beaten. ... Being soft with these barbarians has not stopped the bombing.' The *Daily Mail* stated that 'What happened in Warrington was an act of premeditation and unadulterated terror ... wickedness beyond belief ... the IRA deliberately chose the heart-rendingly softest of targets.'

On the Monday after the explosions a Press Association report noted:

> The scene of Saturday's blasts which felled more than 50 lunchtime shoppers in Bridge Street, and snuffed out the life of three-year-old Johnathan Ball, was bedecked with floral tributes, cuddly toys and heart-rending messages. One from "A Warrington Couple" read: "May God forgive them because we can't." It was an eloquent testament to the sorrow and anger felt within the Cheshire town and throughout the nation.
>
> Another 17 patients were still in hospital in Warrington today. One, 27-year-old Gordon Edwards, was described as "very, very, poorly" with stomach injuries. Five people, mostly teenagers, were seriously maimed in the attack, among them 12-year-old Tim Parry who suffered horrific head injuries. All the others were said to be in a stable condition. They include a 13-year-old girl hit in the knee by shrapnel who was discharged but re-admitted today for surgery.
>
> Johnathan's parents, Marie and Wilf, were said to be at home in Grappenhall, Warrington, overnight where they were being comforted by trained police personnel.
>
> Their little boy had been shopping for a Mother's Day present with a friend of the family, teenager Samantha Thompson, when the litter-bin explosion tore into them both. Samantha (13) was recovering from her injuries in hospital today. She spent yesterday semi-conscious and unaware that her young companion had died from horrific stomach wounds. Her mother, Barbara (54) said; "She is still very poorly. She just keeps coming round and asking for Johnathan."

(*Belfast Telegraph*, 22 March 1993)

After visiting those injured by the explosions the Bishop of Warrington, the Rt Rev. Michael Henshall, said:

Pictures of these people should be sent to America and people there should be told this is what some of you are funding. Look at it, see what you are funding. It is terrible. There is anger in the town, bewilderment and sheer disgust. Those who deliberately target children and young people outside McDonald's—it's absolutely outrageous and disgraceful.

The *Belfast Telegraph* believed that 'in 23 years of terrorist atrocities, the Warrington incident must rate as worst of the worst ever—and, dare we hope, a turning point.' The *Irish News*, which established a fund to help the victims of the bombing, commented:

The death of Johnathan Ball advanced the cause of a united Ireland by not one solitary inch; his death, and the death of countless others throughout the present conflict has cast a shadow over our country.

Johnathan died in Bridge Street, Warrington. There are Bridge streets in a lot of towns in Ireland, on Saturday they too were filled with people, shopping for Mother's day. There is not one person in those streets who remains untouched by the events of Saturday morning.

The IRA says it wants a united Ireland. The majority of the people of this island want one, too. But that does not mean that they support those who go out day and daily to murder and to maim. Every death, every injury further undermines the cause of a united Ireland.

(*Irish News*, 22 March 1993)

In October 2007 Gerry Adams attended a debate organised by the charity Foundation for Peace, where he met Colin and Wendy Parry, the parents of Timothy Parry. At the conference held at Canary Wharf in London, Colin Parry told the audience:

I can say that inviting Gerry Adams to join me here tonight was not, as you might imagine, easy for me or [my wife] Wendy. But it was infinitely easier than holding my son dying. It was infinitely easier than carrying him for the final time in his coffin. It was infinitely easier than saying my final farewell to him with my wife.

(BBC News, 1 November 2007)

Gerry Adams repeated an earlier apology to the Parrys and also repeated an IRA statement made in 2002 regarding the deaths of all 'non-combatants'. He added:

> The fact that two children were killed obviously had a devastating impact, not just on their families and their communities, but on parents including me back in Ireland. ... I have also expressed my personal and sincere regret, and apologised for the hurt inflicted by Republicans, and I do so again this evening.
>
> As we seek to move forward there's a requirement that we address the tragic human consequences of our actions.
>
> (*The Irish Times*, 1 November 2007)

23 OCTOBER 1993: THE SHANKILL BOMB

On 23 October 1993 an IRA bomb exploded in Frizzell's fish shop on the Shankill Road, killing ten people and injuring nearly sixty others. Among those killed were the shop-owner, John Frizzell, his daughter, Sharon McBride, and one of the bombers, Thomas Begley. At 1.10pm the two IRA bombers were seen walking from a car. In an attempt to make it appear that they were making a delivery of goods, they wore white coats and peaked caps and entered the fish shop carrying a cardboard box, which contained the bomb. Four of those who died were women; two schoolgirls were also killed. The Provisionals stated that the bomb had been intended to kill members of the UFF who, they claimed, were meeting in a room in the former UDA office above the shop. The bombing was followed by a spate of attacks on Catholics by loyalist paramilitaries.

The local newspaper, *Shankill People*, which dubbed the day 'Bloody Saturday', told the story of one of the casualties of the bombing:

> Every Saturday Gina Murray and her daughter Leanne went on to the [Shankill] Road to shop for groceries. They were very close and one was rarely seen without the other. Clutching Leanne's fluffy slippers, Mrs Murray painfully recalled the tragic events of the day the IRA murdered her beautiful young innocent child while she was shopping. "Leanne had just left me to go into the fish shop next door for whelks. Suddenly there was this huge bang and I ran

screaming for Leanne. I couldn't find her. No-one had seen her. There were people lying in the street covered in blood. My little girl was underneath all that rubble," she sobbed. Gina Murray clawed at the rubble with her bare hands but it was no use, Leanne was dead.

Thirteen-year-old Leanne had just returned from a cross-community trip to the USA which was designed to bring Protestants and Catholics together. Many kids on these trips make friends. Few stay in touch when they come home. Leanne Murray, however, befriended a young Catholic girl in the States and went swimming with her every week. The two were extremely good friends.

(*Shankill People*, November 1993)

Michael Morrison was shopping for a wreath for his father's funeral when he was killed in the explosion. His partner, Evelyn Baird, and their daughter, seven-year-old Michelle Baird, were also killed. The couple's two remaining children, nine-year-old Darren and six-week-old Lauren, were at home with their grandparents.

On 25 October thousands of workers from Belfast's heavy industries stopped work and marched to the site of the bombing for a memorial service. Local clergymen were joined by Rev. Stephen Kingsnorth from Warrington, who told the crowd: 'In Warrington we know just a little of the suffering in that we recently lost two of our children in a bomb. Our lives and those of our children cannot be built on violence and more violence. I plead in God's name for restraint and not revenge.'

Most of the injured were taken to the Royal Victoria and Mater hospitals in Belfast. Even veterans in the rescue services who had witnessed other atrocities were still shocked by the Shankill bomb. Surgeon Laurence Rock, a consultant at the Royal Victoria Hospital in Belfast, had treated some of the survivors of the Abercorn bomb in 1972. He told the *News Letter*:

"I was in casualty here helping with that [Abercorn bomb], and there are scenes from that I've never forgotten. There are scenes from this I'll never forget either. It doesn't get any easier to deal with. ...

There were people who were killed pretty well outright, and most of those were brought to the Mater by ambulances for formal certification of death. Some of the injuries they had sustained were

horrific to say the least. There were, I suppose, between the two
hospitals, about half-a-dozen people who were clearly critically
injured. Other injuries ranged from severe head and facial injuries
to very nasty injuries caused by flying glass and debris. Some
people had leg fractures, or limb and facial lacerations. Some of
those people needed to go to the Ulster Hospital for plastic surgery
or to come here."

One of the big difficulties was the fact that the hospitals didn't
know the names of the dead, yet relatives were arriving all the time
looking for information. "All we could do was look at the list of
people we knew were alive in hospital and say, look, they are not on
these lists."

There was "nothing easy" about any aspect of dealing with a
bomb, he said, but added that it was more emotionally distressing
speaking to family members who had lost a loved one, than actually
trying to save the injured.

(News Letter, 23 October 1993)

In a bid to help them cope with what they had seen and experienced,
ambulance personnel were given a two-hour stress debriefing after
helping the injured. Alan Murray, Chief Executive of the Eastern
Ambulance Service, praised the work of the rescue services, but
added:

Some of the things they saw yesterday were outside the previous
experiences of most of them—and some of them are so unpleasant
they are not really capable of being repeated because they would be
unsettling for people to read about them.

They were certainly upsetting to those people and it is important to remember that even though they—and when I say "they", I
include the fire brigade, I include the police and I include the local
people in the street—even though they were doing a super-human
job, they are only human beings and, once the adrenalin began to
subside, that is just what they became again.

(News Letter, 25 October 1993)

Shankill People was critical of the 'media circus' that arrived in the
area after the explosion, commenting:

And so they descended. Within 15 minutes of the disaster they began to arrive. The television cameras, the journalists, the photographers, the media-men and women. At first people wanted to turn them away but then someone said: "No let them through, let the world see this." And so they came through, not in their dozens but in their hundreds, from all around the world looking for a story, a fresh angle, almost anything would do.

Within one hour they were already asking the politicians, what about Hume/Adams? The process of forgetting the people had begun. The tragedy was being politicised within the hour. Even then they got it wrong. Any line would do.

(*Shankill People*, November 1993)

Ten years after the bombing the area's new local newspaper, *Shankill Mirror*, reported on a commemoration service for the victims of the bomb. The newspaper reported:

An emotional highpoint of the service was the singing of two songs by girls from Harmony Primary School, Glencairn, including a solo verse by 10-year-old Lauren Baird whose parents Michael and Evelyn and sister Michelle were killed in the bomb.

The congregation broke into spontaneous applause as the girls finished their singing of "Love Shone Down" and "Faithful One." …

In his address Canon Barry Dodds said the aim of the service was that the pain of those who suffered should be acknowledged and should be lessened. He spoke of the broad meaning of the word "victim", saying that many continue to endure the pain and suffering of flashbacks and memories, and for some the "guilt" of surviving.

(*Shankill Mirror*, November 2003)

30 OCTOBER 1993: THE GREYSTEEL MASSACRE

On 30 October two UFF gunmen entered the Rising Sun Bar in Greysteel, Co. Londonderry, and fired at random into the crowd of customers, who were celebrating Hallowe'en. Approximately 200 people were in the lounge waiting for a Hallowe'en night country-and-western dance to begin. One of the gunmen, who were wearing blue boiler suits, shouted 'trick or treat' before opening fire. Seven people, including eighty-one-year-old James Moore, were killed and thirteen wounded; an eighth person died later. The only Protestant killed in the massacre, John Burns, was an ex-UDR member. Oliver McGuckin reported:

> A man who was in the bar at the time said he thought at first the shots were fireworks going off. "We heard one burst of machine gun fire and then three more after that. We all ran to the toilets in the bar and stayed there until they went away."
>
> The man said when he went into the bar about an hour later, "there were bodies everywhere." He added: "The ambulance service didn't bother about the people who were dead—they knew they were already dead and they tried to help the ones who were injured.
>
> Everyone was screaming. I thought that when they were finished there, they were going to come into the bar as well. It was all over in two minutes. Seven people dead; two minutes—that's all it took."
>
> (*Belfast Telegraph*, 1 November 1993)

A UFF statement later claimed that it had attacked the 'nationalist electorate' in revenge for the Shankill bombing.

The Greysteel attack came only a day after two Catholic brothers, Gerard and Rory Cairns, were murdered by the UVF at their home near Bleary, Co. Armagh. The gunmen entered the house through a back door and walked past Roisin Cairns, who was sitting in the kitchen after her eleventh birthday party. The gunmen were wearing masks and Roisin Cairns believed that they were involved in a Hallowe'en prank. After murdering her two brothers the gunmen again walked through the kitchen and out the back door. Roisin Cairns ran to a neighbour's house to raise the alarm.

The mass killing at Greysteel followed a day later. Nuala McCann reported from the Rising Sun Bar shortly after the attack:

> Sunday in Greysteel. The television crews arrived to clutter the roadside with vans carrying satellite discs. Press men with tape recorders, notebooks and cameras with wide-angle lens sought out the grieving relative, the heartbroken friend, the clergyman who might provide a fresh word for mass murder, carnage and slaughter.

Hesitantly, the police lifted the white tape and led the way into the red brick bar. Red for the shining clot of blood on the soft grey corner seat of the lounge; and red for the congealed blood on the wooden floor where broken glasses, dropped in panic, scrunched under the feet.

A red blouse lay in a pool of blood, near a single brown shoe and someone's precious gold ring. White circles surrounded the 30 bullet holes in the walls, painstakingly marked by police forensic officers; and white stuffing bulged from the bullet-torn soft seats. There was a deep hole in the floral-papered cement wall dividing the lounge from the dance floor. A bullet had ripped through to kill someone on the other side. The room was spattered with bullet holes.

On the bar, drinks and beer bottles stood suspended in time. A pile of furniture lay in the corner—tossed aside as people scrambled to reach a loved one in the scene of slaughter.

(*Irish News*, 1 November 1993)

The oldest victim of the attack was eighty-one-year-old James Moore, the father of the owner. His grand-daughter said: 'Granda was standing on his own. There were seven bullets fired at him and four of them hit him. It was no accident, not a case of him being hit by a spare bullet.'

The bar's owner, Jim Moore, said: 'I know my father is dead but I want no revenge for this. I am not bitter. I was never a bitter person. Catholics and Protestants drink in the pub together. They enjoyed their drink together, but it is so sad it had to end up like this.'

Former UDR member John Burns thought the gunmen were part of a Hallowe'en prank; one of the UFF gunmen shot him in the stomach, fatally wounding him. His wife was also seriously injured.

Moira Duddy was on the floor when she was shot dead. Her distraught husband John said: 'We went out on a Saturday night for a wee dance and they blew her to bits. Such men to have done such slaughter—they slaughtered my innocent wife. They were shot all around me and I never got a scratch—I'll never get over it.'

The youngest victim, nineteen-year-old Karen Thompson, was killed along with her boyfriend, Steven Mullan. She regularly stayed with her grandmother, Ella Stirling, who said: 'I asked her if she would be late, and she said she might be. I told her that was all right as long as she came back safe. ... And then her father called to tell me what had happened. I am heart-broken. I have cried all night. Karen was always with me and I am going to miss her terribly.'

In the month of October 1993 twenty-seven people died as a result of the Troubles—the highest number in any single month since October 1976. On the morning after the Greysteel massacre the *Daily Express* commented:

If mainland Britain had suffered a proportionate number of killings as has Northern Ireland in the past eight days we would be burying 810 men, women and children. If the 3,102 deaths since the Troubles began were similarly extrapolated, the toll becomes 109,000. That is a town the size of Blackburn, Gloucester or the population of the Scottish Borders region wiped out.

We in Britain have suffered from the bombers. But it is not belittling what has happened in Warrington and elsewhere to point out that were the nightmare of Ulster perpetrated on the mainland, a solution would have been found long ago.

(*Daily Express*, 1 November 1993)

The *Belfast Telegraph* stated: 'With the massacre at the Rising Sun bar in Greysteel, loyalist paramilitaries have hit rock bottom. Sheer revenge, taken out on the easiest of targets, is their only motivation. Any claim they ever had to a political thought has disappeared.'

Despite the latest atrocity, the *Irish News* still held fast to the belief that peace and a political settlement might now be attainable:

It is vital that all those who call themselves peacemakers—whether they be leading members of Sinn Féin, loyalists, constitutional politicians, ordinary individuals or the two governments—commit themselves to a common purpose. With one voice, we must all cry out for an end to paramilitary violence. Those in the republican community who have the ear of the IRA must demand an immediate cessation of violence, and those in the loyalist community who have influence with its killer gangs must do the same. But cessation or not, we must press on with efforts to bring about a settlement of our problems.

(*Irish News*, 1 November 1993)

15 DECEMBER 1993: THE DOWNING STREET DECLARATION

One of the enduring factors of the conflict in Northern Ireland was the failure to produce a political framework that both unionists and nationalists could support, or at least acquiesce in. Given the mutually conflicting constitutional objectives of the maintenance of the Union and the attainment of a united Ireland, producing such a framework was clearly not a simple matter. Despite this, in December 1993 the joint statement issued by the British and Irish governments appeared to have squared the circle and achieved significant support from both nationalist and unionist political power bases.

The Downing Street Declaration came at a critical moment in the developing peace process. In late September John Hume and Gerry Adams had sent proposals to the Irish government that they believed could provide the basis for peace. A significant factor in the Hume–Adams proposals was that the British government should act as 'persuaders' for a united Ireland—an aspect that was rejected by the British.

At the same time as political discussions were continuing, the IRA maintained its bombing campaign—not least in the form of the Shankill bomb in October, to which there was a loyalist reprisal at Greysteel a week later. In spite of the violence, political negotiations continued. On 27 October Irish Foreign Minister Dick Spring put forward six 'democratic principles' that he said would produce a sustainable peace. Essentially he proposed that there be no talks between the governments and those using, threatening or supporting violence for political ends. If, however, violence was renounced, then 'new doors could open' and the governments would respond 'imaginatively'. Two days later, after a meeting in Brussels, Prime Minister John Major and Taoiseach Albert Reynolds produced a six-point statement along similar lines, which, as in the Spring Principles, declared that there could be no secret agreements or understandings between governments and organisations supporting violence as the price for its cessation.

Despite these proposals rumours continued to circulate that British officials were conducting discussions, if not negotiations, with Sinn Féin—and thus, essentially, with the IRA. The British made numerous denials that this was the case, most famously on 1 November when Labour MP Dennis Skinner told the House of Commons that 'People outside Parliament understand only too well that the government have dealt with terrorists over the decades'. Major's response to this was that 'If the implication of his remarks is that we should sit down and talk with Mr Adams and the Provisional IRA, I can only say that that would turn my stomach and those of most honourable members; we will not do it.'

On 28 November the *Observer* revealed that the British government had, in fact, maintained a secret channel of communications (later referred to as the 'back channel') with Sinn Féin and the IRA for three years and had been in regular contact since the end of February. The story sparked a fresh wave of claim and counter-claim between the British government and republicans as to who had initiated the most recent discussions, as well as revealing some details of the talks. Nonetheless, in the House of Commons Sir Patrick Mayhew faced only limited criticism from British MPs following the revelations; Ian Paisley was ordered to leave the chamber after refusing to withdraw his comment that Mayhew had lied to the House of Commons. It was against this, less than auspicious, background that the final preparations for the Joint Declaration took place.

On 15 December 1993 John Major and Albert Reynolds issued the Joint Declaration on Northern Ireland from London. The Downing Street Declaration proved to be one of the key documents of the peace process. The British and Irish governments made a commitment to work towards a new political framework founded on consent and encompassing arrangements within Northern Ireland, for the whole of Ireland and between Great Britain and Ireland. The British government stated that it had no selfish strategic or economic interest in Northern Ireland and that its primary interest was to see peace, stability and reconciliation established.

In what was arguably the most important section of the document the British government stated that it was for 'the people of Ireland alone, by agreement between the two parts, to exercise their right of self-determination on the basis of consent, freely and concurrently given, North and South, to bring about a united Ireland, if that is their wish'. The document thus provided a delicate balance between the nationalist objective of a united Ireland and the unionist demand for recognition of the right to remain part of the United Kingdom. The *Belfast Telegraph* welcomed the Declaration and believed that it achieved 'a balance between the two traditions, a blurring of the edges, but whether it is to satisfy the extremists and lead to a permanent cessation of violence remains to be seen.'

The Democratic Unionist Party perceived the Declaration as weakening Northern Ireland's status within the United Kingdom. The Ulster Unionists were more supportive of the Declaration—hardly surprising given that James Molyneaux and other unionists had contributed to the text. Additionally, Church of Ireland Archbishop Robin Eames had helped Albert Reynolds in drafting the clauses of the Declaration that dealt with the Republic's attitude towards Northern unionists. In the House of Commons Major also attempted to ease unionist concerns that the Declaration represented a step towards a united Ireland by highlighting what was *not* in the Declaration: the British government would not be 'persuaders' for a united Ireland; the future of Northern Ireland would not be decided by a single act of self-determination across Ireland; there was no timetable for constitutional change nor any arrangement for joint British–Irish authority over Northern Ireland.

Most republicans saw the Declaration as copper-fastening unionists' right to prevent a united Ireland. Significantly, the republican movement did not reject the Declaration out of hand. Instead, Gerry Adams called for clarification of the meaning of the Declaration and for 'direct and unconditional dialogue' with the British and Irish governments.

The prospect for paramilitary ceasefires and a widely acceptable political settlement, however tenuous at that time, also gave renewed significance to another question: what was to be done about paramilitary weapons? This was a question that would continue to dog the peace process over the next decade.

For the most part, however, the Declaration was welcomed as a workable compromise and as such it continued to provide a point of reference in the developing peace process. In the longer term it would help generate the political and philosophical framework around which the Good Friday Agreement could be built.

Two days after the Declaration, Albert Reynolds—who had announced plans for a peace forum in an attempt to tie republicans more firmly into the peace process—gave an upbeat interpretation of its value. He told the Dáil:

In the final analysis this Joint Declaration is particularly addressed to the people and organisations on both sides who can most directly deliver peace. While none of us can ever condone the deeds com-

mitted over the past 25 years, I believe it is right to acknowledge
what I believe are serious and courageous efforts that have been
made for some time by some in the republican leadership to find a
path out of the impasse. I believe when they examine the Joint
Declaration closely, together with the proposal for a peace forum …
they should find that they provide the necessary elements for a
peace process that will create its own dynamic.

18 JUNE 1994: THE HEIGHTS BAR, LOUGHINISLAND

On 18 June 1994 UVF gunmen killed six men and wounded five others
when they opened fire on a group of people watching a televised football match at The Heights Bar, Loughinisland, Co. Down. One eyewitness said the gunmen were laughing as they left the bar. Press
Association reporter Deric Henderson described the scene at the time
of the attack:

> One moment the happy pub crowd watching the Republic of
> Ireland World Cup soccer team were shrieking with joy—then
> came the agonising screams of death. It was all over in a matter of
> seconds. A red Triumph Acclaim pulled up outside. Two gunmen
> got out, walked in on customers whose eyes were fixed on the tele-
> vision screen, sitting with their backs to the door—the only way in
> or out—and while one terrorist stood guard the other opened fire
> with an automatic AK47 rifle.
>
> There was no escape. One man stumbled and fell in panic to get
> away. Another hid in the toilets. Both survived, but by the time the
> killers had abandoned their car with the doors open in a field three
> miles away, five men were dead and another six lay wounded, one
> fatally.
>
> Hugh O'Toole's bar in Loughinisland, where the cheers for a vic-
> tory over Italy had been silenced by UVF gunfire, had suddenly
> become the latest of Ulster's bloody landmarks.
>
> (*News Letter*, 20 June 1994)

On 20 June the *Belfast Telegraph* reported:

> A hail of bullets brought a sudden, brutal end to a night of joy and
> anticipation for the customers of O'Toole's bar. Regulars in the

small country pub had been cheering on the Republic of Ireland in their televised World Cup soccer match against Italy.

It was the second half of the game and the Republic were leading 1-0. The atmosphere in the bar was one of elation. Then suddenly, the whoops of delight turned to screaming and moaning as UVF terrorists sprayed the premises with gunfire.

Nearly half of the 24 people in the pub were hit. Five men died instantly, another a short time later in the hospital. Five more were injured, one of whom was today fighting for his life.

(*Belfast Telegraph*, 20 June 1994)

The UVF claimed that a republican meeting was being held in the bar when it attacked—a claim almost universally rejected as entirely false. The *Irish News* pointed out that Loughinisland's only link to republicanism was that the leading United Irishman Thomas Russell had stayed there in 1798 before his capture and execution.

In many ways the quiet hamlet of Loughinisland was an unlikely target for the gunmen, as Chris Hagan observed:

Loughinisland is barely big enough to qualify as a village. But now its name will be forever associated with a litany of the worst atrocities of the Troubles.

Set deep in the rolling drumlin countryside of Co. Down, time and fame has largely passed the village by over the years. It's difficult for those who don't know where to look to find it off the main Newcastle to Ballynahinch road.

Loughinisland doesn't have a main street. It doesn't even have a footpath running from one end to the other. Indeed it doesn't even have a public phone box within the boundaries of its entrance signs. The parish is made up of scattered farm holdings and the village, such as it is, consists of a chapel, a school and a public house. ...

Villagers were proud of the new St Macartan's primary school and the improvements made to the church. Both gave the village a sense of identity. The other focal point was the Heights Bar, owned by the O'Toole family. It is typical of the many country bars dotted around this part of Down, with its fair share of characters.

The Troubles seemed a million miles away and it was a subject which was taboo in a bar which opened its doors to people of all classes and creeds, or no class or creed at all.

(*Irish News*, 20 June 1994)

Many sources speculated that the attack was the UVF's response to an INLA attack on the Shankill Road, Belfast, two days earlier in which UVF members Colin Craig and David Hamilton were shot dead. A third UVF member, Trevor King, was fatally wounded in the same attack and died on 9 July. Police said they had increased their profile over the weekend in anticipation of a possible paramilitary attack, but that there were hundreds of small pubs scattered across Northern Ireland and it was impossible to guard them all.

At the time of the UVF attack the bar's owner, Hugh O'Toole, and ten other local tradesmen from the area were in Romania helping to refurbish an orphanage and an old people's home. O'Toole returned home immediately after he heard the news of the shooting.

In the wake of the latest atrocity the *Belfast Telegraph* commented:

> After Greysteel and the Shankill comes Loughinisland. Another community has been ravaged by terrorism that came right out of the blue leaving wives without husbands and children without fathers. In killing Barney Green, the UVF notched up another loathsome record—at 87, he was the Troubles' oldest victim.
>
> (*Belfast Telegraph*, 20 June 1994)

The *Irish News* did not believe that the latest loyalist paramilitary attack was entirely a case of retaliation and stated:

> Loyalist violence has its own agenda, it is not reactive to republican violence; and indeed loyalist assassinations predate the foundation of the Provisional IRA. But while republican violence continues, it provides a smokescreen of convenience for loyalists, and an excuse for murders of innocent Catholic people.
>
> An end to the IRA campaign, followed by the incorporation of republicanism into the political process, is likely to stimulate rather than thwart loyalist activity; unless, of course, loyalist paramilitaries join the political process too.
>
> Without doubt, an end to IRA violence would change the atmosphere so enormously that events such as that in Loughinisland would become part of our history rather than part of our present.
>
> (*Irish News*, 20 June 1994)

As was often the case the British tabloid press called for a tougher security policy. *The Sun*, for example, believed that 'We can't go on letting Ulster descend into the pits of hell. The talking has to stop. The security forces know who the UVF and IRA killers are. They must be hunted down and brought to justice. And the death penalty should be brought back so we can be rid of these evil scum forever' (*The Sun*, 20 June 1994). Others, however, such as the *Guardian*, believed that the peace process was and remained the best long-term hope for the people of Northern Ireland.

The *News Letter* asked:

Can there be any doubt that the killers were motivated by a simple desire to murder Roman Catholics, and that a random attack in a pub in a nationalist area, when the Republic of Ireland's World Cup match was being televised, provided the opportunity to strike at a time when the premises would be sufficiently crowded for their evil purposes.

There can be no shortage of condemnation for an act so callous that it immediately evoked memories of the Greysteel pub slaughter, confirming that so-called loyalist gunmen are prepared to plumb new depths of perversity as they scour the countryside for easy targets and innocent victims.

(*News Letter*, 20 June 1994)

31 AUGUST 1994: THE IRA CEASEFIRE

Having pursued a 'long war' policy for nearly two decades, aimed at wearing down British opposition to a united Ireland through the use of force, in August 1994 the IRA announced a ceasefire. Although there had been rumours that such a development was about to take place, the announcement still came as a surprise to most people. Something of the thinking of the IRA's leadership was later revealed in a document circulated among its members in the period leading up to the ceasefire. The document called for the adoption of a policy of the tactical use of the armed struggle (TUAS) and said that although the IRA alone did not have the strength to achieve Irish unity, it could be achieved by allying with other groups to bring about an Irish nationalist consensus. The document stated:

After prolonged discussion and assessment the leadership decided that if it could get agreement with the Dublin government, the

SDLP and the IA [Irish-American] lobby on basic republican principles which would be enough to create the dynamic that would
considerably advance the struggle then it would be prepared to use
the TUAS option. ... Contact with the other parties involved has
been in that context. There are of course differences of opinion on
how a number of these principles are interpreted or applied ...
Nevertheless, differences aside, the leadership believes there is
enough in common to create a substantial political momentum
which will considerably advance the struggle at this time.

The document listed the 'substantial contributing factors' that made
this the right time for an initiative, including John Hume being 'the
only SDLP person on the horizon strong enough to face the challenge',
the Dublin government being 'the strongest government in 25 years or
more' and President Clinton being 'the first US President in decades'
to be substantially influenced by the Irish-American lobby. The
document stated that these factors were unlikely to align again in the
foreseeable future, therefore the IRA leadership recommended that
they proceed with the TUAS option.

Like so much else about the peace process, the meaning and thinking behind the TUAS document remain open to interpretation—did
the IRA leadership really believe that a 'pan-nationalist' coalition
would pressurise the British government into conceding a united
Ireland, or was this merely a cover to end the IRA's military campaign?

On Wednesday 31 August 1994 the course of the Troubles changed
irrevocably with the announcement of a ceasefire by the IRA, or, more
precisely, 'a complete cessation of military operations'. The announcement stated:

Our struggle has seen many gains and advances made by nationalists
and for the democratic position. We believe that an opportunity to
create a just and lasting settlement has been created. We are therefore entering into a new situation in a spirit of determination and
confidence: determined that the injustices which created the
conflict will be removed and confident in the strength and justice
of our struggle to achieve this.

We note that the Downing Street Declaration is not a solution,
nor was it presented as such by its authors. A solution will only be
found as a result of inclusive negotiations. Others, not least the

British government, have a duty to face up to their responsibilities. It is our desire to significantly contribute to the creation of a climate which will encourage this. We urge everyone to approach this new situation with energy, determination and patience.

The significance of the phrase 'complete cessation of military operations' was latched on to immediately and interpreted in differing ways by unionists and nationalists. DUP secretary Nigel Dodds was among many unionists who pointed out that the IRA had not made a permanent renunciation of violence, adding that 'they talk about a complete cessation of violence. But a complete cessation could last a day, a week or a month.' Unionists were concerned as to whether the British government had done a deal with the IRA behind their backs and, if so, what that deal might entail.

In nationalist areas of Belfast and Derry the ceasefire announcement was greeted with triumphant celebrations. This in turn fed into unionist suspicions regarding what had brought about the ceasefire. When Gerry Adams addressed a rally in west Belfast later that day, however, his emphasis appeared to be more on the fact that the IRA had not been defeated, rather than on any claim that they had won. He told the audience:

> I want to say a word or two about the volunteer soldiers of the Irish Republican Army. This is a generation of men and women who have fought the British for the last twenty-five years and are undefeated by the British. We have waited for too long for our freedom. We are demanding of Mr Major's government that he takes decisive steps now to move the situation forward in a fundamental way and that means fundamental political and constitutional change, it means a demilitarisation of the situation, it means our prisoners home from England and home with their families from prisons in Ireland.

The fact that the IRA had announced its cessation against the background of its remaining undefeated, rather than victorious, was lost in the wave of nationalist euphoria. For Taoiseach Albert Reynolds, for instance, the Irish government's view was that 'the long nightmare is over'. John Hume's response was: 'As I said with Gerry Adams, as we said together throughout, our objective at the end of the day was a total cessation of violence. I am very glad that that has been announced today.'

The SDLP's vice-chairman, Jonathan Stephenson, was critical of the British government and unionists for engaging in 'jesuitical nit-picking' over the fact that the IRA statement had not used the word 'permanent', adding that 'The *Collins National Dictionary* defines the word "complete" as "entire, finished, perfect, with no part lacking." I wouldn't expect people to welcome the statement from the IRA un-reservedly, but I would expect the reasonable application of common sense.'

The *Belfast Telegraph* found a balance between the two views. The newspaper's evening edition carried the headline, 'It's Over', but the editorial, entitled 'No more terror?' (with an all-important question-mark), noted:

> Today could be one of the most significant days in the history of Northern Ireland—if not the island of Ireland. It could be the day when the Provisional IRA announced that after nearly 25 years they were abandoning politically-motivated murder and mayhem in favour of politics, pure and simple. Or it could be another false dawn, to add to all the rest. The answer will only become gradually apparent over the next few weeks and months.

Despite the hopes that were invested in it, the IRA ceasefire of August 1994 did not mark the end of violence either from the IRA or from other paramilitary groups. On the day the ceasefire was announced the body of Sean MacDermott, murdered by the UVF, was found; the following day John O'Hanlon was murdered by the UFF. By 10 November the IRA had returned to killing when postal worker Frank Kerr was shot dead by IRA members during a robbery on a Royal Mail sorting office in Newry. The IRA announcement of 31 August 1994 undoubtedly marked one of the most significant days in the course of the Troubles, but it did not, as many hoped, mark the final end of the conflict.

13 OCTOBER 1994: THE CLMC ANNOUNCES A CEASEFIRE

Following the IRA's ceasefire announcement at the end of August 1994, there was an expectation that this would soon be followed by a similar announcement from loyalist paramilitaries. However, there remained a great deal of scepticism, particularly among loyalists, about the IRA's motives in declaring a ceasefire. The results of a *Belfast Telegraph* poll published on 2 September found that 56 per cent believed that the governments had done a secret deal with the IRA, while 30 per cent believed that the ceasefire would not last. In the same month the UVF exploded a car bomb at a Sinn Féin office in west Belfast and also injured two people when the detonator of a bomb exploded on the Belfast–Dublin train.

On 8 September the loyalist paramilitary umbrella organisation, the Combined Loyalist Military Command (CLMC), put forward a list of questions for which it required reassurances before it was prepared to declare a ceasefire These included assurances that there had been no secret deal with the IRA and that the government would 'ensure that there is no "change" or "erosion" within Northern Ireland to facilitate the illusion of an IRA victory. Change, if any, can only be honourable, after dialogue and agreement.'

Subsequent official statements seemed geared towards meeting unionist, and especially loyalist, concerns. On a visit to Belfast on 16 September, Prime Minister John Major said that any political agreement would be put to a referendum: 'My commitment means that no one can go behind your backs. Not today. Not tomorrow. Not at any time. It will be for you to decide.' Two days later Taoiseach Albert Reynolds told the *Observer* that the unification of Ireland would not come about 'in this generation'.

On 10 October the NIO allowed loyalist leaders to enter the Maze prison to discuss a ceasefire with loyalist prisoners. Three days later, at Fernhill House in north Belfast (the headquarters of the pre-First World War UVF), veteran UVF and PUP member Gusty Spence read out a statement by the CLMC announcing a ceasefire:

After a widespread consultative process initiated by representations from the Ulster Democratic and Progressive Unionist Parties, and having received confirmation and guarantees in relation to Northern Ireland's constitutional position within the United Kingdom, as well as other assurances, and, in the belief that the democratically expressed wishes of the greater number of people in Northern Ireland will be respected and upheld, the CLMC will universally cease all operational activities as from 12 midnight on Thursday the 13th October 1994.

The permanence of our ceasefire will be completely dependent upon the continued cessation of all nationalist/republican violence; the sole responsibility for a return to war lies with them.

In the genuine hope that this peace will be permanent, we take the opportunity to pay homage to all our fighters, commandos and volunteers who have paid the supreme sacrifice. They did not die in vain. The Union is safe. …

In all sincerity, we offer to the loved ones of all innocent victims over the past 25 years, abject and true remorse. No words of ours will compensate for the intolerable suffering they have undergone during this conflict.

Let us firmly resolve to respect our differing views of freedom, culture and aspiration and never again permit our political circumstances to degenerate into bloody warfare.

The announcement was welcomed in all quarters, even if many averred that it was overdue. The *Belfast Telegraph* commented:

The decision of the loyalist paramilitaries to declare a ceasefire was inevitable, but no less welcome for that. It made no sense at all for people who profess their loyalty to the Union continuing to bomb and shoot when republicans had put their weapons aside, telling the world they were relying on democratic politics.

The only possible excuse for the loyalists' reluctance to follow the IRA's lead was a fear that a deal had been done with the British government. As time went by, however, it became clear that this was not the case—and that the ceasefire is mainly based on the hope that London will eventually yield to combined nationalist pressure. So long as the pressure is non-violent and democratic, no-one can complain.

(*Belfast Telegraph*, 13 October 1994)

The *News Letter* was also optimistic, if cautiously so, about the CLMC statement:

Running through the statement is a profoundly conciliatory message which bodes well for the peace process. Before we all get too excited, it is best to remember that the statement, like the IRA's, comes from people who play by different rules—people who have been all too willing to murder and maim to further their own aims.

But the tone of the loyalist statement and the words uttered by their political representatives following the announcement in terms of reconciliation and contrition, went far beyond what was anticipated, and certainly went a good deal further in quelling fears of a return to violence than did the Provisional IRA ceasefire statement of six weeks ago.

(*News Letter*, 14 October 1998)

The *Irish News* was also cautious, but slightly more upbeat:

Can it really be true? Is our agony over once and for all? This is not the time for premature celebrations, and anyone familiar with Irish history will be acutely aware that strong hopes have frequently been dashed in the past. However, there is every reason to believe that the violence, which has gripped this society for so long, is now finally at an end.

Now that the loyalists have joined the IRA in stopping their campaign, the last serious obstacle on the road to a permanent peace has been removed.

(*Irish News*, 14 October 1994)

The following evening the *Belfast Telegraph* reported on what it saw as a 'subdued start to an era of new hope'. Darwin Templeton wrote:

When midnight struck across Belfast, there was little sign that history was being made. Battle-weary citizens opted to stay at home with their thoughts, rather than take to the streets in any joyous outpouring.

The low-key response to the loyalist ceasefire was in marked contrast to the scenes of jubilation that followed the IRA truce. There were no flag-waving cavalcades or rallies, with the city centre emptying after brisk late night shopping.

As midnight approached, about 20 peace activists gathered at the City Hall for an impromptu vigil. Many of them were veterans, having faithfully attended such ceremonies in Ulster's darkest hours. As they heralded the new dawn with songs of peace and prayers, they were outnumbered by reporters and cameramen.

Shortly after 12, a crowd of about 200 loyalists, some carrying Union and Ulster flags, marched on the City Hall. They stayed there for a short time chanting and singing before dispersing.

On the Shankill Road about a dozen locals, again carrying flags, milled around the Peter's Hill area under the watchful gaze of the RUC. Yards away loyalist paramilitary slogans stood testimony to how quickly events had turned in Ulster.

Six weeks ago hardliners had daubed "the War has only begun." Now it was over.

(Belfast Telegraph, 14 October 1994)

9 JULY 1995: THE SIEGE OF DRUMCREE

There had been a history of disputed parades for many years before the Drumcree crisis developed in 1995. On 9 July that year confrontations over Orange marches in the area reached a much higher level after the RUC prevented Orangemen from parading along the Catholic Garvaghy Road on the return route from a church service. This incident led to a stand-off between police and Orangemen and widespread rioting in Protestant areas across Northern Ireland. On 11 July a compromise was reached between the police and Orangemen allowing some of the marchers to walk along the road. However, this arrangement did not meet the demands of nationalist groups, which did not want any marchers in the area. In 1996 and 1997 the decision to allow the march to proceed led to rioting in nationalist areas. In 1998 the march was blocked, which action was followed by widespread rioting in loyalist areas. The deaths of three young Catholic brothers, aged nine to eleven, as a result of a sectarian arson attack on their home in Ballymoney, Co. Antrim, on 12 July was followed by a reduction in the level of violence.

The Drumcree dispute highlighted conflicting demands of unionists and nationalists in the area of civil rights. For nationalists, the issue was one of freedom from sectarian harassment; for unionists, the issue was one of freedom to express their cultural identity. The dispute over this specific issue had an impact far beyond the individuals involved and was an element in undermining unionist support for the Good Friday Agreement. Although no march has taken place along the Garvaghy Road since 1997, the Drumcree dispute remains a bone of contention. In September 2006 Orangemen in Portadown held a commemoration to mark 3,000 days of protest against being banned from marching along the Garvaghy Road. In December 2006 members of the Orange Order offered to meet nationalist residents directly for the first time in an attempt to resolve the dispute.

The gulf in unionist and nationalist attitudes towards the issue of parades was clear in the comments of local newspapers at the time of the 1995 dispute. On 10 July the *News Letter* editorial stated:

> The RUC, through its re-routing of the traditional Orange march in Portadown yesterday, has once again allowed itself to be black-mailed by the most undemocratic elements in our society and those who would diligently uphold the law have been pushed into a cul-de-sac.
>
> Sinn Féin thugs and bully boys were allowed to dangerously heighten tension in Portadown, a town that still bears the scars of a vicious IRA campaign ... For weeks, republican elements have been planning a head-on confrontation on the Garvaghy Road and, taking their cue from well-rehearsed compatriots on the lower Ormeau Road, they left the RUC with the dilemma of allowing the Orange parade through and facing the consequences of ugly street disorder.
>
> (*News Letter*, 10 July 1995)

In the view of the *Irish News*, however:

> The Orange Order is turning Drumcree in Co. Armagh into a loyalist version of the West Bank, the lower Ormeau area of Belfast has been on a knife-edge for weeks, and almost everyone is predicting the end of the IRA ceasefire. ... If unionism is about religious and civil liberties, as we are told it is, then it must turn its back, for once and for all, on traditions which result in the alienation of its fellow countrymen and women. And it must try to build traditions capable of embracing everyone who cherishes freedom, democracy and religious tolerance.
>
> (*Irish News*, 11 July 1995)

There was also the danger that the confrontation could lead to the collapse of the entire peace process. Phelim McAleer reported:

> Leading Portadown loyalist Billy Wright has warned that the peace process is at "breaking point" following the RUC's decision not to

allow an Orange march through a nationalist part of the town. Last night the nationalist Garvaghy Road was effectively under siege as hundreds of loyalists gathered at police barricades into the area promising not to leave until a parade from Drumcree Church was allowed to march along its traditional route.

Mr Wright, speaking at the Obin Street entrance to the area, threatened to bring in supporters from other towns to "match the nationalist rent-a-mob." He was referring to protesters who had earlier sat down in the Garvaghy Road and led the police to ban the Drumcree parade.

According to Mr Wright, the behaviour of the protesters made nonsense of Sinn Féin's claim to respect the culture of Protestants.

(*Irish News*, 10 July 1995)

The crisis at Drumcree had brought relations in Northern Ireland to boiling point and nationalists and the Alliance Party were critical of Ian Paisley for making a speech at Drumcree on the night of 10 July in which he said: 'If we don't win this battle, all is lost; it is a matter of life or death, Ulster or the Irish Republic, freedom or slavery, light or darkness.'

On 11 July a compromise was reached between the RUC and Orangemen and later that day 500 Orangemen were permitted to march along the road, but without any bands. Although mediators had been involved in attempting to resolve the dispute, there was an immediate disagreement after the march between Orangemen and residents as to whether the Orangemen had agreed to re-route their march on the Twelfth. Nationalists had also been angered by television images of David Trimble and Ian Paisley's reaction at the end of the march. As Henry McDonald noted:

Trimble walked on to the street and grabbed Paisley by the hand. The Upper Bann MP lifted the DUP's leader's arm together with his and raised them in the air. The sight of the two rival unionist MPs walking, their arms held aloft, between two lines of wildly cheering and clapping loyalists was transmitted by television cameras around the world. This triumphal image caused deep resentment among nationalists across Ireland. Many in Portadown who had reluctantly agreed to a parade through their area were angry that Trimble and Paisley appeared to be rubbing nationalist noses in it: there was a widespread belief that the two unionist politicians were

dancing a jig of victory on the Drumcree deal. That single victorious
gesture compounded local nationalist determination that under no
circumstances would any parade get down that road the following
year.

(Henry McDonald, *David Trimble*, p. 150)

The damage that had been done to community relations by the
Garvaghy Road conflict was clear in the *Irish News* editorial on 12 July:

Yesterday in Portadown the Orange Order had its day. The decision
to allow its members to walk down Garvaghy Road was a victory
for mob rule. Once more unionism used brute force to get its way.

The only people who behaved with any dignity were the small
group of residents who allowed the march to go ahead for the
greater good of the community. Everyone in Northern Ireland—
unionist and nationalist—is in their debt and in the debt of the
mediation network.

It was interesting to compare their willingness to compromise
with the triumphalism displayed by MPs David Trimble and Ian
Paisley as they headed into Portadown to the familiar cries of "no
surrender".

Mr Trimble did his cause no good with a "victory speech" in
which he danced over the feelings of his Garvaghy Road con-
stituents who had allowed the march to pass, and in which he
threatened them with more of the same in the future.

(*Irish News*, 12 July 1995)

Although David Trimble became something of a pariah to nationalists in the aftermath of the siege of Drumcree, his apparent hard line
did nothing to harm his standing among unionists and undoubtedly
played a part in his election to the leadership of the Ulster Unionist
Party just two months later.

30 NOVEMBER 1995: PRESIDENT CLINTON VISITS NORTHERN IRELAND

The arrival of *Air Force One* at Belfast International Airport on 30
November 1995 heralded the beginning of a day unlike any Northern

Ireland had witnessed before. The presidential entourage, with all its pomp and prestige, descended on Belfast and Derry and the charismatic Clinton won over all but the most cynical of observers.

In November 1992 Bill Clinton had been elected President of the United States with the backing of Irish-American groups. His pre-election promise that he would send a presidential peace envoy to Northern Ireland had generally been welcomed by nationalists, but had raised concerns among the British government and unionists. As President, with some notable exceptions, he pursued a pragmatic policy aimed at encouraging all political actors in Northern Ireland to reach agreement.

In December 1993 he supported the Downing Street Declaration, but outraged the British government by granting Gerry Adams a visa to the United States in January 1994. Within the United States this decision was supported by the National Security Council and Irish-American politicians, but opposed by the State Department. Clinton recognised that he had taken a 'difficult decision', but said he hoped it would 'advance the cause of peace in Northern Ireland'.

There was further criticism from Britain in March 1995 when Adams was invited to a St Patrick's Day event in the White House and permitted to raise funds for Sinn Féin during his visit to America. The decision led to a cooling of relations between Britain and the United States, with Prime Minister John Major reportedly refusing to speak to the President for several days. However, such events were exceptions to a general policy of supporting the line taken by the British and Irish governments.

Clinton's appointment of former senator George Mitchell, in 1994, as an economic envoy was to have significant consequences through Mitchell's continuing role in the peace process. Clinton's arrival on a tour of London, Belfast and Dublin in late November 1995 coincided with another period of deadlock in negotiations, particularly with regard to the relationship between political talks and the disposal of paramilitary weapons. A week of intense diplomatic activity involving the British, Irish and American governments finally led to a joint British–Irish communiqué on the way forward in the peace process late in the evening of 28 November, the day before Clinton was due to arrive in London. The communiqué marked the formal launch of a 'twin-track' approach with the London and Dublin governments stating their 'firm aim' of achieving all-party talks by the end of

February 1996. Invitations were sent to all parties to participate in intensive preparatory talks. The second strand of the twin-track approach called for an international body to be established to provide an assessment of the decommissioning issue. The British and Irish governments asked this body to report on the arrangements necessary 'for the removal from the political equation' of paramilitary weapons. The body, which was to be chaired by George Mitchell, was to submit its report by mid-January 1996.

Although the communiqué provided something of a fudge on the subject of weapons and talks, it did provide a degree of agreement between the British and Irish governments and avoided the public relations nightmare of Clinton arriving amid ongoing arguments between the two governments on the issue. In London, Clinton gave his support to the twin-track policy, praised John Major and Taoiseach John Bruton and stated that 'Ireland is closer to true peace than at any time in a generation'.

On the following day President Clinton, his wife Hillary and the presidential entourage flew into Northern Ireland. Clinton received an almost universally warm welcome as his carefully choreographed itinerary took him to the Shankill and Falls Road (where he 'coincidentally' met and shook hands with Gerry Adams) and east Belfast before travelling to Derry. At Mackie's engineering factory in west Belfast he gave a keynote speech in which he stated: 'Here, in Northern Ireland, you are making a miracle ... In the land of the harp and the fiddle, the fife and the lambeg drum, two proud traditions are coming together in the harmonies of peace.' Later in the speech he added:

> Over the last three years I have had the privilege of meeting with, and closely listening to, both nationalists and unionists from Northern Ireland and I believe that the greatest struggle you face now is not between opposing ideas or opposing interests. The greatest struggle you face is between those who, deep down inside, are inclined to be peacemakers, and those who deep down inside cannot yet embrace the cause of peace. Between those who are in the ship of peace and those who are trying to sink it. Old habits die hard.
>
> There will always be those who will define the worth of their lives not by who they are, but by who they are not; not by what they are for but by what they are against. They will never escape the dead-end street of violence. But you, the vast majority, Protestant

and Catholic alike, must not allow the ship of peace to sink on the rocks of old habits and hard grudges.

You must stand firm against terror. You must say to those who still would use violence for political objectives—you are the past, your day is over.

Later, speaking in front of Derry's Guild Hall, Clinton praised John Hume as 'Ireland's most tireless champion for civil rights and its most eloquent voice of non-violence'. Encouraging people to support the peace process he said:

I ask you to build on the opportunity you have before you, to believe that the future can be better than the past. To work together because you have so much more to gain by working together than by drifting apart. Have the patience to work for a just and lasting peace. Reach for it, the United States will reach with you. The further shore of that peace is within your reach.

Returning to Belfast city centre, Clinton switched on the Christmas tree lights before retiring overnight to the Europa Hotel—one of the most bombed hotels in Europe. Clinton himself had clearly been caught up in the atmosphere of the day and leaving the Europa the following morning said he felt 'a great deal of gratitude for such a remarkable day'.

Clinton's visit was widely viewed as politically balanced and providing a significant moment in the developing peace process. When the IRA ended its ceasefire in February 1996, he refused demands to end visas to the United States for Sinn Féin members and encouraged paramilitary groups to end their campaigns.

After the IRA renewed its ceasefire in July 1997 Clinton again encouraged all parties to work towards agreement and spoke directly with some of the groups involved by telephone on the final night of negotiations before the signing of the Good Friday Agreement (GFA). He threw his support behind the campaign in favour of the Agreement and subsequently encouraged the political parties to work towards its implementation. Disillusioned with the implementation of the GFA, unionists began to question Clinton's even-handedness on Northern Ireland over issues such as the apparent down-playing of IRA gun-smuggling from Florida in 1999.

Although Clinton returned to Northern Ireland as President on two further occasions, in September 1998 and in December 2000, neither matched the significance, or the glamour, of his first visit in November 1995.

9 FEBRUARY 1996: THE END OF THE IRA CEASEFIRE

At 5.40pm on 9 February 1996 Scotland Yard received warnings from news agencies and Sky television that the IRA ceasefire was about to end. Several news agencies had received warnings that a bomb had been planted at South Quay railway station, following which attempts were made to evacuate the Canary Wharf area.

Shortly before 7.00pm an IRA statement saying that it was ending its ceasefire from 6.00pm that day was authenticated. The statement commended the leadership of nationalist Ireland and made it clear who they believed was responsible for their decision to end their ceasefire:

> The cessation presented an historic challenge for everyone, and Oglaigh na hEireann [the IRA] commends the leaderships of nationalist Ireland at home and abroad. They rose to the challenge. The British Prime Minister did not. Instead of embracing the peace process, the British government acted in bad faith, with Mr Major and the Unionist leaders squandering this unprecedented opportunity to resolve the conflict.
>
> Time and again over the last eighteen months, selfish party political and sectional interests in the London parliament have been placed before the rights of the people of Ireland. ... The blame for the failure thus far of the Irish peace process lies squarely with John Major and his government.

At 7.01pm a 1,000 lb bomb carried on a lorry near South Quay Station, on the Docklands Light Railway, exploded, killing newsstand workers Inan Bashir and John Jeffries, injuring more than 100 others and causing an estimated £85 million worth of damage. The bomb was clearly intended to cause damage to the tower at Canary Wharf, the tallest building in Britain. The explosion left a crater 14 ft wide and 20 ft deep and was heard throughout east and north-east London.

The attack was almost universally condemned outside republican circles. Northern Ireland Secretary of State Sir Patrick Mayhew responded to the IRA statement by saying: 'Those who have said the government hasn't moved fast enough are really saying, "You haven't responded to our threats fast enough so here's another one to smarten you up."'

For most observers the end of the ceasefire was unexpected. At the time, unionists and republicans appeared to be slowly building bridges. On the day the Canary Wharf bomb exploded, Ulster Unionist MP Ken Maginnis and Sinn Féin Chairman Mitchel McLaughlin took part in a debate on BBC Northern Ireland (the programme was not broadcast because of subsequent events), while on BBC Radio Ulster Gerry Adams spoke of his 'Protestant brothers and sisters' and said that political progress could be made through all-party talks.

Following the launch of the twin-track policy (which attempted to square the circle of all-party talks and removing paramilitary weapons) in November 1995, as well as the champagne atmosphere created by the Clinton visit, political negotiations had once again become bogged down. In early December UUP leader David Trimble refused an Irish government invitation and called on them to remove their territorial claim to Northern Ireland. On 7 December the IRA accused the British government of stalling on inclusive negotiations that would involve Sinn Féin and said there was 'no question of the IRA meeting the ludicrous demand for a surrender of IRA weapons'. Less than two weeks later the murder of Chris Johnston in Belfast, the fifth alleged drug dealer to be murdered by Direct Action Against Drugs (an IRA cover name), highlighted both the limits of the IRA's ceasefire and the fact that the IRA was still prepared to use violence whenever it felt it was necessary. By early January, Direct Action Against Drugs had killed two more men.

The ongoing activity of the IRA often seemed at odds with the more positive noises coming from Sinn Féin. On 10 January the party published its submission to the international arms body (the commission led by George Mitchell). The Sinn Féin document, *Building a Permanent Peace*, stated that the IRA might agree to dispose of its weapons under independent verification, but that this would not be considered until a political settlement had been agreed and then only in the context of overall 'demilitarisation'.

The publication of the Mitchell report on 24 January raised hopes of a breakthrough on the tortuous issue of talks and guns. Mitchell accepted that paramilitary groups were prepared to get rid of their weapons, but that this would not happen before all-party talks had taken place. The report suggested that parties consider decommissioning taking place during all-party negotiations. In addition, the Mitchell report recommended that those participating in talks agree to a set of democratic principles renouncing the use of violence for political ends. Among a number of confidence-building measures the report noted that an elected body with an appropriate mandate might be established.

In the House of Commons Major latched onto this suggestion and announced that the government was ready to introduce legislation for an election to go ahead as soon as practicable on the grounds that this would show that parties involved in the talks had a democratic mandate. Nationalists across Ireland reacted furiously to this suggestion, seeing it as a stalling tactic and a concession to unionists. John Hume went as far as to suggest that the government might be trying to buy Unionist votes in the Commons in order to hold on to power. The nationalist belief that the Conservative government was now working to a unionist agenda was strengthened on the following day when Sir Patrick Mayhew announced that a Northern Ireland Grand Committee was to be established—something unionists had been demanding for some time. However, if the British government was to drop its policy of decommissioning before talks, as the Mitchell report suggested, then an alternative strategy needed to be found that would keep most unionists involved in the process.

By early February the political process was again going through a traumatic period, though few would have predicted the events that followed a week later. On 2 February fifty-seven shots were fired at the home of a police officer in Co. Tyrone, giving a worrying sign of paramilitary intentions. On the same day the Forum for Peace and Reconciliation published its report in Dublin. Sinn Féin did not agree to the clauses of the report that provided what it saw as a 'unionist veto', i.e. that the consent of a majority in Northern Ireland was required for any new agreement.

The British and Irish governments meanwhile attempted to resolve the arguments that had emerged as a result of the decision to hold elections in Northern Ireland. On 7 February Sir Patrick Mayhew met Dick Spring for talks in Dublin. Spring later suggested that the peace process could be moved forward by calling a conference for the purposes of 'intensive multilateral discussions'. This proposal was generally welcomed by nationalists, but rejected by unionists. By this time, however, the patience of the IRA was exhausted and it was no longer prepared to continue the long process of negotiation. On 9 February the IRA announced the ending of its ceasefire, followed almost immediately by the bombing of Canary Wharf. Another worrying point was the subsequent revelation that the IRA had been planning the London attack since the time of the Clinton visit to Northern Ireland late in 1995. Had the prospects for peace created by the IRA and CLMC ceasefires of 1994 raised hopes for a peaceful future that would never be met?

27 DECEMBER 1997: BILLY WRIGHT SHOT DEAD IN THE MAZE

On 27 December 1997 leading loyalist paramilitary Billy Wright was shot dead by republican prisoners inside the Maze Prison. Wright was born in Wolverhampton, England, in 1960 but raised in Co. Armagh. In 1976 he joined the UVF, partly as a response to the Kingsmill massacre. In 1977 he was sentenced to six years' imprisonment for hijacking and firearms offences. On his release he moved to Scotland briefly, but soon returned to Portadown and resumed his connections with the UVF. During the 1980s he was repeatedly arrested in connection with terrorist offences, but not convicted.

Wright's paramilitary lifestyle inevitably meant that he was also a target. On 4 June 1994 a bomb exploded under his car when he turned on the ignition. The blast threw him into the street, but he was not seriously injured. He later claimed that the RUC had been negligent in asking an untrained person such as himself to check for explosive devices. He also claimed, in an interview with the *Sunday Times*, that the Irish secret service was plotting to kill him. In all, Wright had survived at least six attempts on his life before he was killed by the INLA.

Steven Moore reported on the facts surrounding the murder of Billy Wright in what was supposed to be one of the most secure prisons in Europe:

Wright, 37, was shot dead at 10 am as he was escorted through the prison to the visitor centre. He was gunned down in what was supposed to be a secure yard next to his accommodation at the jail.

The attack took place at H-Block 6, which houses lvf [Loyalist Volunteer Force] prisoners in wings C and D and inla inmates in the opposite side in wings A and B. A number of inla men clambered onto the roof of H Block six's A-wing and waited for their victim to emerge from D-wing. They were lying in wait and only moved once they heard Wright's name being called to get into the white van which was to carry him and a fellow prisoner to the visitors' centre, where his girlfriend was waiting.

The warder had just closed the van's back doors and was climbing in alongside his colleague in the front when the gunmen struck. At least two jumped down from the A-wing roof and rushed over to the vehicle, pulled open the doors and opened fire on Wright. He was struck at least five times in the back and died instantly.

The inla men then climbed back onto the A-wing roof and dropped back down into their own exercise yard, where three gave themselves up to prison officers. Two guns were recovered and a Prison Service inquiry launched, centring on how the weapons were smuggled into the jail.

(*News Letter*, 29 December 1997)

As commander of a uvf brigade around Portadown, Wright is believed to have organised nearly twenty sectarian murders. In 1996 he broke away from the uvf when the organisation failed to take action in support of Orange marchers at Drumcree. The murder of two Catholics in the area by Wright's unit without uvf approval led to his expulsion from the organisation and death threats against him. In response, Wright formed the Loyalist Volunteer Force (lvf), which drew support from former uvf members in the area and others opposed to the peace process.

Despite continuing lvf activity, Wright was not imprisoned until March 1997 when he was jailed for threatening to kill a woman. In April 1997 he was sent to the Maze Prison, where lvf prisoners were kept in the same H-Block as inla prisoners, although in separate wings.

Journalist Paul Connolly recalled his experiences of interviewing Wright:

The words were softly spoken, but said with iron determination. "I was born Billy Wright, and I will die Billy Wright." Wright was telling me how he despised the nickname "King Rat," and blamed "republican elements" in the media for it.

But he also knew the media attention had given him almost mythical status among young militants in the tough loyalist housing estates of mid-Ulster. With his piercing eyes and ice-cold manner, Wright could come across full of menace and hate. But, paradoxically, he was also religious. He frequently ended telephone conversations with the words "God Bless" and had banned swearing and other "un-Christian" behaviour in his wing of the Maze.

But there is no doubt his extreme views led to many murders, and that, in his alter ego as "King Rat," he personally pulled the trigger on an unknown number of victims. In his short life, the trail of widows and orphans he left behind him stands like a testament to his personal capacity for cruelty and, in a wider context, of man's inhumanity to man.

(*Belfast Telegraph*, 29 December 1997)

Hours after Wright was killed, Seamus Dillon was shot dead by the LVF at a hotel in Dungannon where he was working as a doorman. What was almost certainly intended to be an attack on the hotel disco was foiled when Dillon and two other hotel security men approached the car in which the gunmen were sitting. The loyalist gunmen fired nearly twenty times, killing Dillon and wounding the two other security men and a teenage waiter. Despite being a former IRA prisoner Seamus Dillon was not believed to have been a specific target of the gunmen. At the funeral on 30 December, Fr Seamus Rice said he felt that many young people in Tyrone owed their lives to Dillon:

When Seamus Dillon was brutally murdered several days ago he gave his life saving the lives of others. I have no doubt about that. … We don't come to judge, to praise, to condemn or anything like that. We come here to pray for the soul of the deceased. We don't do anything but pray. God does the rest.

The following month the LVF was responsible for further sectarian murders with the killing of community worker Terry Enright on 11 January 1998 and Fergal McCusker a week later.

On the Monday following the murders of Billy Wright and Seamus Dillon, the *Irish News* commented:

> For all the talk of peace processes, politically inspired violence has never been off the agenda in Northern Ireland.
>
> On Saturday, we printed the photographs and names of the 13 victims of paramilitary violence in 1997, by the end of the day another two names had been added to the list.
>
> The murder of Loyalist Volunteer Force leader Billy Wright, in the Maze Prison, was almost unbelievable. The murder of Seamus Dillon, and the attempted murder of others, at the Glengannon Hotel, was no less horrifying for its grim predictability.
>
> The path Wright chose to take during his short and bloody life is a matter of public record. He, and those who followed him, were responsible for some of the most horrific sectarian murders in Northern Ireland's recent history.
>
> But his murder was wrong and without justification. Nobody has the right to take away the life of a fellow human being. Wright was entitled to the protection of the law in exactly the same way as every other individual in our society.
>
> (*Irish News*, 29 December 1997)

In 2004, in the wake of a report by Judge Peter Cory, the Northern Ireland Secretary of State announced an inquiry into possible collusion in the events surrounding the killing of Billy Wright. In November 2005 it was announced that the inquiry would be converted so that it would be held under the terms of the Inquiries Act 2005. The inquiry began in Belfast in October 2006.

10 APRIL 1998: THE GOOD FRIDAY AGREEMENT

The Northern Ireland peace process had always been a political roller-coaster and the period that followed the ending of the IRA ceasefire in February 1996 until the signing of the Good Friday Agreement in 1998 was no exception.

In May 1996 elections were held for a Northern Ireland Forum, which was also to provide a mandate for the ten largest parties across Northern Ireland to participate in all-party negotiations. In June multi-party talks commenced at Stormont under less-than-auspicious circumstances: Sinn Féin was barred from participating because of the ongoing IRA campaign, while unionists objected to the British and Irish governments' appointment of George Mitchell as chairman of the talks.

On 7 October two IRA bombs exploded inside Lisburn Army barracks, injuring more than thirty people, including warrant officer James Bradwell, who died from his injuries four days later. On 12 February 1997 lance-bombardier Stephen Restorick was shot dead by an IRA sniper at a checkpoint in Bessbrook, Co. Armagh. He would be the last soldier to be killed while serving in Northern Ireland.

The election of a new Labour government with a clear majority in the House of Commons in May 1997 added fresh impetus to the peace process. Prime Minister Tony Blair sought to encourage republicans of the merits of political negotiation, while at the same time reassuring unionists that the Union was not under threat. In Belfast, on 16 May, he told an audience that his agenda was not a united Ireland, adding: 'None of us in this hall today, even the youngest, is likely to see Northern Ireland as anything but a part of the UK. That is the reality, because the consent principle is now almost universally accepted.' At the same time he offered immediate talks between government officials and Sinn Féin, but said that the 'settlement train' was leaving with or without them. Despite Sinn Féin's Martin McGuinness meeting senior civil servants less than a week later, the conflict was still far from over. On 16 June two RUC officers were killed by the IRA in Lurgan, but despite this and official reassurances to the contrary, contacts between the NIO and Sinn Féin continued.

On 18 July the government revealed that Sinn Féin could participate in talks in advance of any IRA decommissioning of weapons provided the Mitchell Principles were adhered to. The British climb-down on the arms issue was attacked by unionists as an attempt to buy a cease-fire at any cost. However, the following day saw the IRA announcement of a 'complete cessation of military operations', to come into effect from midday on 20 July. Predictably this announcement was greeted with less enthusiasm than had been the case at the time of the 1994 ceasefire.

On 21 July Sinn Féin joined the talks process (although the actual all-party negotiations did not begin until September), leading the

DUP and Robert McCartney's United Kingdom Unionist Party to walk out. Crucially, however, the UUP remained in the talks process.

The following months saw continuing political negotiations but also continuing activity from paramilitaries opposed to the peace process, increasing internal loyalist paramilitary conflict and growing opposition to the talks within the ranks of the UUP. In January 1998 the British and Irish governments presented the parties with a 'heads of agreement' document, which set the framework for the Good Friday Agreement. Despite this, and despite their ceasefires, murders by the UDA and IRA continued. These activities led to the UDA-linked Ulster Democratic Party and Sinn Féin being expelled temporarily from the talks process.

By April the talks were heading towards the deadline that had been set for the ninth day of that month. On 8 April, having just attended his mother's funeral, Taoiseach Bertie Ahern joined the other participants in the talks at Castle Buildings in the Stormont estate in Belfast. On 9 April the talks continued to make slow progress, although at one point Sinn Féin appeared to be on the verge of walking out over the issues of early prisoner releases and decommissioning.

Tensions within unionism over the negotiations were also played out in the public gaze. At 11.00pm nearly 150 DUP protesters entered the grounds of Parliament Buildings to protest against the talks. Less than an hour later, Ian Paisley and other DUP leaders were harangued at a press conference by PUP supporters.

Overnight concessions to Sinn Féin on the issues of early prisoner releases and the use of vaguer language on the requirement for decommissioning kept the party involved in the talks. David Trimble requested, and received, a letter from Tony Blair stating that decommissioning should begin in June and that those parties associated with paramilitary groups that had not decommissioned weapons (essentially Sinn Féin) would be excluded from office. Despite this reassurance, a worrying sign for the future of the Agreement was that UUP negotiator Jeffrey Donaldson refused to endorse the agreement.

The Belfast Agreement, more popularly known as the Good Friday Agreement, was signed by the British and Irish governments and the Northern Ireland political parties at Stormont on 10 April 1998. It contained proposals for both a political settlement based on the three-strand approach outlined in the earlier Brooke–Mayhew talks and elements of a 'peace' settlement dealing with prisoner releases, decommissioning of paramilitary weapons, police reform and human rights.

The GFA included a provision for a 108-member Northern Ireland Assembly, to be elected by proportional representation. The Assembly would be headed by an Executive Committee with legislative powers. The Executive's first responsibility would be to establish a North-South Ministerial Council to direct co-operation on a number of issues. In the Assembly votes on important decisions would require a majority of both unionist and nationalist members voting in favour or a weighted majority of 60 per cent, with 40 per cent or more of both nationalists and unionists present voting in favour.

As part of the Agreement the Irish government also agreed to amend the Republic's constitutional claim to Northern Ireland to make the objective of a united Ireland aspirational rather than a constitutional imperative. The British government in turn agreed to replace the Government of Ireland Act. A British-Irish Council was to be established, which would have representatives from all the major parliaments and assemblies in the British Isles. An independent commission was to report on future arrangements for policing. The number and role of armed forces in Northern Ireland would be reduced and emergency powers removed.

The announcement that an agreement had been reached was well received, albeit with more enthusiasm internationally and among neutral and nationalist circles than among unionists. The potential difficulties for the GFA were outlined in the newspaper headlines of 11 April. The *Irish News* showed cautious optimism, noting 'Today is only the beginning, it is not the end'. Both the *News Letter* and *Belfast Telegraph* focused on the difficulties that David Trimble could face in selling the agreement to his party, with the *News Letter* giving the ominous warning, 'Trimble facing revolt'. The *Irish Times* took the time to ponder the historic significance of the day, noting in its editorial, entitled 'Easter 1998':

> Perhaps, in time, the date will resonate in the collective memory of our children and grandchildren, just as 1916 or 1912 or 1689 or 1798 have done for those of earlier generations. Where the inherited historic icons were the rebels of 1916 or the Larne gunrunners of 1912, or the victors in ancient battles, perhaps those of the coming times will be the peacemakers who buried the quarrel of 400 years

inside the grey, prefabricated huts of the Castle Buildings at Stormont, in the days running up to Easter 1998. Perhaps.

(*The Irish Times*, 11 April 1998)

15 AUGUST 1998: THE OMAGH BOMB

On 15 August 1998 a car bomb planted by the republican splinter group the Real IRA exploded in Omagh, Co. Tyrone, killing twenty-eight people and injuring 300 others. Another victim died from his wounds three weeks later. Among those killed in the explosion were a twenty-month-old baby girl, two Spanish visitors, a grandmother, her daughter and grand-daughter from the same family and unborn twins. The 300–500 lb bomb explosion occurred at 3.04pm on a Saturday afternoon during the town's civic festival, with the result that many of those killed in the explosion were women and children. The first of three bomb warnings was received by Ulster Television in Belfast just before 2.30pm. It said that a 500 lb bomb had been placed at the courthouse in Omagh's Main Street; the third warning said that the bomb was 200 yards up from the courthouse. The result was that police inadvertently directed people towards the car bomb, parked 500 yards away outside a school uniform shop, instead of away from it. The Omagh bomb was the largest number of deaths of any single event of the Troubles.

Witnesses saw two men park a Vauxhall Cavalier in Market Street at approximately 2.00pm. The explosion, shortly after 3.00pm, left a scene of chaos and devastation.

Constable James Morrell said in his police statement that he saw "injured and bodies littering the streets." His statement added: "I saw a woman sitting in the middle of the wreckage. I saw that her right leg was blown apart around the knee area. The lower part of her right leg was still attached. There was not much blood as the flesh and bone looked to be partly cooked."

He attended a young boy who had suffered multiple injuries, including puncture wounds to the stomach. When Constable Morrell tried to speak to the boy he replied, "I Spanish, I Spanish." There was a group of Spanish students visiting Omagh that day and two were among the dead.

Constable Morrell was forced to use nappies from a chemist in the town because they had run out of bandages. Police and other emergency services began loading the injured into vehicles which they were using as makeshift ambulances. However, when they reached the Tyrone County Hospital it had been overwhelmed and they were redirected.

(*Belfast Telegraph*, 21 December 2007)

RUC officer Gary McClatchey stated: 'I recall seeing a body on the road, in the middle of the road. The whole of the bottom of his jaw was missing. It was obvious that he was dead. I saw a girl under the remains of a burning car, I think it was a front axle. The girl was trapped and was conscious. She was screaming.'

(*Belfast Telegraph*, 21 December 2007)

Barry McCaffrey of the *Irish News* later noted:

The names of the dead read like a microcosm of those killed during the Troubles. No religion or community was left untouched. The dead included Catholics, Protestants, republicans, unionists, young and old. Among those killed were father and son Brian and Frederick White. Grandmother Mary Grimes, her daughter Avril Monaghan and 18-month-old grandchild Maura were all killed. It also included Spanish schoolboy Fernando Blasco and his teacher Rocio Ramos who had been on a bus trip from Buncrana in Co. Donegal.

The scene at Omagh Hospital was compared to a scene from a Second World War battlefield with blood running down the steps of the entrance. Off-duty hospital staff rushed back to work to help the injured. Helicopters were used to fly the most seriously injured victims to other hospitals across the North as emergency services in the County Tyrone town struggled to cope. A British Army camp at Lisanelly had to be opened as a temporary morgue.

Tony Blair, Bertie Ahern, Hillary and Bill Clinton, President Mary McAleese and Prince Charles all visited Omagh in the days after the bomb. At the time Mr Ahern refused to rule out internment against dissident republicans. The day after the atrocity the Real IRA admitted responsibility and said it was ordering an immediate halt to "military operations".

(*Irish News*, 21 December 2007)

Twelve-year-old James Barker was one of those who died as a result of injuries caused by the explosion. He had made a last-minute decision to join a tour group from Buncrana, in Co. Donegal, to Omagh. His mother later said: 'He would have survived if operated on earlier, but they were totally overwhelmed in the hospital. Our life took a different road on August 15, 1998—it was as if a bomb went off in our family. I cannot forgive. I should have been there protecting James. We went to Ireland for a better quality of life and look what it did to us.'

(*The Times*, 21 December 2007)

In December 2007, after a ten-month trial, a south Armagh man was cleared of fifty-six charges against him, including the murders of those killed in Omagh. The case was notable for the scathing comments made by the judge regarding the lack of thoroughness in the evidence presented on behalf of the prosecution.

In January 2008 Sir Ronnie Flanagan, who had been Chief Constable of the RUC at the time of the Omagh bomb, said he was sorry that no one had been brought to justice for the attack and apologised to the families of the Omagh victims and those who were injured. The editorial of the *News Letter* reflected the view of many newspapers on the situation nearly a decade after the explosion:

Whatever the ramifications of the judgment, grieving Omagh families are still searching for closure to the torment which they have had to endure for almost a decade, but, regrettably, the chances of achieving this now are not considered high.

(*News Letter*, 21 December 2007)

The Times, at least, found something more positive to take from the Omagh atrocity:

If there is the remotest consolation in this saga it is that it is so firmly of the past, not the future. The Omagh assault was meant to be the "Real" IRA's call to arms, a warped protest against the mainstream IRA's willingness to enter the political process. It was intended to rally all dissident republicans to the hardliners' cause. It failed miserably. Public opinion on each side of the border was revolted by the senseless slaughter. Omagh was thus the Real IRA's first and last "spectacular." After nine long years, the political process has reached its fruition. Few in 1998 would have thought it possible that less than a decade later the Rev. Ian Paisley and Martin McGuinness would preside together over a power-sharing executive. The search for justice for Omagh must continue unabated. The wider pursuit of peace, though, has been won.

(*The Times*, 21 December 2007)

The 2000s

18 JUNE 2001: THE HOLY CROSS DISPUTE

Although a number of commentators (particularly outside Northern Ireland) believed the signing of the Good Friday Agreement signalled the end of the Troubles, many community relations problems remained at local level. This was clearly illustrated by the dispute surrounding the Holy Cross Girls' Primary School in the upper Ardoyne area of Belfast in June 2001.

Population movement that had come about as a result of the Troubles had left the Holy Cross girls' primary school in what was now a largely loyalist area. At the same time, the loyalist Glenbryn area was surrounded by Catholic residential estates. Sectarian tensions increased in late June when loyalists putting up UDA flags for the Twelfth of July celebrations were attacked by republicans, including, according to local loyalists, some of the parents of Holy Cross pupils. The importance of the fine detail in the interpretation of territory was highlighted in the different views of loyalists and nationalists as to whether the area in which the flags had been erected constituted a 'loyalist' or a 'neutral' district.

Following a weekend of tension, on Monday 18 June loyalists picketed the front gate of the school. The following day riot police were deployed to escort the children into the school. The situation quickly deteriorated into one in which loyalist picketers harassed schoolgirls and their parents as they made their way to school. Loyalists argued that pupils could be taken in by the school's back door, but for some of the schoolgirls' parents the right to enter the school by the front gate was a matter of principle. The stand-off continued until the end of the school year, on 29 June.

Among other things the dispute highlighted a chasm in the different views of many Protestants and Catholics towards the meaning of the dispute. Protestant community worker Mark Coulter believed that the dispute was being used by Sinn Féin for propaganda reasons:

We now have a situation where these children are being escorted to school and Sinn Féin are saying that this is like Alabama in the

1950s and '60s. Well if you want to know about Alabama then come to our side of the peace line and see how we're living behind steel grilles, then go and see the lovely new houses they have.

Republicans took a very different view, however, placing the dispute within the broader issue of civil rights: 'Unionism is crumbling and the situation is becoming very volatile. They have to realise that we have a right to walk where we want and get our children to and from school in peace' (*Daily Telegraph*, 22 June 2001).

Several days into the dispute the *Irish News* commented on the situation at Holy Cross and the danger it presented to a stable political settlement:

> The scenes from north Belfast and beyond over recent days have been as disturbing as they are grimly familiar. Crying children prevented from going to their primary school, nationalists and loyalists rioting in the streets, families driven from their homes and Protestant and Catholic churches burnt to the ground—these were all images which should have been confined to the history books.
>
> (*Irish News*, 22 June 2001)

The loyalist protest recommenced on 3 September when the new school year began. On this occasion there was a substantial police and Army presence in the area and approximately fifty of the schoolgirls and their parents were able to force their way past the protestors and through to the school's front entrance. On 4 September a loyalist blast bomb injured a member of the RUC and more blast bombs were thrown the following day.

The death of sixteen-year-old Thomas McDonald in a hit-and-run incident on the same day, which loyalists believed had sectarian overtones, added to the tension. Clare Murphy described the situation in Ardoyne on the following day:

> It may have been rubble on the road or wet tarmac that caused the little girl in the red coat to trip. But she fell clutching her lunchbox as she tried to escape the loud boom to her right. A cloud of smoke rose from the spent pipe bomb just yards from where she sat screaming. Her mother quickly backtracked, encouraging the child to run the remaining distance.

Another blonde child appeared to break from her mother and forge ahead in the confused crowd, her face reddened from wailing. Father Aidan Troy of Holy Cross school stood in the corridor of armoured cars lining the road, urging on the crouched-over parents.

As over 100 Catholic parents and children entered the loyalist area just after 9 am it appeared the Protestant protestors had changed their tactics. The abusive crowds were gone, replaced by a handful of slow-clapping women with their backs turned, lining the road near burnt-out cars. "Yous should be ashamed of yourself," was the single catcall.

It was not until the procession reached Glenbryn Parade that rocks rained down and the children screamed. The explosion moments later proved tactics had changed for the worse. The parents huddled around the school door, tears streaming down the faces of mothers and children. One woman pledged she would never send her child back. Her daughter looked up wide-eyed.

(*The Irish Times*, 6 September 2001)

For a week in early September, before the September 11 attacks in the United States took their attention elsewhere, the Holy Cross dispute became the centre of world media attention. Suzanne Breen noted that the loyalist protest had done little to win sympathy for any grievances they might have:

Most observers find it impossible to accept that Protestant grievances are in any way alleviated by yelling and spitting at children and calling their mothers "whores" and "sluts". The contrast of little Catholic girls with tears running down their faces and grown adult Protestants shouting abuse at them does nothing to advance unionism. E-mails to local newspapers from abroad have described the protesters as "savages", "degenerates" and "mentally unstable."

(*The Irish Times*, 5 September 2001)

On 22 November the First and Deputy First Ministers of the Northern Ireland Executive, David Trimble and Mark Durkan, met upper Ardoyne residents to discuss the Holy Cross dispute as well as an investment package for north Belfast being drawn up by the NI Executive. The loyalist protestors agreed to call off their protest the following day.

In January 2002 there were renewed confrontations outside the school, leading to further fears of widespread violence in north Belfast, but the violence subsequently subsided.

Journalist Henry McDonald commented on the Holy Cross controversy within the context of what he saw as the greater shortcomings of the Good Friday Agreement:

> If the Holy Cross crisis teaches us anything it is that the Agreement's principal design fault has been its architects failure to address the structural sectarianism prevalent in Northern society.
>
> The Agreement celebrated, no, in fact exalted, ethnic difference and division. It rather too neatly compartmentalised us all into categories of unionist and nationalist, republican and loyalist with no encouragement to the centre ground. In short, the Agreement institutionalised sectarianism. This is, in part, why we find ourselves in the present mess because finding agreement in Castle Buildings is easy compared to reaching an existential compromise between the two communities in, say, Castle ward of North Belfast. And that is why so much of the media who heralded the Agreement as the only panacea to the Troubles have worked themselves up into such an exaggerated hysteria over Holy Cross—their theory no longer fits the facts on the ground.
>
> (*The Observer*, 9 September 2001)

23 OCTOBER 2001: THE IRA PUTS WEAPONS BEYOND USE

As paramilitary organisations began to scale down their campaigns, the political parties associated with them sought to be accepted as fully democratic parties. One of the major questions this raised was what was to be done about the weapons being held by the paramilitary organisations. For loyalist organisations the issue, theoretically at least, should have been easier to deal with than for republicans as the loyalist parties (the Progressive Unionist Party and Ulster Democratic Party) accepted being associated with their respective paramilitary groups (the Ulster Volunteer Force and Ulster Defence Association). Sinn Féin (SF), however, stated that it was not the Irish Republican Army (IRA) and did not accept that IRA activities should lead to any penalties on the party. Furthermore, as the IRA claimed to be the legitimate army of Ireland, it felt under no obligation to disarm, particularly since such a move might be interpreted as the IRA accepting that it had been defeated militarily. In addition to this, both republican and loyalist paramilitaries faced practical difficulties in tracing all their weapons, as well as concerns about internal feuds or feuds with other paramilitary groups. There was also the broader question of whether these groups wished to keep their weapons as a way of retaining their control in certain areas.

In late 1993 and early 1994 there were disputes between the various political actors as to whether the decommissioning of weapons in connection with political negotiations had even been raised as an issue. The British insisted they had been clear on the need for decommissioning before talks, while republicans said no such preconditions had been mentioned.

By March 1995 the republican position had shifted somewhat, with SF President Gerry Adams stating that decommissioning would happen at the end of negotiations, not at the beginning. In November 1995, after a long period of stalemate, a 'twin-track' approach was launched, with political talks set to begin in February 1996 while an independent commission, under Senator George Mitchell, would examine the weapons issue. In January 1996 Mitchell suggested that decommissioning begin during talks, but subsequent developments, such as Prime Minister John Major's decision to hold elections that would lead to all-party talks, were not well received by republicans and the IRA ended its ceasefire in February with the Canary Wharf bomb in London.

The arrival of the Labour Party to power in May 1997 was followed by the British government's dropping of the demand for decommissioning before talks and the IRA's reinstatement of its ceasefire. In September Sinn Féin signed the Mitchell Principles and joined the talks process. Later that month the Independent International Commission on Decommissioning (IICD) was launched, but it made slow progress on the issue.

Even the signing of the Good Friday Agreement in April 1998 failed to resolve the issue, with UUP leader David Trimble asking for, and receiving, a written assurance from Tony Blair that the Prime Minister's view was that decommissioning should begin immediately. For the next eighteen months the UUP pursued a policy of 'no guns, no government', repeatedly asserting that the UUP would not enter government with Sinn Féin until the decommissioning of IRA weapons had taken place. Decommissioning of loyalist paramilitary weapons was given less attention because loyalist parties had not won enough seats in the Northern Ireland Assembly to be represented in the Executive.

In December 1999 Trimble and the UUP changed their position and entered the Executive with Sinn Féin, although only on the basis that IRA decommissioning would commence by the end of January 2000. No IRA decommissioning took place, and in February 2000 Trimble used the threat of his resignation to force Secretary of State Peter Mandelson to suspend the institutions. In May an IRA statement said it was committed to putting its arms 'completely and verifiably' beyond use, leading to the restoration of devolution. Two IRA arms dumps were inspected independently the following month, but there was no further movement on IRA weapons after this. As a result, Trimble resigned as First Minister in July 2001.

In October 2001 the IRA finally began to put its weapons 'beyond use', though this was viewed as being motivated, at least partly, by the changed attitude of the United States towards paramilitary/terrorist groups holding weapons in the wake of the September 11 attacks. The arrest of three Irish republicans in Colombia, in connection with the alleged training of guerrilla groups in that country, was also a contributing factor.

The first act of decommissioning by the IRA was signposted by Gerry Adams in a speech at Conway Mill, in west Belfast, on 22 October. Adams stated that 'Martin McGuinness and I have also had discussions with the IRA and we have put to the IRA the view that, if it could make a groundbreaking move on the arms issue, that this could save the peace process from collapse and transform the situation.'

An IRA statement on 23 October denied that decommissioning had been part of the discussions with British and Irish government representatives, but noted that: 'The political process is now on the point of collapse. Such a collapse would certainly, and eventually, put the overall peace process in jeopardy. There is a responsibility upon everyone seriously committed to a just peace to do our best to avoid this. Therefore, in order to save the peace process, we have implemented the scheme agreed with the IICD in August.'

The IICD confirmed this:

On August 6 2001, the Commission reported that agreement had been reached with the IRA on a method to put IRA arms completely and verifiably beyond use. This would be done in such a way as to involve no risk to the public and avoid the possibility of misappropriation by others.

We have now witnessed an event—which we regard as significant—in which the IRA has put a quantity of arms completely beyond use. The material in question includes arms, ammunition and explosives.

The UUP re-entered the Executive, but the arms issue continued to be significant in turning unionist opinion against the GFA, under the terms of which, they believed, decommissioning should already have been completed.

In April 2002 the IRA put a second batch of its weapons beyond use, but other IRA activity continued, such as intelligence-gathering, leading to a further threat from the UUP to withdraw from the Executive and another suspension of the institutions in October. In October, in conjunction with the announcement of fresh Northern Ireland Assembly elections, a third act of IRA decommissioning of weapons took place, but a dispute surrounding details of the amount of weapons involved angered unionists and served to weaken Trimble's increasingly tenuous leadership of the UUP.

January 2004 saw the establishment of the Independent Monitoring Commission (IMC), which was perceived as taking a more proactive approach on the issue of paramilitary activity than the IICD. The IRA's principle of not decommissioning weapons had now been breached, so that the question became one of when, rather than if, decommissioning would be completed.

In July 2005 the IRA announced an end to its armed campaign and in September the IICD stated that the IRA had decommissioned all of its weapons. Nonetheless, the protracted nature of the issue of the decommissioning of IRA weapons undoubtedly played a significant role in souring unionist–nationalist relations in the wake of the GFA and harming the prospects for devolution. Even after the completion of IRA decommissioning the question of when loyalist paramilitaries would begin to move on the issue still remained to be dealt with. Despite this, as political commentator William Graham noted at the time, 'On the arms issue, a point has now been reached of republicans thinking the unthinkable and doing what they would never have considered doing in the past' (*Irish News*, 23 October 2001).

4 OCTOBER 2002: STORMONTGATE

On 4 October 2002 Police Service of Northern Ireland (PSNI) officers raided Sinn Féin party offices in the Northern Ireland Assembly buildings. The PSNI claimed that the IRA was operating a spy-ring from Stormont. Three men, including Sinn Féin's Northern Ireland Assembly office administrator Denis Donaldson, were subsequently arrested. Although documents were discovered at Donaldson's home, only two computer disks were reportedly taken from the Sinn Féin offices and these were later returned. Sinn Féin members claimed that the raid had been instigated by Special Branch and by 'securocrats' in an attempt to undermine the peace process.

Barry McCaffrey described the somewhat bizarre series of events:

> It should have been a sleepy Friday morning at Stormont when politicians and civil servants slowed down for the weekend. Few people were even at Parliament Buildings at the time of the early morning police searches.
>
> A group of city centre traders stood in front of the imposing pillars at the entrance to the building, waiting to take part in a press launch to encourage shoppers to stop using plastic bags. A bus load of schoolgirls disembarked at the bottom steps eager to start their trip around the seat of Northern Ireland government.
>
> But this was not any normal Friday morning at the Assembly. Only a TV film crew had been present when the PSNI raid on Sinn Féin offices began shortly before 8.30 am. Later, as news spread of the police action, the media gathered outside Parliament Buildings.
>
> Seven PSNI Land Rovers sat parked close to the left hand side entrance to the building. Ulster Unionist Assembly Member David McNarry stood chatting to reporters, apparently as amazed as anyone else that police were raiding political offices within government buildings.
>
> (*Irish News*, 5 October 2002)

Sinn Féin Assembly member Gerry Kelly sought to use the attention of the media and invited the news reporters and camera crews to follow him up to the party offices. As the media personnel headed up the stairs, they were passed by PSNI officers heading in the opposite direction on their way out. The police search only appeared to have led to the confiscation of a small number of papers and computer disks. Inside the party offices Gerry Kelly told the press: 'It's about blackening Sinn Féin to let David Trimble off the hook—it is politically unbelievable.'

While many reports focused on the police raid at Stormont, there were a number of searches elsewhere. Chris Thornton reported:

> The serious lurch in the peace process became public today when police Land Rovers pulled up at Stormont with a warrant to search a Sinn Féin office. But the brief search of a desk turned out to be the closing phase of an operation that stretched back over a year and is said to have raised government concerns about IRA intentions.
>
> Today's raids began before dawn with searches of six houses in west and north Belfast. Security sources described the exercise as "a major operation" involving 200 officers, including detectives and tactical support units. … Documents were seized during the house raids this morning, which began around 5 am. Police said the raids were part of an investigation into "the activities of republican terrorists in Belfast."
>
> Security sources said the investigation is intelligence related, but is not connected to last March's break-in at Castlereagh Special Branch offices.
>
> The raid at Stormont appeared to be a direct result of Mr Donaldson's arrest. Police said it concentrated on a single desk in one office and the search was watched by an Assembly official. Two computer disks were taken away by police.

(*Belfast Telegraph*, 4 October 2002)

The PSNI raid and associated events, nicknamed 'Stormontgate', increased hostility between unionists and nationalists in the Assembly. The UUP had already threatened to withdraw from the Executive because of continuing IRA activity, including the suspicion of IRA involvement in a break-in at Castlereagh police station in March, and the failure of the IRA to decommission weapons. The police action against an alleged republican spy-ring operating in Stormont was effectively the final straw for unionists. The *Belfast Telegraph* also showed little sympathy for Sinn Féin's position, commenting:

> Since the Good Friday Agreement was signed more than four years ago many unionists have backed the accord but remained sceptical about Sinn Féin's commitment to the peace process.
>
> The events of recent days suggest that it was wise to exercise such caution. Today, all those who were prepared to make a leap of faith and take the republican movement at face value are entitled to feel sorely let down.
>
> The Agreement faces its biggest crisis ever, and may well be in melt-down mode. Regrettably it seems that Sinn Féin paid scant regard to the yellow card issued by the Secretary of State in July when he made it clear that there was no room for double standards in the peace process.
>
> Now that the Sinn Féin mask has slipped again, the onus is on [the Secretary of State] Dr Reid to take firm action. Sinn Féin has failed so far to decide between democracy and violence, but now there can be no further obfuscation.
>
> (*Belfast Telegraph*, 7 October 2002)

In the wake of the raid David Trimble demanded that Prime Minister Tony Blair act to exclude Sinn Féin from the Northern Ireland Executive, or else UUP ministers would resign. Instead, the government suspended the devolved institutions on 14 October.

In spite of this, efforts to create a stable political framework continued to stumble forward. In April 2003 a joint British–Irish plan for the complete implementation of the Good Friday Agreement was postponed because the governments considered the IRA's response insufficient. In October, Blair announced new Assembly elections. A third act of decommissioning of IRA weapons was carried out, but unionists were unhappy that there were no specific details of the type and amount of weapons involved.

Unionist voters were clearly unhappy with how the UUP had performed and in the Assembly elections, held on 26 November, the DUP received 25.6 per cent of first-preference votes and thirty seats, thereby becoming the largest party in the Assembly. The Ulster

Unionists' position was further weakened in December when UUP MP Jeffrey Donaldson and two other Assembly members resigned from the party. On 5 January 2004 all three joined the DUP.

At the same time the Stormontgate affair seemed to have done little to harm Sinn Féin's standing among nationalist voters. The party received 23.5 per cent of first-preference votes and twenty-four seats in the Assembly, making it the largest nationalist party.

The aftermath of the Stormontgate affair was played out more than a year after the Assembly election. On 8 December 2005 the Northern Ireland Public Prosecution Service announced that charges against the three men had been dropped because they were 'no longer in the public interest'. The announcement brought conflicting claims from unionists and republicans as to whether it was a concession to republicans in the wake of IRA decommissioning or the fact that there was no evidence against the three. A week later, however, Gerry Adams revealed that Donaldson had been a MI5 informant for more than two decades, raising questions as to whether more highly placed informants were still active within the republican movement. Donaldson subsequently moved to a cottage in Co. Donegal, but was found shot dead there on 4 April 2006.

20 DECEMBER 2004: THE NORTHERN BANK ROBBERY

On the night of 20 December 2004 the Northern Bank building in Belfast city centre became the location of the largest bank robbery in UK history when £26.5 million was stolen in a raid. The fact that the IRA was soon associated with the robbery inevitably had political repercussions.

In many ways the robbery came at an unusual time, with the DUP and Sinn Féin apparently moving towards a deal that could lead to the Northern Ireland Executive being re-established. On 7 December Gerry Adams had suggested that Sinn Féin accept the latest proposals from the British and Irish governments. The DUP remained concerned over the issue of the decommissioning of IRA weapons, however, and the talks collapsed on 8 December. The following day the IRA issued a statement that it hoped might keep negotiations alive, but its assurances were not considered strong enough by the British and Irish governments to restart the process.

The scale of the Northern Bank raid led most commentators to the conclusion that there were very few organisations capable of carrying out such a robbery, therefore the IRA soon became the chief suspect. On 7 January 2005 the PSNI stated that the IRA had carried out the robbery. Two days later Taoiseach Bertie Ahern went further and claimed that Sinn Féin leaders knew the IRA was planning the Northern Bank raid. Although the IRA denied any involvement, a report from the Independent Monitoring Commission on 10 February supported the view that senior Sinn Féin members authorised the Northern Bank robbery. The IMC report stated:

> It was a complex crime that was clearly the result of long and careful planning. Two employees of the Northern Bank and their families were abducted on Sunday 19 December by individuals threatening violence with firearms, one at Poleglass on the outskirts of Belfast, and the other at Loughinisland, Co Down, some 20 miles away. Under the threat that serious harm would be done to their families, these employees were coerced into delivering the money to the robbers during the course of the following day. They and their families were released after the robbery.

Sinn Féin spokespersons and the IRA denied any involvement in the robbery, and there appeared to be no obvious reason why the IRA should carry out such a robbery at that time. Some commentators, however, viewed it as the IRA's way of reminding the British and Irish governments that they were still an effective organisation and should not be taken for granted. The robbery could also be interpreted as a signal to republican supporters that they would not weakly concede to the demands of other political actors.

Beyond the significance of the incident in itself, the robbery raised the broader issue of whether the IRA had given up criminal activity. To most observers the answer seemed to be, no. The collapse of political talks in early December had been followed by a series of IRA punishment attacks in republican areas of Belfast. Taoiseach Bertie Ahern criticised the IRA in the Dáil over these issues on 26 January 2005, stating:

> It is not a question of the size of the bank raid, and it was a big bank raid. I did not show anger regarding earlier events—for example the raid on the Makro store in Dunmurry last Easter during which

£1 million worth of goods was taken and staff were tied up by armed men. The International Monitoring Commission blamed the IRA for that. We in this House took that coolly enough.

What I find really offensive—and I say it here in the House with members of Sinn Féin present … is that there was an ability to turn off all punishment beatings while negotiations were in progress but as soon as the negotiations failed there was a string of them. They were again a nightly occurrence. I will give Sinn Féin full marks for discipline, but not for anything else.

Then, on 30 January 2005, Belfast man Robert McCartney was murdered allegedly by IRA members following an argument in a bar in central Belfast. IRA members quickly cleared the bar of any forensic evidence and warned those present not to give any information to the police. However, the public outcry against the murder of Robert McCartney was so great that on 25 February the IRA stated that it had dismissed three of its members associated with the murder. Despite this, pressure continued to be exerted by some republicans against the sisters of Robert McCartney, who campaigned for his killers to be brought to justice. In March an IRA statement said the killing '… was wrong. It was murder. But it was not carried out by the IRA, nor was it carried out on behalf of the IRA.' On the ground, however, things were less clear, as Robert McCartney's sister, Catherine McCartney later noted:

> The statement went on to criticise those who refused to accept the IRA's lies, bemoaning the fact that regardless of what the organisation did, "some people" would never be happy. The question was, what had the IRA done apart from destroy the evidence and intimidate witnesses?
>
> The statement was followed up by a death threat, delivered to us by the police with some advice and the assurance that, "It's the ones that don't warn you that you have to worry about." Although we treated the threats with nothing more than contempt, they proved that the IRA's own supporters or volunteers didn't believe in its statements of support either.
>
> (Catherine McCartney, *Walls of Silence*, p. 159)

On 17 February 2005 gardaí discovered £2.4 million at the home of a financial advisor in Co. Cork, which they believed to be part of £4.9

million sent by the IRA to Cork for money laundering. Follow-up raids led to a further £605,000 being recovered. More than £1 million more was believed to have been burned by another individual who thought that gardaí were about to arrest him.

Such was the seriousness of the situation that the *Sunday Tribune* believed that:

> The Good Friday Agreement is in tatters after the events of the past few weeks. The Sinn Féin leadership has excluded itself indefinitely from political power, North and South, because of the activities of its paramilitary wing. … The astonishing scale and reach of the IRA operations, as revealed by the Northern Bank robbery, has almost been capped by the emerging disclosures about the level of involvement in its activities by leading members of the professional classes in the Republic. The scale of the IRA money-laundering operation was a threat to democratic standards every bit as serious as the bank robbery itself.
>
> (*Sunday Tribune*, 20 February 2005)

By February 2005 the prospects for a devolved administration appeared bleak—the Northern Bank robbery, the McCartney murder and other IRA activity seemed to remove the prospect of Sinn Féin's role in an Executive for the foreseeable future. The IRA's actions also raised questions about the very existence of the organisation. Journalist Chris Thornton commented:

> Most republicans agree that there will be no return to war. It would cripple Sinn Féin's growth and, anyway, the peace process was founded on the basis that the war couldn't be won. Danny Morrison, Sinn Féin's former director of publicity, wrote in *Daily Ireland* that "the reason why a return to armed struggle would be foolhardy is because it would be a return to military stalemate." Which leaves republicans grappling with an awkward question while the peace process stews: if it is incapable of waging war and incompatible with peace, what is the IRA there for?
>
> (*Irish Independent*, 5 February 2005)

28 JULY 2005: THE IRA ANNOUNCES AN END TO ITS ARMED CAMPAIGN

In May 2005 the Westminster general election saw the DUP strengthen its position as the largest party in Northern Ireland by winning nine of Northern Ireland's eighteen seats. Sinn Féin had become the second largest party by winning five seats. It was against this background that, on 28 July 2005, the IRA announced the end of its armed campaign.

The IRA statement, read out to the media by former republican prisoner Seanna Walsh, announced:

The leadership of Oglaigh na hEireann has formally ordered an end to the armed campaign. This will take effect from 4pm [1600 BST] this afternoon. All IRA units have been ordered to dump arms. All Volunteers have been instructed to assist the development of purely political and democratic programmes through exclusively peaceful means. Volunteers must not engage in any other activities whatsoever.

The IRA leadership has also authorised our representative to engage with the IICD [Independent International Commission on Decommissioning] to complete the process to verifiably put its arms beyond use in a way which will further enhance public confidence and to conclude this as quickly as possible. We have invited two independent witnesses, from the Protestant and Catholic churches, to testify to this.

The Army Council took these decisions following an unprecedented internal discussion and consultation process with IRA units and Volunteers. We appreciate the honest and forthright way in which the consultation process was carried out and the depth and content of the submissions. We are proud of the comradely way in which this truly historic discussion was conducted. The outcome of our consultations show very strong support among IRA Volunteers for the Sinn Féin peace strategy.

The statement went on to say that the failure of the British and Irish governments and unionists to engage fully in the peace process had caused difficulties. It made clear that the decision had been taken to advance republican objectives, including achieving a united Ireland, ind that there was now an alternative to the use of violence by which these objectives could be achieved. The IRA restated the view that the armed struggle was entirely legitimate, but recognised that many people had suffered in the conflict. As a result, 'there is a compelling imperative on all sides to build a just and lasting peace.' The IRA statement concluded by saying:

> Every Volunteer is aware of the import of the decisions we have taken and all Oglaigh are compelled to fully comply with these orders. There is now an unprecedented opportunity to utilise the considerable energy and goodwill which there is for the peace process. This comprehensive series of unparalleled initiatives is our contribution to this and to the continued endeavours to bring about independence and unity for the people of Ireland.

The *Irish News* saw the IRA statement as bringing Northern Ireland one step closer to the goal of lasting peace:

> The long-awaited IRA statement declaring an end to the armed struggle is another enormously positive step which brings that goal closer. The IRA remains in name but in effect lies dormant. IRA members have been told to dump their arms and not to engage "in any other activities whatsoever." In other words, no more murders, punishment attacks, targeting, robberies or anything else which is unacceptable in a democratic society. These activities could never be justified and should have stopped long ago. However, we must deal with where we are now and republicans can expect rigorous scrutiny in the weeks and months ahead to see if they are adhering to the spirit and letter of this statement.
>
> (*Irish News*, 29 July 2005)

The *News Letter* took a highly cautious stance, however, reminding its readers that the IRA had killed more than 1,800 people over the previous thirty-five years and commenting:

> The IRA statement, while a seismic shift in Irish republican policy and ideology on the "armed struggle" concept, contained too many gaps and omissions for law-abiding people in Northern Ireland to take comfort. They did not say the war was over nor apologise to the victims, while the IRA structure is to remain in place. They still

hold themselves outside the law and offer no support for policing while their decommissioning scheme falls short of the minimum demands of unionism.

(News Letter, 29 July 2005)

The *Belfast Telegraph* saw the announcement as creating 'day one of the new Northern Ireland', while the government announcement that a number of military installations were to be closed added to the overall view of 'tearing down the past' (*Belfast Telegraph*, 29 July 2005).

The *Irish Times* believed that the IRA statement had been 'a long time coming and somewhat diminished for that', but added:

It will be a seminal day nonetheless, if the republican movement does what it says it will do now. And there is reason to believe it may. The worldwide war on terror has changed the political climate for Sinn Féin and the IRA in ways that could not have been imagined a few years ago. Suicide bombings have devalued the so-called "armed struggle" as a means of achieving political aims. And there is less willingness among the people of Ireland—nationalist and unionist—to tolerate ambiguity on paramilitarism, money-laundering and criminality any longer.

(The Irish Times, 29 July 2005)

Political commentator Mark Hennessy reflected on the general air of cautious optimism:

In 1994, cars travelled down west Belfast and many other nationalist areas in Northern Ireland, horns blaring, wrapped in Tricolours, in the hours after the IRA declared its ceasefire.

There was less of a sense yesterday that the hand of history was spread upon the land. Too many false dawns have made politicians and the public cautious. Caution, perhaps, may prove to be a better servant.

If backed up by deeds over coming weeks and months, the IRA's statement is historic, one that will greatly challenge the organisation and those in it who may have bridled at the leadership of Gerry Adams and Martin McGuinness.

Undoubtedly, it is as clear and unambiguous as could have been expected in any document signed "P. O'Neill"—certainly far more so than the effort it produced last December. ... The IRA yesterday went further than last December by ordering its members to dump arms, act through "exclusively peaceful means" and not "engage in any other activities whatsoever."

The language used offers little room for manoeuvre. Punishment beatings are out, intimidation is out, protection rackets are out, smuggling is out and robberies are out.

(*The Irish Times*, 29 July 2005)

Although the road towards the formation of a new executive continued to be a rocky one, progress was made. On 1 August the British government announced that within two years the number of troops in Northern Ireland would be reduced from over 10,500 to 5,000. In September the IICD said it believed the IRA had decommissioned all of its weapons. Five months later, in February 2005, a report from the Independent Monitoring Commission stated that although all paramilitary groups were still involved in illegal activity, the level of violence was decreasing. A political settlement had not yet been achieved, but the environment in which talks were taking place was, arguably, becoming more conducive to such an outcome.

26 MARCH 2007: PAISLEY AND ADAMS ANNOUNCE THE DATE FOR DEVOLUTION

On 8 May 2007 a power-sharing Northern Ireland Executive once again took responsibility for local departments of government. Unlike earlier local administrations, however, the main parties were not the Ulster Unionists and the SDLP, but instead the unlikely combination of the DUP and Sinn Féin.

At the time the Good Friday Agreement had been signed in 1998 such a situation would have appeared to be a recipe for disaster, yet by 2007 many saw a DUP–Sinn Féin axis in the Assembly as a natural development and perhaps the best chance to provide a stable Executive.

In 2003 Assembly elections confirmed the DUP and Sinn Féin as the largest unionist and nationalist party, and the more cohesive nature of the parties compared to their rivals suggested that this was likely to remain the case for at least the next decade. After this the British and Irish governments, much to the chagrin of the other parties, appeared to focus increasingly on brokering a deal between the two, even though other parties were sidelined.

In late 2004 the parties came close to a deal before it fell apart over DUP demands for photographic evidence of the decommissioning of IRA weapons and an end to IRA criminality. The prospect of a deal also collapsed as a result of the IRA's raid on the Northern Bank and the murder of Robert McCartney. Although the discussions had come to nothing, there was still a feeling on the ground that, unlikely as it appeared, a deal between the DUP and Sinn Féin was almost inevitable at some time in the future.

The Northern Ireland election results of May 2005 cemented the DUP and Sinn Féin positions as the leading unionist and nationalist parties, and in July the IRA's announcement that its campaign was over opened the door a little further to some sort of political understanding between the two parties. Although the government set a devolution deadline for late 2006, this failed to produce a breakthrough. Further talks involving local political parties and the British and Irish governments were held at St Andrews, in Scotland, in October and the governments subsequently set a target of March 2007 for devolution. Nonetheless the feeling persisted that the DUP would agree to enter an Executive with Sinn Féin only when they believed the time was right.

In 2007 the apparent 'de-greening' of Sinn Féin continued when, on 28 January, the party voted to support the PSNI. Two days later a report from the Independent Monitoring Commission stated that the IRA had abandoned violence and terrorism. On 7 March fresh Assembly elections confirmed the DUP as the largest party in Northern Ireland and Sinn Féin as the second largest and speculation began to grow as to the possibility of the two parties agreeing to work together in an Executive.

Although the government had set 26 March as the latest deadline for devolution, that deadline was not met. The events of the day were in many ways more remarkable, however. Ian Paisley and Gerry Adams met for direct talks for the first time and agreed that their parties would participate together in an Executive from 8 May. Sitting at adjacent tables in the Members' dining room in Stormont, Paisley and Adams each read statements announcing the agreed date for

devolution. The speeches bore remarkable similarities in the issues
they highlighted, particularly the objectives of restoring devolution,
delivering the best future for the people of Northern Ireland/Ireland
and remembering the cost of past conflicts while also looking to the
future. Paisley stated:

> After a long and difficult time in the Province, I believe that enor-
> mous opportunities lie ahead for Northern Ireland. Devolution has
> never been an end in itself but is about making a positive difference
> to people's lives. I want to make it clear that I am committed to
> delivering not only for those who voted for the DUP but for all the
> people of Northern Ireland.
>
> We must not allow our justified loathing of the horrors and
> tragedies of the past to become a barrier to creating a better and
> more stable future.

Gerry Adams said:

> We have all come a very long way in the process of peace making
> and national reconciliation. We are very conscious of the many
> people who have suffered. We owe it to them to build the best
> future possible.
>
> It is a time for generosity, a time to be mindful of the common
> good and of the future of all our people.
>
> I am pleased to say that collectively we have created the poten-
> tial to build a new, harmonious and equitable relationship between
> nationalists and republicans and unionists, as well as the rest of the
> people of the island of Ireland.

The decision was generally well received, though not widely cele-
brated. The DUP received some criticism for the decision from within
its own ranks, and on 27 March the DUP's MEP, Jim Allister, resigned
from the party followed by a number of district councillors. Aside
from that upheaval, internal divisions were remarkably low-key for
such a major step.

The *Irish News* saw the announcement as the 'final pieces in the jigsaw':

> Among the many emotions which surrounded yesterday's dramatic
> proceedings at Stormont, perhaps the most dominant was relief. A
> final deal has been within touching distance for some months, and

there was always the fear that a last-minute reversal could take place. Instead, we had the compelling image of Ian Paisley and Gerry Adams sitting shoulder to shoulder in what amounted to a spirit of full agreement.

(*Irish News*, 27 March 2007)

The *News Letter* saw the events at Stormont as 'taking first tentative steps into a new era':

During the twists and turns of the peace process, the people of Northern Ireland have seen many days come and go which were billed as historic, but the events of yesterday at Parliament Buildings truly justify the description.

The announcement that the DUP and Sinn Féin had met and agreed a date for devolution was significant enough, but the sight of Ian Paisley and Gerry Adams delivering the message together was enough to stop even the most hardened cynic in his tracks. Forget the frosty body language, it was undoubtedly an image many thought they would never live to see.

(*News Letter*, 27 March 2007)

In a more cynical vein, the *Daily Mirror* believed that 'The Ian and Gerry show is proof pigs can fly after all'. The report added that:

... after decades of misery and mayhem, after all the bombs and bullets, the tears and terror, after the political pawns and Secretaries of State, the same old faces finally came to a conclusion that everyone will be able to live with.

Their jowls may be heavier and their hair greyer but yesterday Ian Paisley and Gerry Adams helped turn Northern Ireland's political Groundhog Day into the country's first flying pig.

(*Daily Mirror*, 27 March 2007)

8 MAY 2007: DEVOLUTION—PEACE AT LAST?

In the run-up to the date for devolution Ian Paisley, now the First Minister Designate, met Fianna Fáil leader and Taoiseach Bertie Ahern at Farmleigh House in Dublin on 4 April. The two men greeted each other like old friends before discussing issues such as tourism and investment. Later Ahern, recognising the significance of the event, commented: 'At this important time in our history we must do our best to put behind us the terrible wounds of our past and work together to build a new relationship between our two traditions.' Ian Paisley responded with a speech in which he sounded more like Terence O'Neill or Brian Faulkner in previous decades: 'Some say hedges make the best neighbours, but that is not the case. I don't believe we should plant a hedge between our two countries.' Then, in another important reference to history, he continued: 'We both look forward to visiting the battle site at the Boyne, but not to re-fight it. I look forward to future meetings and trust that old suspicions and discords can be buried forever under the prospect of mutual and respectful cooperation.'

In advance of devolution coming into effect there were further positive developments. On 16 April a Sinn Féin delegation met the Policing Board for the first time and on 3 May the UVF announced it was taking a non-military role and had put its weapons 'beyond reach'. One senior UVF member said:'we are flicking off the switch on the UVF as a paramilitary body, a war machine. Today the lights have gone out on the UVF as a military force. It's over. The UVF and Red Hand Commando now only exist as a civilian, non-combatant body of men. Non-criminal, moving strictly into community activism and support' (*News Letter*, 4 May 2007).

On 8 May Assembly Members met in the same chamber where the former Northern Ireland Parliament and Assemblies had met, and Ian Paisley and Martin McGuinness affirmed their pledges of office as First and Deputy First Ministers of Northern Ireland. Significantly, if somewhat unusually, the 'atmospherics' between Paisley and McGuinness appeared to be more positive than had been the case between the former First and Deputy First Ministers, David Trimble and Seamus Mallon. (Some of Northern Ireland's notorious cynics soon began referring to Paisley and McGuinness as 'the Chuckle Brothers'.) For the *Irish Times*, the ceremony marked the end of the Northern Ireland conflict.

As had been the case during the Northern Ireland Assembly election, the event appeared to arouse more excitement among foreign journalists than among the peace process-weary public. While there was a feeling that a significant event had taken place, a more general opinion was that the politicians should now get on with the job of sorting out problems in health, education, water charges and other issues and forget about the constitutional question for the future.

In his inaugural speech as First Minister, Ian Paisley reminded the audience of those who had been killed or injured in the conflict. He then said:

> In politics, as in life, it is a truism that no one can ever have one hundred per cent of what they desire. They must make a verdict when they believe they have achieved enough to move things forward. Unlike at any other time I believe we are now able to make progress. ... I believe that Northern Ireland has come to a time of peace, a time when hate will no longer rule. How good it will be to be part of a wonderful healing in our province. Today we have begun to plant and we await the harvest.

Also speaking in Stormont's Great Hall the new Deputy First Minister, Martin McGuinness, thanked those who had helped in the peace process:

> We will continue to rely on that support as we strive towards a society moving from division and disharmony to one which celebrates our diversity and is determined to provide a better future for all our people. One which cherishes the elderly, the vulnerable, the young and all of our children equally. Which welcomes warmly those from other lands and cultures who wish to join us and forge a future together. A society which remembers those who have lost their lives. ...
>
> We know that this will not be easy and the road we are embarking on will have many twists and turns. It is, however, a road which we have chosen and which is supported by the vast majority of our people.

Taoiseach Bertie Ahern said:

> The events that we have had the privilege of witnessing are a powerful statement that peace is not impossible and conflict is not inevitable. We cannot undo our sad and turbulent past. And none of us can forget the many victims of the Troubles. But we can, and

are, shaping our future in a new and better way and in doing so we can put the divisions of the past behind us forever.

The significance of the day was best captured by Tony Blair (now in the final weeks of his Premiership), who spoke to the audience in the Great Hall but also addressed his remarks to the people of Northern Ireland:

> You have lived through the pain and suffering of the past. Many of you each day will pause to remember someone very close and very special who you lost. And for many the pain of that memory will be as real today as it was the hour in the day they were told of that loss. You will never forget. For some it is impossible to forgive. For the rest of us we too need to remember what it was like in order to marvel at how it has changed.
>
> Northern Ireland was synonymous with conflict, it was felt to be intractable. The Troubles were not so much a dispute as a fact of life. Irreconcilable differences, people felt that it could not be done, indeed sometimes even that it shouldn't be done, that the compromises involved were too ugly. Yet in the end it was done and this holds a lesson for conflict everywhere to define the right political framework since only through politics can come peace that lasts.

Long-time Troubles reporter David McKittrick was one of many who expressed surprise at the turn of events:

> It is the closest thing to a miracle that Belfast has seen: the sight of two veterans, Protestant patriarch and iconic republican, standing shoulder to shoulder to vow that they will leave the past behind … Over the years I heard them, repeatedly and routinely, send out the message that there would be no compromise, no sell-out, no surrender. But now there is a new rhetoric and all of the old certainties are disappearing.
>
> (*The Independent*, 9 May 2007)

The *Belfast Telegraph* hailed the formation of the Executive as 'The day no-one thought would ever happen'; the *News Letter* as 'shaking off the chains of history'. The *Irish News* sounded a more cautious note:

Some will have been totally impressed by everything they witnessed, and felt swept along by the excitement of the occasion. Others will have experienced varying degrees of cynicism at the more obvious attempts to stage-manage emotional phrases and imagery during the course of the day. Marginal figures on either side of the divide will have simultaneously rejected the entire initiative as a sell-out to their perceived opponents. However, the majority reaction is likely to have been one of sheer relief that, at last, all the elements necessary for a new political beginning in Northern Ireland have comprehensively fallen into place.

(*Irish News*, 9 May 2007)

Veteran reporter James Kelly wrote:

The big day at Stormont was obviously stage-managed as a historic event but all the participants are well aware that tough challenges face them in the days ahead. History, according to Edward Gibbon, is "a register of crimes, follies and misfortunes." Let's hope Tony Blair is right when he spoke of Ireland "breaking the chains of history".

We have waited nine years. Time to end the false dawns and the old foolishness which sent more than 3,500 men, women and children to an early grave.

(*Irish News*, 9 May 2007)

Bibliography

— Ballymacarrett Research Group, *Lagan Enclave: a History of Conflict in the Short Strand 1886–1997*, Belfast: Ballymacarrett Research Group, 1997.
— Bew, Paul and Gillespie, Gordon, *Northern Ireland: A Chronology of the Troubles 1968–1999*, Dublin: Gill & Macmillan, 1999.
— Currie, Austin, *All Hell Will Break Loose*, Dublin: The O'Brien Press, 2004.
— Curtis, Nicky, *Faith and Duty*, London: Andre Deutsch, 1998.
— Deutsch, Richard and Magowan, Vivien, *Northern Ireland: A Chronology of Events*, Vols. 1–3, 1968–74, Belfast: Blackstaff Press, 1973, 1974, 1975.
— Gillespie, Gordon, *The Historical Dictionary of the Northern Ireland Conflict*, Lanham, Maryland: Scarecrow Press, 2008.
— Hughes, Will, *Citybus: Belfast's buses 1973–1988*, Newtownards: Colourpoint, 2005.
— Jackson, Sir Mike, *Soldier: the Autobiography*, London: Bantam, 2007.
— Mason, Roy, *Paying the Price*, London: John Hale, 1999.
— McCann, Eamonn, *War and an Irish Town*, London: Pluto Press, 1974.
— McCartney, Catherine, *Walls of Silence*, Dublin: Gill & Macmillan, 2007.
— McDonald, Henry, *David Trimble*, London: Bloomsbury, 2000.
— McGuffin, John, *Internment*, Tralee: Anvil Books, 1973.
— McGuffin, John, *The Guineapigs*, Harmondsworth: Penguin, 1974.
— Mullan, Don, *The Dublin and Monaghan Bombings*, Dublin: Wolfhound Press, 2000.
— Mullin, Chris, *Error of Judgement: The Truth about the Birmingham Bombs*, Dublin: Poolbeg Press, 1980.
— Needham, Richard, *Battling for Peace*, Belfast: Blackstaff Press, 1998.
— O'Doherty, Malachi, *The Telling Year: Belfast 1972*, Dublin: Gill & Macmillan, 2007.
— Swan, Sean, *Official Irish Republicanism 1969 to 1972*, United States: Lulu.com, 2007.
— Warner, Geoffrey, 'The Falls Road Curfew Revisited' in *Irish Studies Review*, Vol. 14, No.3, 2006, pp 325–42.
— Whitelaw, William, *The Whitelaw Memoirs*, London: Aurum Press, 1989.

REPORTS
— Great Britain, Ministry of Defence, *Operation Banner: An Analysis of Military Operations in Northern Ireland*, London: Ministry of Defence, 2006.
— *Report of the Independent International Panel on Alleged Collusion in Sectarian Killings in Northern Ireland*, Notre Dame, Indiana: The Authors, 2007.

— *Violence and Civil Disturbances in Northern Ireland in 1969: Report of Tribunal of Inquiry* [The Scarman Report], Belfast: HMSO, 1972.
— International Military Commission: Reports.

NEWSPAPERS AND MAGAZINES
— *An Phoblacht*
— *Belfast Telegraph*
— *Cork Examiner*
— *Daily Express*
— *Daily Ireland*
— *Daily Mail*
— *Daily Mirror*
— *Daily Telegraph*
— *Derry Journal*
— *Evening Argus*
— *Financial Times*
— *Fortnight*
— *The Guardian*
— *The Independent*
— *Iris*
— *Irish Independent*
— *Irish News*
— *Irish Press*
— *The Irish Times*
— *Living Marxism*
— *Mail on Sunday*
— *News Letter*
— *News of the World*
— *The Observer*
— *Shankill Mirror*
— *Shankill People*
— *The Star*
— *The Sun*
— *Sunday Express*
— *Sunday Mirror*
— *Sunday News*
— *Sunday People*
— *Sunday Press*
— *Sunday Times*
— *Sunday Tribune*
— *The Times*

— BBC News on-line: http://news.bbc.co.uk

Index